Mastering Technical Art in Unreal Engine
Materials and VFX

Greg Penninck and Stuart Butler

CRC Press
Taylor & Francis Group
Boca Raton London New York

CRC Press is an imprint of the
Taylor & Francis Group, an **informa** business

Designed cover image: Greg Penninck and Stuart Butler

First edition published 2025
by CRC Press
2385 NW Executive Center Drive, Suite 320, Boca Raton FL 33431

and by CRC Press
4 Park Square, Milton Park, Abingdon, Oxon, OX14 4RN

CRC Press is an imprint of Taylor & Francis Group, LLC

ISBN: 9781032663845 (hbk)
ISBN: 9781032649689 (pbk)
ISBN: 9781032663852 (ebk)
ISBN: 9781032663869 (eBook+)

DOI: 10.1201/9781032663852

Typeset in Times
by codeMantra

Access the support material: http://www.routledge.com/9781032649689

Contents

Preface

Introduction to the Series

Welcome to this book series: *Mastering Technical Art in Unreal Engine*. In this first book, we will be exploring Materials and VFX, creating exciting Technical Art content and systems directly in Unreal Engine 5. You will begin by working with the Unreal Engine Material Editor, learning how to create Materials from scratch for a provided Game Environment and eventually realizing materials for in-game VFX with the Niagara Particle Editor.

This book represents over 20 years of teaching and development experience that has helped educate and develop many game artists working in the UK games industry today. We will share straightforward and engaging exercises for you to practice and test yourself against to help you master your Unreal Engine Technical Art skills.

Materials and VFX

In this book, we'll begin by creating Game Materials to help render 3D Models. You'll develop skills that allow you to create optimized materials and explore ways of creating parameterized Master Materials. You'll then utilize your skills to help create engaging VFX with Niagara learning to create Real-time particles utilizing materials. This book will give you the introductory skills to begin your mastery journey in the field of Technical Art.

World Building

In our second book, you'll learn the art of creating Real-time landscapes. You'll master both technical and artistic skills to create stunning Real-time worlds that make use of modern engine workflows. Worlds in games now require multiple developers to populate complex ecosystems; with this title, you'll learn how to work with all kinds of different developers and systems to realize Unreal Landscapes.

How to Use This Book

There are a couple of things you need to know about this book and how we have presented the activities, in order for you to get the most out of each chapter.

Reading Step-by-Step Instructions

Each chapter features multiple step-by-step tutorials to guide you through making materials and VFX systems; the following formatting styles have been used, and understanding these will help you speed through each activity with ease:

- **Bold Text** – When you see bold text, this is something to look out for on screen. These include labels on the user interface, such as the **Details** panel, parameters such as **Sort Priority**, names of nodes such as **Multiply(0,1)** and many more.
- **Italic Text** – When you see italic text, this is something for you to enter by typing, such as *Diffuse Texture* when renaming nodes, values to enter such as *1.25*, something to search for in a search box such as *OneMinus* or something to select from a dropdown.

As we go through the book, we will provide parameter values in tutorials. Many of these can be adjusted to achieve different end results, and we encourage you to play with these values to see what they do and how changing them affects the end result. Don't worry if your final result isn't 100% perfect. That is all part of the process of learning Technical Art.

Unreal Engine Version

The tutorials in this book have been created using Unreal Engine version 5.3. If you don't already have this installed on your computer, there is a quick guide included in Chapter 4.

Project Files

At the start of Chapter 4, we will also ask you to download some project files we have created for you to use throughout the book. When using these, it's a good idea to keep a copy of the original levels, just in case you want to jump back to start again without needing to create a whole new project.

Practice, Practice, Practice!

Many of the tools and techniques we discuss in this book may feel complex, confusing and sometimes challenging when you first start out, don't worry! Over time, as Unreal and its many tools become more familiar, the processes themselves will become second nature as you develop a deeper understanding of the engine and its various editors.

Crashes!

Games Engines are continually evolving software that are always in development. So, they will often suffer from crashes, errors and other issues that may feel frustrating; don't worry, it happens to all of us and it's rarely something you will have done.

For that reason, we will often prompt you to save your work, while Unreal does have an Autosave, it's always worth manually saving each time you create/refine or finish an asset so when the inevitable does happen, you can simply restart the software, reload the project and level and continue where you left off.

Acknowledgments

I would like to thank my family and colleagues for their time and love during the creation of this book. I'd also like to thank Bobbie Fletcher, Nader Alikhani and Cris Robson for their guidance and support during the early parts of my career. Lastly, I'd like to thank Stu for coping with the severe level of Gregisms and nonsense throughout this book and beyond. – Greg Penninck

I would like to thank my family for their endless amounts of support and my colleagues, both old and new, for their words of guidance and support. I'd also like to thank Bobbie Fletcher for affording me many professional opportunities and for always being a great mentor and Justin Mohlman for giving me my first opportunity to develop educational content for an international audience. Lastly, I'd also like to thank Greg for inviting me to join him on this journey of sharing our love and knowledge of Unreal Engine. – Stuart Butler

Author Biographies

Greg Penninck has worked and taught in the Games Industry sector since 2006, creating many world-leading games courses and modules from Foundation to Masters Level. He is an Authorized Unreal Instructor Partner for Epic Games and has been teaching Unreal Engine for over 15 years. In 2016, he was awarded an Epic Developer Grant through his company Thundersteed Ltd., which helped him continue to spread the joy of Unreal Development. He works as a Marketing Artist for REALTIME, a BAFTA-nominated VFX Studio.

Stuart Butler is the Dean of Creative Industries at CG Spectrum Institute. He has taught in the HE sector since 2009, creating many games courses and modules from Foundation to Masters Level, and he was formerly the Course Director of Games Technology at Staffordshire University. He is an Authorized Unreal Instructor Partner and Educational Content Creator for Epic Games and has been teaching Unreal Engine since the launch of UDK. He has contributed to projects as a Vehicle Artist, Animator, Game Designer and Technical Designer/Artist; his broad skillset and understanding provide insight into all aspects of Games Development. Alongside Greg, as part of their Company Thundersteed Ltd, he was awarded an Epic Developer Grant in 2016.

1

What Is Technical Art

In this chapter, we are going to talk about the role within the games industry which is Technical Art. You will learn about:

- What Technical Art is.
- What technical artists do.
- What software a technical artist should learn.
- What skills a technical artist should have.
- How technical artists fit into a development team.
- What fields there are within Technical Art.

We will finish the chapter with a short quiz to test your understanding of what we've discussed.

Introduction to Technical Art

In this chapter, we are going to explore Technical Art, but what is Technical Art you ask? Technical Art is an exciting field of Games Development that revolves around three core concepts:

1. **Creating Solutions to Help Other Artists** – Whether that's a tool to help speed up a workflow or a template material to keep consistency, technical artists are first and foremost focused on helping others work smart.
2. **Developing Systems and Art that Run Effectively at Run Time** – You'll know when something is hurting performance and guide others to produce content that looks great but doesn't hurt gameplay.
3. **Researching and Creating Novel Solutions** – Technical artists are always at the forefront of developing and looking for new techniques and systems to help create better content for others.

If you enjoy building Game Art and want to take your understanding to the next level to support those around you, then Technical Art might be for you. The field of Technical Art is very broad, the jobs and tasks you might need to complete require mastery of a large set of Game Engine Tools. As you progress through this book, and other books in the series, we will explore some of the most exciting areas. For now, let's look at a couple of these areas at a high level.

DOI: 10.1201/9781032663852-1

What Do Technical Artists Do?

Technical artists in game development act as a bridge between art and code, helping both the art team and the code team to deliver the requirements of the artistic vision while maintaining performant solutions that align with any technical restrictions. The main tasks a technical artist might undertake are:

- **Solve Problems** – You will work with artists and programmers to find solutions to game art problems, your work will cover a wide range of in-game-related issues such as rigs not working, materials not rendering properly, poor naming or tool usage.
- **Facilitate Artists** – You will help others work smarter and faster. As a technical artist, you will often help remove blockers and enable artists to complete their tasks effectively.
- **Devise Workflows** – Part of facilitating others will be ensuring good workflows are followed. You will communicate across departments and create effective planning documentation and guides to help the work of others. This may mean populating wikis, creating technical documents or producing workflow videos.
- **Create Art** – From time to time, you may be expected to create art assets. Technical artists often have a broad specialism and may be called up to help with Asset Generation during a project.
- **Develop Tools** – Technical artists often create tools inside and outside of Game Engines to improve the effectiveness of Game Art Pipelines.

Communication Is Key

Another key part of the role, which is true for any game developer, is communication with other team members. For a technical artist, this is especially important as you will often be the interface between the art and technical teams, having a good understanding of both teams' priorities and language. As part of that communication element, you will also be tasked with producing documentation to explain how things work (for the technical team to be able to review and refine) and how they should be used (for the art team to be able to use them on their assets), this side of communication, which includes visual and written elements is an important part of any technical artist's week.

What Software Should I Learn?

A technical artist's understanding of software packages and workflows is usually quite broad, even if their job role is quite specific. While this book focuses on Unreal Engine, you can expect to work with many other pieces of software to help support your team. Some of the most common pieces of software used by technical artists are:

- Houdini to create VFX and Procedural assets.
- 3D Studio Max/Maya to create game ready assets.
- Adobe Suite including Photoshop, Substance Designer and Substance Painter, to create textures and imagery.

The above is by no means a complete list and as a technical artist you will always be on the forefront of the latest and greatest tools to help push pipeline efficiency in your team.

It is also common for technical artists to work with a variety of programming and scripting languages using an IDE (integrated development environment) such as Visual Studio or JetBrains Rider. The languages you might benefit from exploring include:

- C++ to create tools, plugins, gameplay and or logic.
- MaxScript/Mel Script to help prepare assets in 3DS Max/Maya.
- Python for pipeline development and scripting in software such as Houdini, Maya and some game engines.
- JavaScript to assist with asset integration with games.

Also, if you are working with Unreal Engine, it is worth having a solid understanding of Blueprints to allow you to prototype tools and ideas in visual script before converting your solutions to C++. Unreal Engine's Blueprint Utilities system allows for the development of asset and actor tools using the Blueprint scripting language and Unreal Motion Graphics (UMG), which can help to quickly produce tools for teams to use in the Unreal Engine Editor.

What Skills Should a Technical Artist Have?

Outside of software, there are many skills a studio might look for in a technical artist and these need to be demonstrated in your portfolio. We recommend having a portfolio on communities such as ArtStation. They are a great place to host your content easily without needing to also learn HTML, CSS and other web-based technologies. A personal website is also fine; however, ensure that the functionality of any portfolio doesn't get in the way of your content. Clear, concise media is a must to keep the focus on your work. Try to ensure your portfolio can demonstrate many of the following to help improve your chances when trying to get into the Games Industry.

Technical artists are often required to have **exceptional attention to detail** and **great communication skills**. Both skills can be evidenced through the polish of your own game assets but also in your presentation of breakdowns, project summaries and write-ups, as well as anywhere you publicly share and demonstrate your projects. When presenting work, it is a great idea to include a bit of detail about the production process and the lessons learned from projects; this helps a studio understand a bit about you and your projects. Visual communication is also key, including diagrams and flow charts to explain process and tools workflows will help show your ability to communicate complex elements to a development team.

As a technical artist, it's key to hold a **broad understanding of game art pipelines** and the **development software and tools** which support them. Understanding how artists work is very helpful. You can demonstrate this by including examples of digital game art assets in your portfolio (characters, environments, vehicles, weapons, etc.) and by ensuring your portfolio entries have a focus on workflows and processes used to achieve the end results, particularly where any clever solutions have been deployed. It's beneficial to maintain this understanding with modern tools. If a new piece of software gets released or begins to become more popular, as a technical artist, you will be expected to explore the opportunities it might provide.

As suggested earlier when discussing software, **understanding scripting and high-level programming languages** can be beneficial for technical artists. You might not always be expected to program in languages such as C++, but the utilization of scripting languages such as Lua, Python, Java or Blueprint is more common. The more you know, the further you can liaise between Art and Programming teams. This can be demonstrated by showing an **ability to develop small tools or scripts**. Demonstrating any example utilities that help to speed up production or solve problems is a fantastic skill. These could be an in-engine tool or in a tool for a Digital Content Creation package (DCC). Remember to show the problem/challenge that the tool solves, explain how it does so and then evidence how the tool has been built with the end user in mind.

It is also important that technical artists display **core, fundamental art skills** within their work. This doesn't mean that you need to be an amazing traditional artist with a portfolio full of sketches or watercolor paintings; we advise instead, that you try to demonstrate strong artistic principles in the projects you include in your portfolio. Try to focus on being able to evidence strong color theory, composition and layout. It's important to be well-versed in the terminology and language of art to be able to communicate with the art team. Combined with those art skills, it's beneficial to show **creative problem solving**, through examples of where you have overcome problems. A common interview question for artists, and particularly technical artists is "What is the most difficult technical challenge you have faced and how did you overcome it?"

And the final skill that is key to evidence is the ability to complete **full pipeline projects**, try to demonstrate where you have taken a concept through to a fully completed game project. This gives you the opportunity to showcase a variety of technical challenges such as materials, rigging, physics, asset setup, rendering, and much more. When you first create your portfolio, such as when you are completing a university degree or starting to apply for roles after studying via online courses, different learning resources and books such as this one, it's quite likely your work will feature a range of different styles based on the learning resources you have been using. This is okay if you are applying to work at a studio that works on a wide variety of titles, such as an outsource or co-development studio but if you are applying to larger companies with popular, established intellectual properties (IPs), you might need to be more specific with the work you use to demonstrate your skills. Targeting your portfolio to show that you can work with styles similar to those of the games the studio produces; for example, a hard surface artist applying to work on Rare's *Sea of Thieves* would be better to focus on stylized assets with a nautical theme than highly realistic military weapons more akin to Activision's *Call of Duty* series and vice versa.

So, now we know what you need to get into a team, let's look at what that team might look like on the inside.

How Does a Technical Artist Fit into a Development Team?

As we have already mentioned, the Technical Art discipline acts as a bridge between programming and art. With that in mind, you are probably wondering what a team structure might look like with a technical artist in it? This will often depend on the company, as not all studios operate in the same way with Technical Art sitting more closely with code or art, so, let's explore a couple of example studio setups.

Figure 1.1 shows two possible placements for a Technical Art team within a smaller studio/development team, being managed by the Art Manager, therefore sitting alongside art a bit more closely, or being led by the technical manager, resulting in the team sitting more closely with programming. In these instances, the expected skills may also be biased toward the team they are sitting within. Regardless of where the team sits, a technical artist will be expected to support multiple different teams including animation, art and design, so they could be responsible for many aspects of development such as rigging, VFX, materials and general pipeline duties.

Figure 1.2 shows a larger studio with a dedicated team. In larger studios, there might be multiple Technical Art areas. In these studios, the technical artists may align with a more focused field, we will explore those next.

Before we move on, however, it's important to realize that while Figure 1.2 might visually suggest that Technical Art is a bigger department than the other areas, the number of staff in each of the roles within the Technical Art team will be much lower than, for example, each level of the design or programming team. We also haven't split each of the other development areas down into their smaller parts, such as art is commonly split into environments, characters, vehicles or hard surfaces.

What Fields Are There Within Technical Art?

There are multiple disciplines that exist within Technical Art, you may be required to master some or all the following areas, and this is certainly not a definitive list.

- **Technical Artist** – In this more generalist role, you would be expected to support the art team with many technical challenges spreading across the development process. You would be an exceptional communicator who works closely with both programming and art to drive workflows and solutions to technical challenges.
- **VFX Technical Artist** – Technical artists in this more specific role would work with the systems that integrate into the VFX Pipeline. You would have expert knowledge of materials, textures, lighting, physics and particle systems to support artists to create fantastic visuals with great performance.
- **Pipeline Technical Artist** – A Pipeline Technical Art will work closely with the programming team to ensure the appropriate tools are available to create game assets. You may support both the asset creation and game

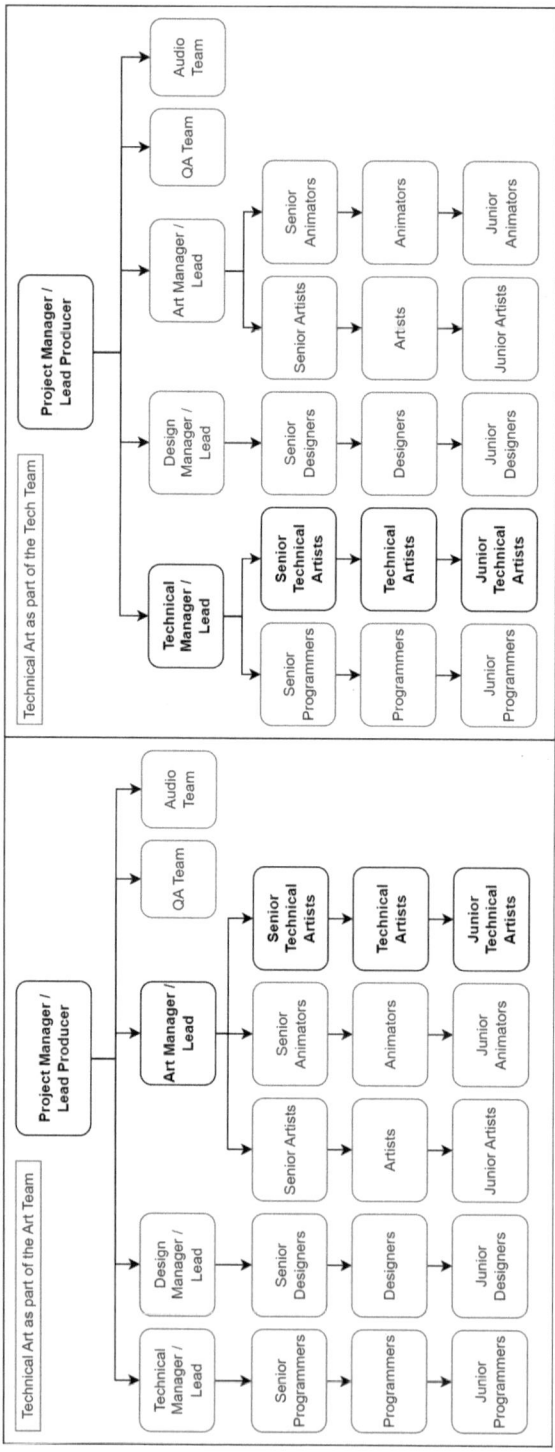

FIGURE 1.1   Organization charts showing two possible structures including Technical Art within a development team/studio.

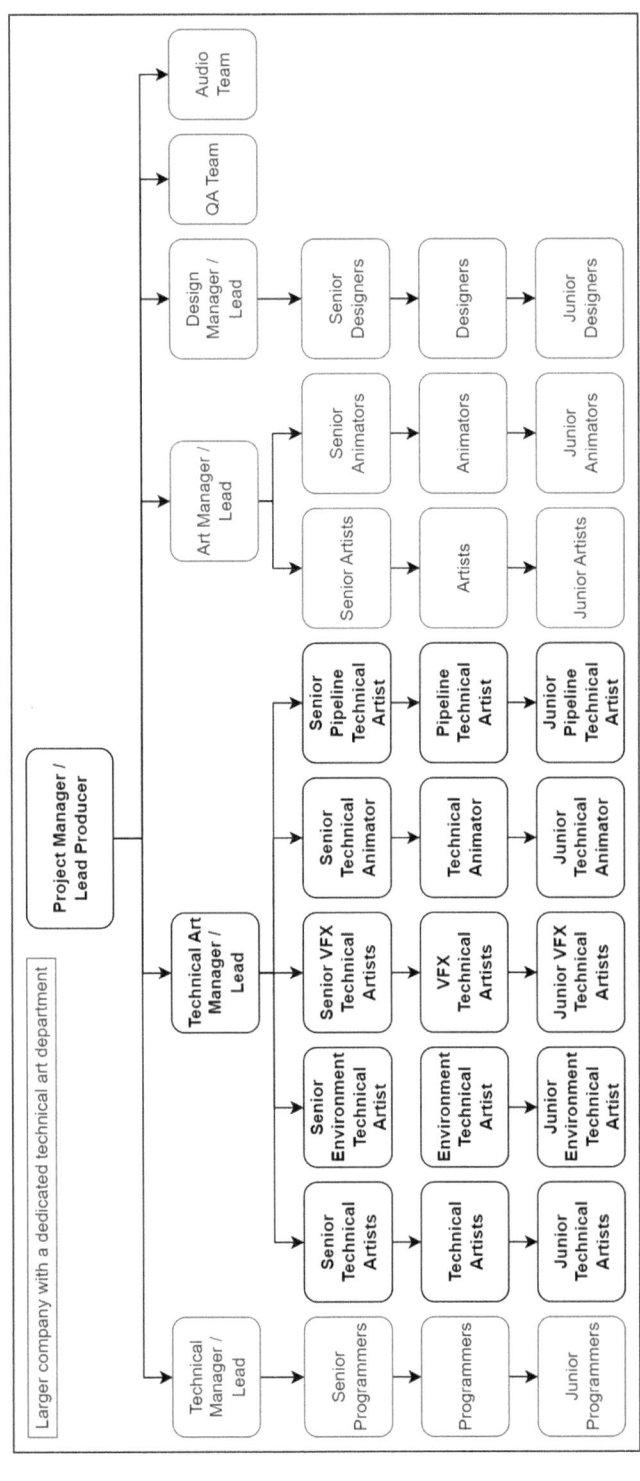

FIGURE 1.2   Organization chart showing a larger, dedicated Technical Art team within a development team/studio.

deployment side of the pipeline working with a variety of different software and platforms.

- **Technical Animator** – As the name suggests, this role is much more aligned with animation. You would likely focus on rig setup, animation pipelines, and animation systems setup. You would regularly work alongside the animators in your team, as well as gameplay programmers, to ensure that the animations function effectively and there are no blockers in the animation workflow. In larger studios, you might also work with hardware such as a motion capture stage to help support the integration of recorded motion capture performances including both body and facial performance capture.

- **Environmental Technical Artist** – As games get bigger so do the technical challenges. Environmental Technical Art focuses on the creation of massive, stunning worlds. You are likely to work with procedural landscapes, world atmosphere, lighting, foliage tools and the population of vast detailed environments.

- **Virtual Reality/Virtual Production Technical Artist** – Some platforms require very dedicated technical artists. In areas such as Virtual Reality (VR), Virtual Production (VP) or even Augmented Reality (AR), technical artists are likely to be working on a multitude of different hardware setups as well as different software. Your expertise could cover things like cameras, motion capture studios, in camera VFX pipelines, mobile platforms, VR headsets and more.

Conclusion

In this chapter, we've learned all about the role of a technical artist including what they do and how they might contribute to a game's development. We've also covered some key considerations for creating portfolios as a technical artist applying for your first role and we have taken a quick look at some of the other more niche roles within Technical Art.

Chapter 1 Quiz

Question 1: What Game Studio Departments do technical artists not work closely with?

    a. Art

    b. Programming/Engineering

    c. Marketing

    d. All of them, technical artists work alone

Question 2: Which of the examples below are fields within Technical Art? (select 3)

    a. Environmental Technical Art

    b. Technical Art

    c. Character Art

    d.   Gameplay Design

    e.   Technical Animation

Question 3: Which of the following are examples of what a technical artist might do? (select 3)

    a.   Coordinate the Production Team

    b.   Create Materials

    c.   Build Tools for Artists

    d.   Budgeting for Marketing

    e.   Setup and Test Rigs for Animators

Question 4: Technical artists devise workflows for the art team?

    a.   True

    b.   False

Answers

Question 1: c

Question 2: a, b, e

Question 3: b, c, e

Question 4: a

2

An Artist's Guide to the Rendering Pipeline

Introduction

This chapter introduces you to the Rendering pipeline in Unreal Engine, you'll learn about:

- Rendering Methodologies such as Deferred Rendering.
- How Physically Based Rendering is implemented in Unreal Engine.
- Material and VFX Optimization tools and features.

Introduction to the Rendering Pipelines in Unreal Engine

Unreal Engine 5 uses a Deferred approach for Rendering. The rendering engine breaks down the process into passes, resulting in the creation of a G-Buffer. The G-Buffer contains information such as Color, Depth, Metallic, Roughness, Normals and other properties that are then utilized in a lighting pass. The Deferred approach in Unreal Engine has many specialist stages and processes, which Epic has detailed in their Begin Play | Rendering online learning available here. https://dev.epicgames.com/community/learning/tutorials/vyZ1/unreal-engine-begin-play-rendering

Epic's Begin Play | Rendering also features a useful schematic which is a great reference for Technical Artists to refer to when troubleshooting effects and understanding the order at which features are processed.

Unreal's Deferred Rendering methodology is able to render a large number of lights with complex materials while maintaining stable performance. The advantage of processing many lights and render features makes it a successful renderer that recreates detailed and physically accurate scenery. It is for this reason that Deferred Rendering is utilized by many of the games we play today.

Unreal also has the option to utilize Forward Rendering which does not create a G-Buffer/defer lighting calculations. Forward Rendering is better suited to platforms such as VR where speed is very important and rendering feature sets are generally less expansive.

Let's explore the overall Strengths and Weaknesses of Deferred Rendering in a little more detail:

DOI: 10.1201/9781032663852-2

Strengths of Deferred Rendering

- Deferred Rendering can render many more lights than other methods. Lighting is only calculated on visible objects; this results in less draw calls.
- Deferred Rendering in Unreal affords many Post Processing Effects (Lens Flare, Vignette, Colour Grading, Screen Space Effects, Bloom).
- The G-Buffer stores all the necessary passes and information for Unreal to utilize for lighting and rendering.

Weakness of Deferred Rendering

- Deferred Renderers have a large upfront memory cost for the G-Buffer. This memory usage can cause issues on older graphics cards which have a smaller amount of RAM. This is further complicated by large 4k screens that require a lot of pixels to be rendered, further increasing the demand on GPU bandwidth.
- Transparency and Antialiasing often require work around combinations of rendering strategies.

Physically Based Rendering

Physically Based Rendering, also known as PBR, is a rendering methodology that tries to accurately represent how Materials and Lighting interact in the real world. Representing real-world physical lighting is complex and expensive in terms of game performance.

As a Material Artist, we will commonly use Epic's Material Model, which affords four key physically based attributes, these are:

- Base Color
- Roughness
- Metallic
- Specular

We will break down the above terminology in the coming chapters as we begin to create our materials. For now, it is important to note that the four attributes above are common across all Unreal Engine 4 and Unreal Engine 5 versions up to version 5.3, and it is likely to evolve with the advances of Epic's Substrate system which is currently in an experimental stage.

Regardless of which model is used, the goal of the Material Attributes is to create Game Art that performs consistently in all lighting situations and environments. This helps development teams avoid creating too many assets and relies less on artistic interpretation. Art generated using a PBR workflow can be targeted to different aesthetics, whether it be realistic art styles or non-photorealistic rendering, as seen in Disney/Pixar movies.

You are likely to find other rendering pipelines in game development, such as older Specular/Diffuse workflows. Knowing where to start with any workflow is important to working efficiently. As a starting point, Epic have provided many example properties on their documentation, which can help us create Parametric Materials quickly. Some examples can be found here: https://docs.unrealengine.com/5.3/en-US/ physically-based-materials-in-unreal-engine/

As a Technical Artist that specializes in Materials, you will need to know how to leverage PBR values in Material Creation while also providing flexibility for team members to tweak and adapt values. It is important to note that while PBR is focused on recreating reality, artists will still be able to tweak colors and adjust values which we will explore in later chapters. Nothing is set in stone, real-world rules should be treated a bit more like guidelines depending on the target art style.

Areas for Optimization

Optimization is a massive topic, we'll explore some common issues that can occur when working with Materials and Particle Effects later in this book. The single best strategy for this process is to ensure your development team has a consistent documented approach that developers follow when carrying out work in their relevant discipline. In addition, this area is ever evolving, particularly as rendering technologies change and adapt.

Draw Calls

To render geometry, Unreal creates "Draw Calls" that instruct the Rendering Engine how and what to draw on screen. A Draw Call contains information such as Transforms, Materials, Textures and Buffers. This information is gathered and prepared by the CPU before being passed onto the GPU for rendering. Unfortunately, it's very easy to create a bottleneck by creating many thousands of these calls if you are approaching asset creation or scene design incorrectly. Common problems and things to watch out for are:

1. 3D Models/Assets with too many Material IDs. For example, creating large meshes with hundreds of materials, could become a blocker.

2. 3D Models/Assets built out of too many small components, for example, a castle built out of individual stones would create many thousands of draw calls. Whereas a Castle built from modular walls and trims would result in much fewer draw calls.

3. Not using instancing tools such as Foliage Instancing or Procedural Volume tools that help to render many copies of the same mesh.

4. Not using Hierarchical Level of Detail (HLOD's). This system will reduce a group of meshes into a proxy object with 1 Draw Call. This is particularly handy for background meshes.

5. Underutilization of Nanite, Nanite can improve draw call limitations dramatically in Unreal Engine 5. Typically, it has a small CPU cost with 1 draw

call per material present in the scene. Epic note that disabling Nanite on some of the larger demos such as Valley of the Ancients can lead to tens of thousands of traditional Draw Calls.

If we are not careful with Draw Calls, it is possible for the engine to become CPU bound, meaning the engine is too busy completing CPU processes that it won't be able to pass information to the GPU fast enough.

So, how do we find out if this is a problem? We can view Draw Calls in a couple of ways in Unreal using one of two console commands: "stat scenerendering" or "stat RHI". To activate a console command, press the tilde (`) key on your keyboard and type either *stat scenerendering* or *stat rhi* and press enter. To remove the stat commands, simply re-enter the command via the console. Figures 2.1 and 2.2 show the type of information generated by the console commands.

How many Draw Calls are too many? It's very difficult to say that rendering is dependent on so many factors and features. Some rough numbers would be:

- Mobile Devices: a few Hundred
- PC & Consoles: 3000–5000
- High Spec Workstation: 10000

A better approach would be to ensure that workflows within your team's asset creation and rendering pipelines are well understood and distributed to ensure everyone pulls together to make a game/real-time product in the most optimal way.

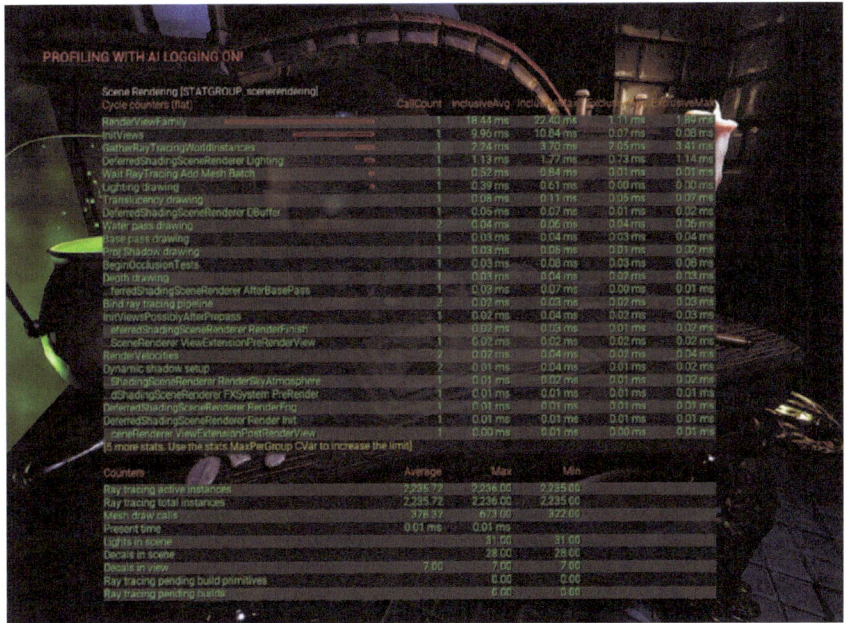

FIGURE 2.1 The Editor viewport with "stat scenerendering" debug text activated.

FIGURE 2.2 The Editor viewport with "stat rhi" debug text activated.

Shader Complexity

All materials are not equal. It's important to keep track of how expensive certain materials are. Both the Material Editor and Viewport Viewmodes will give you some rough ideas, the engine allows you to see Instruction Counts as well as Shader Complexity. Higher Instruction counts normally means a Material will be more costly however, it's not always that simple. Sometimes, some instructions will cost more than others, and it's not always obvious. For example, loading textures with texture samples will be slower than simple math instructions but may be counted as the same number of instructions. The Instruction Count provides a rough starting point to get you started as you investigate your work.

Viewing Instruction Count in the Material Editor

To view Instruction Counts in any open Material; navigate to the Windows menu and select Stats. This will populate a small bar of the UI at the bottom of the Material Editor. An example of this UI can be seen in Figure 2.3. This will give you an indication of things like the Instructions at different parts of your Material pass (Base Pass/Vertex Shader) as well as information such as the number of Texture Lookups/Samplers.

Viewing Shader Complexity in the Viewport

To view shader complexity in the viewport, we can use the Shader Complexity Overdraw. To enable this, click on the **Lit** button in the 3D Viewport. From the options

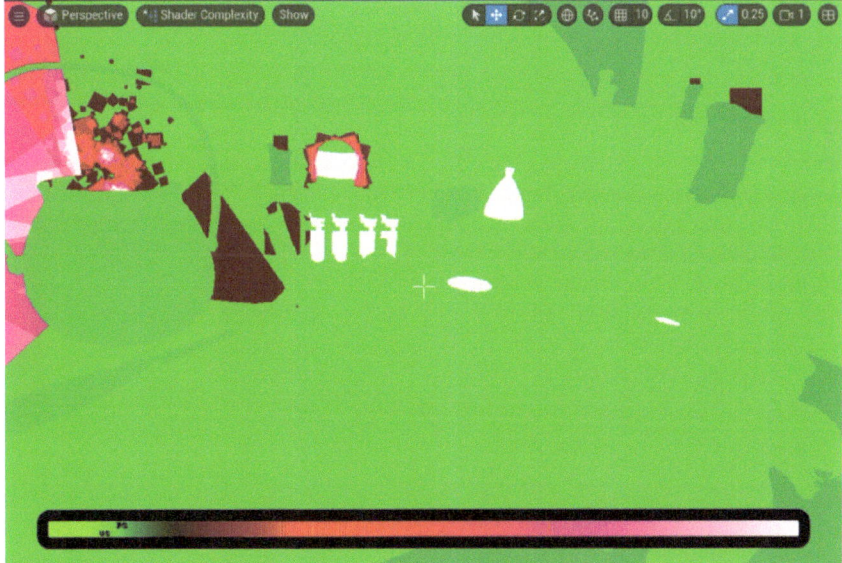

FIGURE 2.3   Material Stats visible in the material editor UI.

FIGURE 2.4   Editor viewport with shader complexity enabled.

menu, scroll down to **Optimization Viewmodes | Shader Complexity**. Your view-port should look somewhat similar to Figure 2.4, depending on where your camera is in the level. To return the Viewport back to Lit mode, click the same button (the text will now say **Shader Complexity**) and select the **Lit** option from the menu.

How Can We Reduce Shader Complexity and Instruction Counts

Now that you have some understanding of how to identify when a shader has become too expensive, we can explore a few approaches to reduce that impact. Consider the following:

- Avoid costly nodes, noise nodes for example are better replaced with textures.
- Avoid using nodes like Sine and other complex Math nodes unless needed.
- Don't always go for the most expensive Transparency settings. Materials like Glass, Water and Fog can easily increase shader complexity and also lead to overdraw, which we'll look at next.

Overdraw

Overdraw occurs when objects are rendered on top of one another many times. This happens when we have many transparent objects and is often caused by materials/particles that feature things like glass, water and fog. For lower end platforms, Overdraw can dramatically reduce performance so it's important to limit the amount of Overdraw where possible. In Unreal, we can view Overdraw by using the Quad Overdraw option in the Editor. An example of this can be seen in Figure 2.5.

Viewing Overdraw

To enable Quad Overdraw, click on the **Lit** button in the 3D Viewport. From the menu, select **Optimization Viewmodes | Quad Overdraw**. Your viewport should look somewhat similar to Figure 2.5 depending on where your camera is in the level. To return the Viewport back to Lit mode, click the same button (the text will now say **Quad Overdraw**) and select the **Lit** option from the menu.

The Quad Overdraw Viewport mode allows us to see where a pixel is being drawn multiple times due to things like transparency. If a pixel is dark blue, there is no Overdraw, as the colors progress through the scale shown at the bottom of the screen through green, yellow, red and eventually white, potential problems become more obvious, with white showing where a pixel is drawn many times due to many overlapping transparent objects.

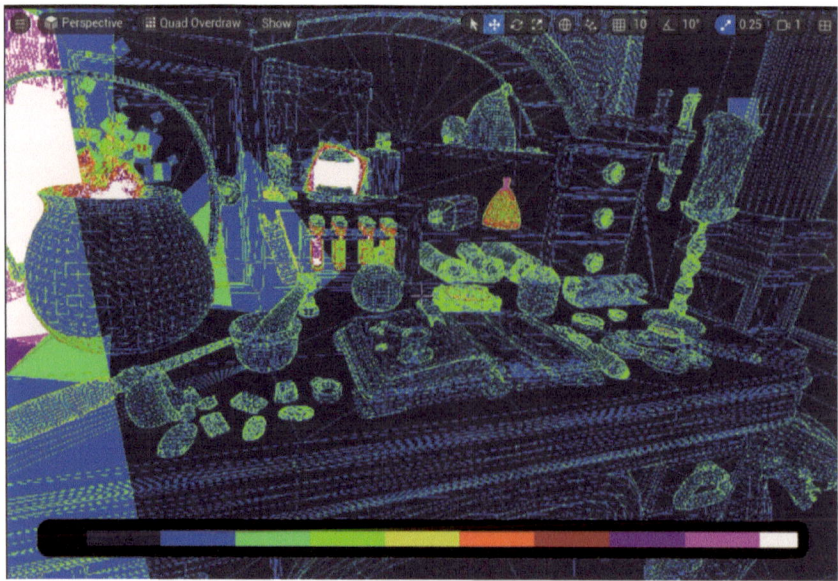

FIGURE 2.5   Editor viewport with quad overdraw enabled.

How Can We Reduce Overdraw?

There are a few different approaches we can use to help reduce Overdraw in Unreal, let's take a look at a few of those.

1. Reduce material complexity where possible. This may mean avoiding Transparent Materials and trying to rely on Masked or even Opaque Materials. In some cases, this sadly won't be possible for example, Particle Effects that require soft transparent rendering like smoke.
2. Use LODs in both Meshes and Particle Effects; try to limit when Unreal draws the highest LOD.
3. Reduce the amount of spawned particles; try to achieve a strong visual result with as few particles as possible. Just because we can spawn 100 smoke particles doesn't mean we should.
4. Optimize the size of transparent objects, the larger an object is on the screen will increase the Overdraw potential.
5. Explore using geometry for some models instead of Transparent Textures, for example we could model grass meshes instead of using opacity textures.

Memory

One of the common issues with artwork in games is the amount of memory it requires. Textures in particular account for a large part of a game budget both in terms of storage and video runtime RAM. Materials and Visual Effects almost always need textures, thus our goal should be to use textures as effectively as possible to avoid causing problems for our games and real-time projects.

In this book, many textures have been provided for you to work with, they are not optimized so provide an opportunity for us to explore what options we have within Unreal to improve texture memory.

Viewing Texture Memory and Sizes

To explore a Texture's resolution and usage, we need to explore an imported Texture Asset in the Texture Properties window. Let's do this now.

1. In the **Content Browser**, navigate to the folder **Content | Textures | Book**.
2. Double click on the **Book_BaseColor** texture asset to view its properties.
3. With the texture open, navigate to the **Details** panel.
4. You will see that the Texture is **4096 * 4096** pixels in resolution, for all of the following Status' **Imported**, **Displayed** and **Max-In-Game**. The **Texture Resource Size** is also listed as **10923 kb**, roughly **10 mb**. Not every texture will require such resolution and it's important to be able to reduce this where required.
5. Using the Search Box at the top of the **Details** panel, type the word *Max*.
6. Set the **Maximum Texture Size** Parameter to *1024*.
7. You will now see the Texture Resource Size reduced to *683 kb*. The resolution parameters will also be updated to reflect the **1024** change. This

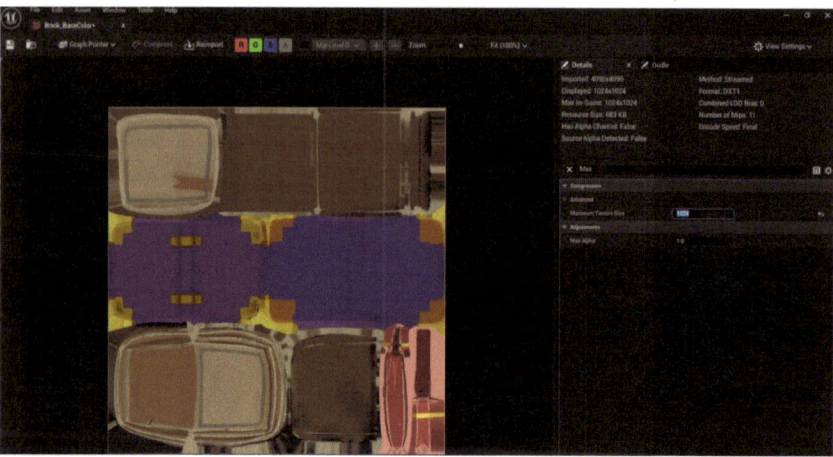

FIGURE 2.6   Texture settings.

small change across many textures will save a lot of memory and the cost of texture detail. An example of this change can be seen in Figure 2.6.

8. This change is not required to be saved; you may now close the Texture Properties Window.

NOTE

If you need to make changes like this across multiple Textures, you can select the assets in the Content Browser and then right click on them. Navigate to **Asset Actions | Edit Selection in Property Matrix**. You'll then be able to adjust the Resolution across multiple textures in one rather than opening them individually.

Typically, a Technical Art Director/Lead Artist will dictate what resolution game assets should be; for example, a basic prop might have a texture of 1024, whereas a hero character may have textures of 4096. There are several factors to consider when making these decisions, for example, where is the object in relation to the game camera (further away=lower resolution) or is there a set Texel Density for example 512 pixels per meter squared.

Another very useful Memory tool in Unreal Engine is the Statistics Viewer. To open the Statistics Viewer navigate to **Tools** Menu | **Audit | Statistics**. This Window/ Viewer gives you oversights over a number of options. By default the tool shows the Primitive Stats in the level which allows you to understand triangle counts which is useful to understand model budgets.

To use the Statistics Viewer to understand Textures, click the top left button and pick **Texture Stats** from the dropdown menu. Next, click the top right dropdown menu button and change the options from **Current Stream Level** to **All Streaming**

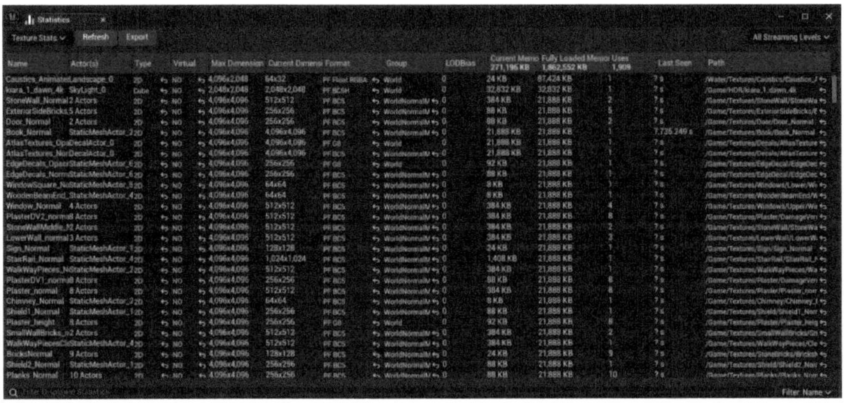

FIGURE 2.7 The statistics viewer.

Levels. You will now get a large table that shows you the Texture Dimensions and Memory allocations. What's great about this tool is that you can click the column headers to sort the table to help isolate any large imagery. The Statistics Viewer is a great first steps tool to understand model and texture budgets within levels, an example of the UI can be seen in Figure 2.7.

Unreal GPU Profiling

To see a more detailed breakdown of frame render time, we can also use Unreal's GPU Visualizer. You can launch this feature by pressing Ctrl + Shift and Comma in the Editor or by typing *ProfileGPU* into the console. An example of the information provided can be seen in Figure 2.8. The Visualizer shows various stages of the rendering pipeline and their costs, this goes beyond the scope of this book; however, it's incredibly helpful if you are trying to understand where the GPU section of rendering is being spent.

Try expanding the lighting sections you'll find many of the level actors inside, the tool is incredibly helpful for quickly highlighting actors and features that may need further optimization.

Conclusion

We've made an Introduction to the Rendering pipeline and some of the key terminology involved in its operation. From this starting point, you'll be able to reference how key factors of the rendering pipeline mesh together. We have also explored several areas of concern where we might need to intervene and optimize our approach.

This is but an introduction to many issues that may arise during rendering, material creation and particle effects design. From here, try to utilize some of the debug commands, modes and options to understand the provided project. There is much left to optimize and debug inside Unreal, and the provided assets have many avenues for possible optimization.

FIGURE 2.8   GPU visualizer.

Chapter 2 Quiz

Question 1: What is Physically Based Rendering?

    a. Physically Based Rendering is the strenuous heavy lifting the render engine computes.

    b. Physically Based Rendering is when a mesh is rendered at a physical location in game.

    c. Physically Based Rendering is a game engine methodology that tries to represent how Materials and Light interact in the real world.

Question 2: What are Draw Calls?

    a. A Draw Call is a button inside of Unreal Engine that calls the render to compute.

    b. A Draw Call is a set of instructions that prepare geometry to be rendered within a game engine.

    c. A Draw Call is when a level in a game ends in a tie.

Question 3: What are examples of tools that can help us understand rendering performance in Unreal?

    a.   The Statistics Bunker, Shader Flex and Triangle Overdraw are helpful optimization tools within Unreal.

    b.   The Statistics Window, Shader Complexity Viewmode and Quad Overdraw Viewmode are helpful optimization tools within Unreal.

    c.   The Optimization View Navigator is a helpful hub within Unreal.

Question 4: Which statement best defines Deferred Rendering?

    a.   Deferred Rendering is when a game engine calculates all a frame in one pass.

    b.   Deferred Rendering is when a game engine calculates all mesh positions and transforms and then runs a light pass.

    c.   Deferred Rendering is when a game engine breaks down the process into passes, resulting in the creation of a G-Buffer.

Answers

Question 1: c

Question 2: b

Question 3: b

Question 4: c

3

What Are Materials?

In this chapter, we are going to discuss the world of materials and how they fit into the art pipeline for games. You will learn about:

- Materials assets and their uses within games.
- Texture assets and the different types of textures.
- Texture formats and texture compression.
- UVW Coordinates and how materials are applied to 3D Models.

Introduction to Materials

Materials control the visual representation of a mesh or object in a 3D scene. They are a key component of how any rendered 3D looks including films, pre-rendered images and, importantly (for this book), games. As a Technical Artist, it is one of our tasks to set up materials, configuring many properties to build a visual representation that fits with the art style required for each project. We control color, roughness, metallic, transparency, emissive and many other features to achieve the stunning visuals we are accustomed to in today's games. As part of our role, we work to empower other developers by creating and setting up the required material functionality and maintaining good performance for our games & applications with the solutions we build.

To create the visual aesthetic of an object, a material completes lots of calculations. In Unreal Engine these calculations are created in the Material Editor. Before opening the editor it's important to understand what features are available and what might be needed for a material.

Material Resources

Materials are built up from many ingredients such as textures, masks (greyscale textures), parameters, gradients and much more. Understanding the options available to you will help you make the important decisions around what resources are needed prior to material creation, although sometimes, you will find yourself needing to create some new elements when you find something new or have a great idea.

Textures

Textures are 2D images imported into Unreal Engine that can be incorporated into materials.

 DOI: 10.1201/9781032663852-3

FIGURE 3.1 A range of different textures.

Textures can be created in a range of different software; most commonly, however, they are created in software such as Adobe Photoshop, Substance Painter or Substance Designer. Textures can be utilized in many ways; they can define color or roughness, or to be used as a mask for selecting and/or blending values together. As we begin to build Materials we'll use lots of textures, however, they are one of the largest memory costs in games and real-time applications. It's important to use textures carefully and learn when they are necessary and when they can be replaced with parameters.

Texture Types

We can use textures for many different purposes and with all those different uses, it's sensible to assume that each different use will require a different type of texture.

Figure 3.1 shows a selection of textures which you will find in the Unreal Project and provides an example of a range of different texture types. They are, from left to right, a Color, Normal and a Merge Map, let's explore these and a few others.

- **Color Texture** – Alternatively referred to as an albedo texture, these textures are the easiest texture to look at and visually understand. The color texture provides the surface color for the model. For a character this would include skin tones, freckles, scars and tattoos. For an environment texture, you might expect to see brick patterns or wood grain For a racing car, you can expect to see the livery, sponsor logos and badges. When using modern games engines, such as Unreal Engine 5, color textures contain very little lighting information resulting in the texture containing very little tonal variation unlike older style diffuse textures which would contain highlights and shadows.

- **Grayscale Textures** – There are two main uses for grayscale textures in materials; as inputs to the material or as masks. Many of the inputs in a material can only use a single channel of information, unlike the color input (and resulting texture) which use all three channels of a texture, Red, Green and Blue (RGB). This means that if we are producing textures directly for one of these inputs, such as roughness, metallic or ambient occlusion, we would produce a grayscale texture where all three channels for each pixel are the same. When used as a mask, these form part of a blending system or are used for adjusting how a section of the texture is affected by which instructions in the material. Depending on the material and the usage of the mask, some grayscale textures may only contain either white or black pixels, these are referred to as Binary Masks. An example of using such a Binary Mask could be in a leaf material, where the model is a rectangular plane and the section of polygons which needs to be not visible, would be black on the mask whereas the leaf area would appear white.

- **Merged Map Textures** – This type of texture has multiple different names, you may also find them referred to as mix maps or combined mask textures, with artists and studios using different names and labels, but all of these are used in the same way, to provide multiple images (or maps) for use in the material contained within a single texture file, saving precious memory. These textures are often very odd to look at when viewing all three channels (RGB), in order to understand what the texture is bringing to the material, we need to view the different channels as grayscale textures. These are typically used to replace the use of three separate grayscale textures used as inputs into the roughness, metallic, or ambient occlusion or may contain three binary masks to provide additional control to the material. Often, the naming convention with merge maps will depend on what textures are being saved in them.

- **Normal Map Textures** – Normal maps are used in games to add extra lighting detail to materials, often to give the sense that we are viewing a higher polygon model than we actually are. The texture itself stores the direction perpendicular to the surface for each pixel. The directional data is stored in the RGB data of the texture with each channel corresponding to the world axes XYZ. It is important to remember that normal maps do not change the physical geometry of the model they are applied to, just how light interacts with the surface. Typically, normal maps are either generated from grayscale textures called height maps or baked from a high polygon model in a Digital Content Creation (DCC) tool such as 3D modeling software like 3DS Max, Maya, or Blender or texture generation software like Substance Painter or Substance Designer.

- **HDR Textures** – High Dynamic Range (HDR) textures are a special type of texture with a higher bit depth than normal texture. HDR files can be saved with up to 32 bits per channel and aren't restricted by the typical, limited number of values. The values for each channel are also stored as floating-point numbers (floats) instead of integers, allowing for values to exceed the normal 0–1 range in Unreal and it's this characteristic which separates HDR textures from normal textures. File formats for HDR textures are typically either the RGBE format (.hdr) or OpenEXR (.exr), both of which can be imported into Unreal Engine. In Unreal, we typically use HDR textures for lighting of scenes and backdrops when presenting assets.

Texture Formats and Compression

When we author textures, it's beneficial to understand how textures are formatted and saved and what different file types we have available to us. Not all image (texture) file formats are created equally; some formats, such as JPEGs (including .jpeg and .jpg), are more suitable for use on websites due to their 10:1 compression ratio, which is relied upon to reduce the file size of images and subsequently reduce the loading times. This reduction in file size, however, doesn't come without a cost; the JPEG file format is what is known as a lossy format, this means that when the image gets compressed during the saving process, there is inevitable data loss, which causes a reduction in image quality. This is why photos you post on social media platforms are often blurrier than the original on your smartphone or contain visible noise and artifacts, as they are stored and delivered to your device as JPEGs.

In game development, we prefer to use lossless formats where the image we save is the image stored and re-delivered to us when we open them again, load or import the texture into the engine. The main file formats we use are:

- **Bitmap (.bmp)** – The humble bitmap is the stable texture type of many art pipelines and is the simplest format that we use. Bitmaps in older pipelines from sixth-generation consoles, such as the PlayStation 2, used 8-bit bitmaps where each pixel was represented by 8-bits of memory, limiting the number of available colors in the texture to a maximum of 256, offering an extra challenge to texture creation. For modern pipelines, bitmap textures are now saved as 24-bit bitmaps (referred to as true color bitmaps), providing 24-bit of memory per pixel (8 bits per channel) resulting in approximately 16 million possible colors with each channel (red, green and blue) being represented with 256 possible values.

- **Targa (.tga)** – The .tga file format, similar to the .bmp offers 24 bits of color information; however, what makes it unique and beneficial to art pipelines is that the .tga can be saved with 32 bits per pixel. The additional 8 bits provide an alpha channel which is typically used as a transparency channel but can be used as a fourth channel for masks in a merge map or as a mask added to a color map to be used in another element of a material such as masking which part of a texture should be tinted. When saving a .tga texture with an alpha channel, we must ensure that we select the 32-bit option else the alpha channel won't be saved.

- **Portable Network Graphic (.png)** – This file format is very popular for high quality graphics for websites with lossless compression resulting in a smaller file size than a .bmp and for that reason, can also be quite useful for game textures. We do need to be careful when using .png files for importing textures as .png files can be saved with 16 bits per channel instead of the typical 8-bits per channel which will result in the colors appearing washed out as the values get squashed into an 8-bit range (256 values) when imported into Unreal. The .png file format also supports transparency in an alpha channel; however, unlike a .tga file, the transparency does not need to be specifically set in an alpha channel when working in Photoshop. The default export format for both Substance Painter and Substance Designer is .png.

Texture Sizes

The size of a texture is something we should also consider as the texture resolution can have a significant impact on the memory requirements for a material; knowing when you need a high-resolution texture and when you can use something smaller is key to maintaining optimized solutions. Common sizes for game texture are 1024 ´ 1024, 2048 ´ 2048 or 4096 ´ 4096. Textures when authored for use in Unreal Engine must be sized so both the pixel width and height are to the power of 2 (2, 4, 8, 16, 32, 64, 128, 256, etc.). Whilst the size is limited to dimensions to the power of 2, textures aren't required to be square so you can have texture sizes such as 1024 ´ 2048 although square textures are more typical. A good example of a non-square texture is a texture used for the main section of a tire.

UVW Coordinates

UVW Mapping (often referred to unwrapping) is the methodology of turning a 3D model's geometry or surface into a 2D format that relates to a position on a texture. Each vertex in a model has XYZ coordinates, which denote its position in 3D space. Each vertex also has UVW coordinates, which denote their position on a texture. The existence of the W coordinate may seem a little odd as there are only two axes on a texture, the W can be used to flip the orientation of a map or be used as part of 3D procedural materials, but for the most part, we don't need to worry about the W. UVW mapping coordinates are important to material creation in several ways.

Firstly, they are key in achieving the accurate display of our textures, a good set of UVW coordinates (otherwise known as a good unwrap) with little to no distortion ensures our textures render correctly on the model in Unreal. Good unwrapping is usually the focus of a 3D modeler or 3D artist in a development team and is unlikely to be something a technical artist would generally work on when focusing on materials. As a general rule, we need our game assets well-prepared prior to creating materials.

The second reason our mapping coordinates are important is because we can use them to manipulate our textures' appearance in the engine. We can directly move, rotate, scale, and animate the UVW coordinates in our materials, which allows us to produce a range of effects including panning, rotating and zooming effects. This affords us the ability to create effects in materials such as smoke or scrolling street signs, all by manipulating the UVW coordinates of the model, affecting how the textures are displayed. When beginning material creation, it's likely that you'll need to work with coordinates to control tiling before broadening out into animating textures.

And finally, the other key use of the UVW coordinates when creating materials is to control the repetition (or tiling) of a texture on surfaces (either 3D models or landscape elements) and allow us to make sure the texture detail in our scenes maintains a consistent texel density (a measure of pixels of texture per centimeter in a 3D world) and a balanced level of texturing detail. We can also manipulate the use of the UVW coordinates differently in different parts of the material, allowing us to add additional normal map detail using tiling on top of a baked normal from texture-baking software such as Substance Painter or Designer.

Issues with UVW Coordinates such as unwanted distortions or inverted faces (causing the textures to appear flipped) can be quite troublesome when creating materials. When these issues do arise, we often need to export our models back to other DCC packages to fix any errors.

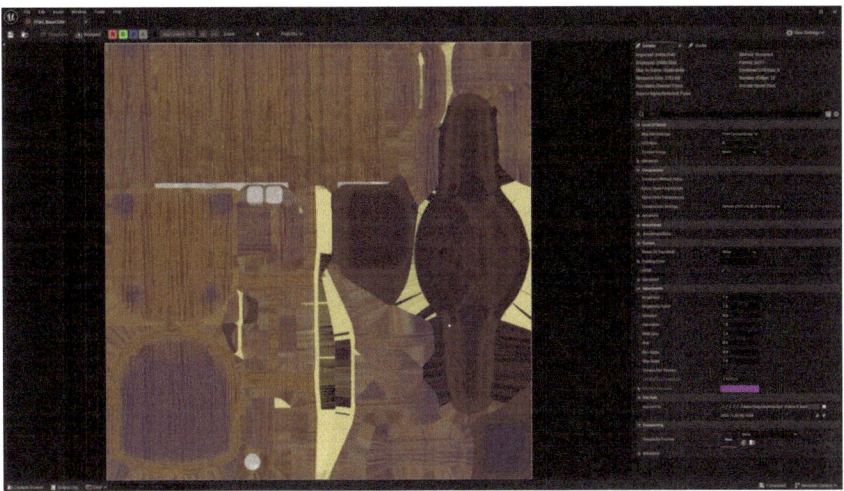

FIGURE 3.2 The texture asset editor in Unreal Engine.

Texture Settings in Unreal Engine

When we import textures into Unreal Engine, they are converted into texture assets, which have a plethora of settings on them which control how they are stored, compressed and handled within the engine. These can be explored by opening a texture asset, providing a window as shown in Figure 3.2. This window has the ability to preview each of the channels (using the R, G, B, and A buttons across the top menu bar) and the texture settings in the Details panel.

We already explored textures sizes in Chapter 2, the other key settings to understand are:

- **Mip Gen Settings** – This determines how the textures are downscaled with the scalability settings. Typically, this remains on **FromTextureGroup** but has options to handle downsizing differently, or to not downsize at all when using **NoMipmaps**.
- **Texture Group** – This provides a series of predefined textures groups which will impact the Mip Gen Settings when we package our games. As default, a lot of these options don't have any effect as the default settings for each group are the same. The benefit comes when optimizing a project for different platforms and devices as these groups can be manipulated from config files for use when the game is packaged.
- **Compress without Alpha** – This setting allows us to ignore the alpha channel on a texture. If it was imported with an alpha channel which we don't intend to use, or was blank but not turned off at export, this allows us to ignore the channel, reducing the memory usage when using the texture.
- **Compression Settings** – This dropdown determines how the textures are compressed and stored. Some of the more commonly used ones are **Default**

(for most textures), **Normalmap** (for normal map textures) and **Masks no sRGB** (for merged map textures).

- **sRGB** – This Boolean variable denotes which color space a texture should be considered in and if the values should be sampled as color or linear color.

Certain texture types must be set up in a certain way for them to be handled correctly in materials. When using a merged map, we must ensure that sRGB checkbox is turned off as this causes the material to treat each of the three channels as separate mask textures and samples them as linear color. When using normal maps, we need to make sure we select the Normalmap Compression Setting; this changes how the texture is stored, ignoring the blue channel, which is derived from the green and the red and changing the compression type.

Material Uses and Material Domains

Materials are a key part to the visual style of our games, cinematics, scenes, animations, films or whatever it is that you are using Unreal Engine for, we can build and apply materials to lots of different things in engine, so as technical artists, we will create materials for different uses. The main things we make materials for are:

- Static Meshes
- Skeletal Meshes
- Landscapes
- User Interfaces in UMG (Unreal Motion Graphics)
- Visual Effects (VFX)
- Light Functions
- Post Processes

Each usage uses different input options dependent on the material domain selected for a material, some uses require a specific material domain, such as when creating materials for use in a post process volume, we use the Post Process material domain, or when creating User Interfaces, we use the User Interface Material Domain. The available material domains are:

- **Surface** – The most common domain, used for meshes, landscapes and VFX.
- **Deferred Decal** – Used for decals, either for a Decal Actor, which places a decal in the world, useful for adding things like graffiti or damage overlays to surfaces or for Mesh Decals where a decal material is applied to parts of a model.
- **Light Function** – These materials are applied to lights to manipulate their intensity and color. Common uses include animating lights to flicker or pulse.
- **Volume** – These materials are used to manipulate behavior in a 3D volume for use in a particle system.

- **Post Process** – Used to apply screen space effects after the scene has been rendered. These uses of these materials include adding outlines to objects when they are within an interactable distance or highlighting enemies through a wall.
- **User Interface** – As the name suggests, these materials are for use in UMG to create materials for the UI.

Each of the materials domains adjust which input pins are available on the material, for example, when selecting the Post Process material domain, all pins except for the Emissive Color input become unavailable but the material node looks the same as when using the Surface material domain. However, when using the User Interface material domain, we are presented with a completely different set of inputs including Final Color, Opacity or Opacity Mask (only one is available at any time, dependent on blend mode), and Screen Position. Because of this, it is important to learn which material domain and blend mode to use in a material. So, let's take a look at the different Blend Modes.

Blend Modes and Shading Models

Each material domain has a selection of blend modes and shading models (not always available) which further determine which inputs are available for the material.

Blend Modes

The blend modes available depend on the material domain but the main ones we will look at for now are the available blend modes for the Surface material domain. These are:

- **Opaque** – This is the standard material type, it, as the name suggests, is designed for opaque surfaces, surfaces where the light doesn't pass through or enter.
- **Masked** – This mode provides us with access to the **Opacity Mask** input. This allows us to define areas of the material which are completely transparent using a black and white mask. Using this mode, each pixel can either be completely opaque or completely transparent, there is no range of opacity. The Details panel has a variable called Opacity Mask Clip Value which is used to convert any gradients in a texture (or math based input) connected to the Opacity Mask input, Anything above that value will be considered as white (opaque) anything below will be considered as black (transparent).
- **Translucent** – This mode provides the range of opacity that the masked mode does not. With this mode, the Opacity Mask pin becomes grayed out and the Opacity pin becomes available. This mode allows for 256 levels of transparency using a grayscale mask input.
- **Additive** – This mode takes the material and applies it on top of whatever is behind it (from the camera's perspective). This works the same way as the

Add blend mode in Photoshop. This mode has a reduced number of inputs with the key available pins being Base Color Emissive Color and Opacity. This blend mode is ideal for creating sci-fi materials such as holograms or a material for a ghost in a more fantasy setting.

- **Modulate** – This blend mode multiplies the value of the material against the pixels behind it, similar to how a Multiply layer works in Photoshop. This mode only offers the Emissive Color input pin.
- **Alpha Composite** – This mode is used for materials that have textures with a premultiplied alpha and often used instead of the translucent or additive modes when creating brightly colored VFX.
- **Alpha Holdout** – An alpha holdout material allows you to define transparency on one object to be carried over to the object behind it (provided that object is not using an opaque blend mode). This can be used to create what appear to be holes in surfaces but are only visible if the alpha holdout material is in front of the other material from the camera's perspective.

Shading Models

Just like blend modes, the shading models available will depend upon the material domain. The shading models, as well as providing different rendering options and results, also change the available inputs on a material. There are a lot of different models, let's explore some of the more common ones:

- **Unlit** – This model only outputs emissive for color, this model is typically used for either emissive objects such as light bulbs (where the emissive value will need to be multiplied to a value much greater than 1 to achieve a glow effect) or for a retro/mobile art style where you want to paint the lighting and shadow into your models and not allow them to be lit by in game lights (in this case the values are kept in the 0–1 range to avoid glows).
- **Default Lit** – This is the default shading model, it is the standard option for PBR materials.
- **Subsurface** – This shading model allows light to penetrate the surface of the object and diffuse through it. This is the shading model we would use to replicate skin, ice, wax and other surfaces where they appear to have depth or where, if you place a light behind them, you'd expect to see some light transmission through the object. An alternative to this model for skin which is more performant but slightly less accurate is the Preintegrated Skin model. A high end rendering version is also available, called Subsurface Profile, which utilizes Screen Space Rendering as it's more effective in representing the subtleties of things like human skin.
- **Clear Coat** – This model is used to represent materials where a clear layer needs to be represented on top of the normal surface. Materials such as car paint, where a top coat of clear lacquer is applied in the real world, typically make use of the clear coat shading model.
- **Two Sided Foliage** – This shading model is used, as the name suggests to represent foliage. Foliage presents a unique challenge in that light can be

transmitted through leaves, similar to skin, but due to how thin leaves are, using the subsurface shading model doesn't provide the most accurate result. This shading model shows lighting on the underside of the surface as if light had traveled through the surface, unlike when you turn on the two sided option in the default lit shading model which would show the underside as almost black.

You can learn more about Shading Models in Unreal from Epic's documentation: https://docs.unrealengine.com/5.3/en-US/shading-models-in-unreal-engine/

Conclusion

In this chapter, we've explored a lot of theory relating to materials including the resources we need to make them, the different types of textures we use, the various types of compression both inside and outside of the engine, as well as the various options we have when creating materials including different material domains, blend modes and shading models. Answer the following questions to see how much you've learned.

Chapter 3 Quiz

Question 1: Which of the following statements is NOT true?
   a.   Texture sizes are required to be in the power of 2.
   b.   Merge maps contain multiple normal map textures.
   c.   Textures help us apply materials to a model.
   d.   UVW coordinates can be animated in the engine.

Question 2: Merge map textures are used for what?
   a.   To determine how other textures will be merged in a material.
   b.   To create animated materials.
   c.   Containing other textures to be used in a material.
   d.   To scale the UVW coordinates to control tiling.

Question 3: How many values does an 8-bit channel have access to?
   a.   8
   b.   10
   c.   256
   d.   16 000 000

Question 4: Which of the following shading models is most suitable for rendering skin?
   a.   Default Lit
   b.   Translucent
   c.   Clear Coat
   d.   Subsurface

Answers

Question 1: b
Question 2: c
Question 3: c
Question 4: d

4

Creating Your First Material

In this chapter, we are going to guide you through creating the first material for the wizard's desk. You will learn about:

- How to create a new material.
- The Material Editor and Material Graph.
- The use of textures in materials.
- Applying materials to meshes in the scene.

Before we can begin making things, we need the project files which include textures for all of the assets in the wizard's desk scene. We will guide you through downloading and exploring the project before we begin with setting up a material for a simple asset, the collection of coins on the right-hand side of the desk.

Getting Started with the Project Files

To follow the practical tutorials in this book, you are going to need to download the project files which are available from the Taylor & Francis website at http://www.routledge.com/9781032649689. You will also need to have Unreal Engine 5.3 installed on your computer.

Installing Unreal Engine

You can download Unreal Engine via the Epic Games Launcher (available from https://unrealengine.com) in the Unreal Engine section (left hand side), Library tab. All project files are provided for use in Unreal Engine 5.3, they should work in newer versions (however some issues may occur) but will not work in any version lower than 5.3. If this is the first time you've installed Unreal Engine, your Epic Launcher after version 5.3 has been installed should look similar to Figure 4.1.

Extracting the Project

The project download is provided as a .zip archive. This will need extracting (or unzipping) using either the tool built-in to your operating system or with a program such as 7-Zip.

When extracting the project, ensure that you maintain the folder structure and do not move any files around as this will prevent the Unreal Engine editor from opening the project correctly.

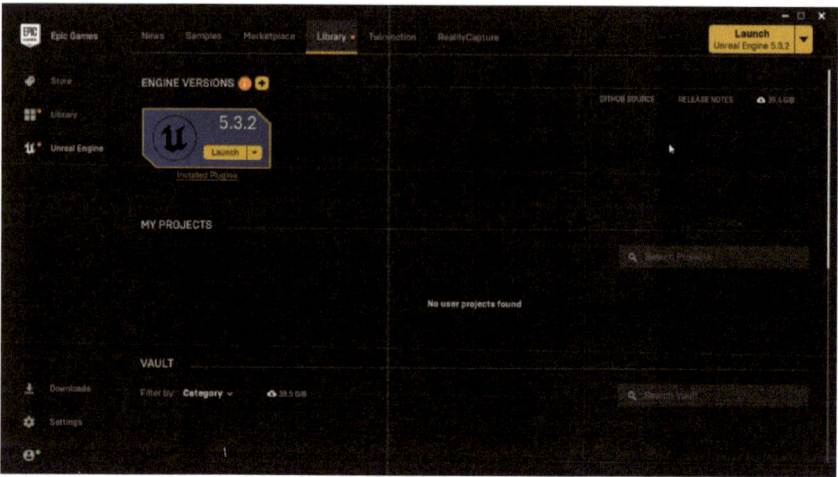

FIGURE 4.1   Epic Games Launcher with Unreal Engine 5.3 installed as an available Engine version.

Once extracted, you should have a root directory called **WizardsDesk**, inside of which you should find two directories (**Config** and **Content**) and a **WizardsDesk. uproject** file.

Opening the Project

With the project extracted (ensure you are not looking at the files in a compressed folder), double click on the **WizardsDesk.uproject** file. This will launch the project in the Unreal Engine editor. If you have multiple versions of the engine installed on your computer, you may be greeted with a popup asking you to select an engine version. Ensure you select Unreal Engine 5.3 or newer as mentioned earlier.

The first time you open the project (and any time you open it after a driver update), the loading sequence may appear to stall around the 45% region, don't worry, this is the point in which the engine does its first phase of compiling the shaders for the project and this can take a little time, so having to wait is quite normal. You should see the number of shaders still to be compiled in the bottom left of the splash screen after the loaded percentage indicator, as shown in Figure 4.2.

Exploring the Project

When the project opens, you should be greeted with the WizardsDesk_Start level which should be displaying the outside of a stone keep, as shown in Figure 4.3.

You should also find that we have docked a **Content Browser** at the bottom of the window. This is not the normal layout you would get if you were to create a new Unreal Project from scratch. If you ever want to replicate this (or you can't see a docked Content Browser), click the **Content Drawer** button in the bottom left corner of the Unreal Engine Editor, and once it has opened, click the **Dock in Layout** button in the top right corner of the content drawer.

FIGURE 4.2 The WizardsDesk splash screen with shaders compiling.

FIGURE 4.3 The default opening view when first launching the WizardsDesk project.

Bookmarks

In the scene, we have set up a series of bookmarks; these are saved locations for the viewport to be positioned and help environment artists or level designers return to sections of a world to review and make changes based on set views. We've provided nine bookmarks that show a variety of locations around the scene. The view you see when you first open the project is bookmark 1. You can return to this location in the viewport at any time by pressing the 1 key on your keyboard.

Explore the other bookmarks by pressing the other number keys; note, however, that this only works on the number keys across the top of your keyboard, not those in the numpad area.

Bookmark 2 shows the desk that we will be focusing on for the start of the book; later, we will move outside to explore some other areas to build materials and visual effects for which can be seen in the high-numbered bookmarks.

Free Movement

You can move around the scene using your mouse as the WASD keys in the same way you would a first-person shooter game. To enable this, you first need to click and hold a mouse button down over the viewport. While holding down the mouse button, you can fly around the world by pressing W (forward), A (left), S (backward) and D (right), and depending on which mouse button you are holding, you can either move forward and backward with the left mouse button held down or look around/change direction by moving the mouse when you have the right mouse button held.

You can also zoom in and out in the viewport using your mouse's scroll wheel. You don't need to click on the viewport to enable this behavior.

In the top right corner of the viewport, there is a camera icon with some numbers next to it, and this allows you to control how fast the camera moves in the viewport. Clicking on it will give you a popup with **Camera Speed** and **Camera Speed Scalar**, the higher these values are, the faster your camera will move when you press the WASD keys, which is beneficial when you need to navigate around the very large worlds that Unreal Engine is capable of rendering. The lower these values are, the slower the camera will move, allowing for more refined movement when needing to focus on smaller details.

Selecting Objects

Take some time to have a look at some of the objects around the scene. You can select any of the elements within the scene by left clicking on them. Click on some of the meshes in the world such as the items on the desk to see what awaits you...

If you want to take a close look at some of the models, when you have them selected, on the right side of the screen, you should find the **Details** panel, a tab in the user interface that shows all the information about the selected actor in the world. With a model (or static mesh as they are called in Unreal Engine) selected, you should see a **Static Mesh** variable with a dropdown. Underneath the dropdown, there is a small folder icon with a magnifying glass; clicking this will select the Static Mesh Asset in the **Content Browser** at the bottom of the screen. Once you have found the mesh in the **Content Browser**, double click on the icon to open it in the Static Mesh Editor. If you were to do this with the upper section of the desk, you should see the mesh with a material applied, as shown in Figure 4.4. We've removed all of the materials in the WizardsDesk_Start map to form the exercises in this book.

When you're done having a look around, we can get started on making the first material for the scene.

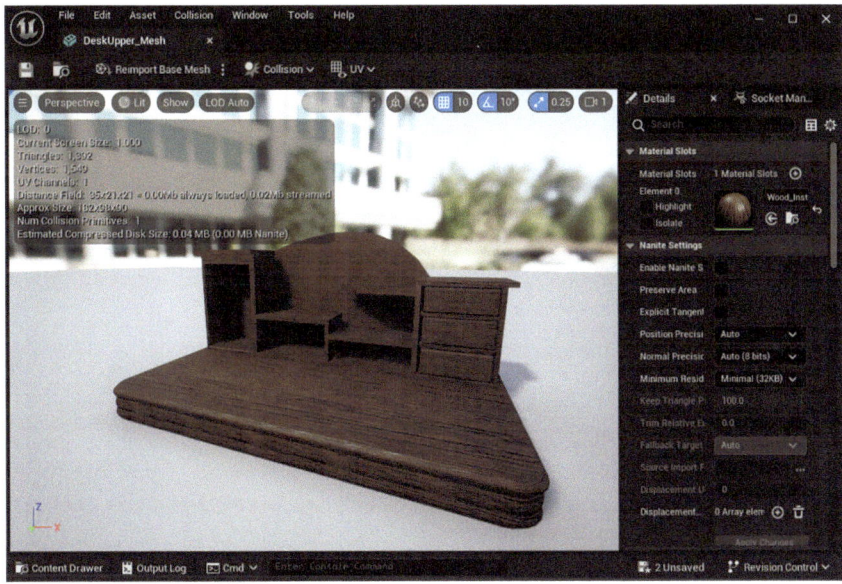

FIGURE 4.4   The DeskUpper_Mesh open in the static mesh editor.

Creating a New Material Asset

To begin creating your first material, first we need to create a suitable folder structure. It's important when working on a project to keep the folders in the Content Browser organized to make finding and working on assets a more user-friendly experience. We are going to keep all our materials in a *Materials* folder, currently, this doesn't exist so let's go ahead and create it.

1. In the **Content Browser**, navigate to the **Content** folder.
2. Click the **+Add** button in the top left corner of the **Content Browser**.
3. Select **New Folder** from the popup menu.
4. Name the folder *Materials.*

Now we have our folder, we can create our first material asset, which is going to be used on some of the coins on the desk. Later, we will create some additional folders to separate the different types of materials we will create (master materials and materials instances), but for now, we will create our first material in this folder to do this:

1. Right click anywhere in the **Materials** folder and select **Material** from the popup menu.
2. Call the new material asset *M_Coins.*
3. Click the **Save All** button in the top of the **Content Browser** to make sure the asset is saved.
4. Double click the **M_Coins** asset to open it in the Material Editor.

Introduction to the Material Editor

Now you have opened the M_Coins materials, you should see the material editor window, which should appear very similar to Figure 4.5. This is how all new material assets look when we create them.

The material editor window is split into four sections by default:

- **Viewport** – This is in the top left portion of the window and by default should show a gray sphere with an office building in the background. This shows us the result of our material as we create it.
- **Material Graph** – This is the main portion of the window and will include a single node with many input pins including Base Color, Metallic, Specular and so on.
- **Details Panel** – This is the bottom left portion of the window and has a second tab labeled **Parameters.** The details panel is where we can modify various settings about our material including its Material Domain, Blend Mode and Shading Model.
- **Stats Panel** – This is the bottom section of the window, underneath the graph and also has a second tab, labeled **Find Results**. Here we can see how many instructions our material has and the number of textures we've used.

Introduction to the Material Graph

The main development area of the Material Editor is called the Material Graph. In a newly created material, the graph will have only the Result Node visible, which will show the name of the material in the node title, so in our case, it should read **M_Coins**, as shown in Figure 4.5. The Result node has many potential inputs that

FIGURE 4.5   The M_Coins material open in the material editor with the default layout.

will help you create the look of a Material. We will explore many of these inputs over the coming chapter, however in this first example we will only utilize **Base Color**, **Roughness** and **Metallic**. So, what do these three input pins represent?

- **Base Color** is the overall color of a Material. It's often represented by either a Texture or a Parametric R, G, B value.
- **Roughness** controls a Materials scattering of reflected light. With a value of 0 being a mirror and a value of 1 a very rough/matte surface.
- **Metallic** allows us to control whether a Material should look like a metal or not. A value of 0 could be more useful for plastic or stone and a value of 1 could be used to represent material surfaces such as Gold or Silver. It is possible to use values in between to help replicate damaged or aged metals that might have dirt or dust on their surface.

Adding Textures to the Material

The first thing we are going to do with our material is add some textures. The project files include a lot of textures which we will apply to each of the different meshes. For the coin material we have three texture maps; a Base Color map, a merged Occlusion, Roughness, Metallic map labeled as ORM and a Normal map.

To use textures in our materials, we need to use Texture Sample nodes. These nodes contain a reference (or link) to a texture asset from your Content Browser and a selection of settings, most of which we can leave alone for now. It is, however, worth being aware of the Sampler Type.

The Sampler Type dropdown contains options which select how the selected texture is handled. The three we need to be aware of for this chapter are; Color, Normal and Linear Color. We will be using a Color sampler for our base Color texture, a Normal sampler for our Normal Map and a Linear Color sampler for our ORM texture. Typically, when you add a texture to your graph, Unreal will select the most suitable Sampler Type for your selected texture based on its Compression Group and Texture Group settings.

Base Color Texture

To begin with we are going to add the Base Color texture to the material.

1. Click the **Content Drawer** button in the bottom left of the screen, this should open a popup just like the content browser, the difference with the drawer is it only stays open while you are interacting with it. Alternatively, you can press CTRL + Space to open it.
2. Navigate to **Textures | Coins | Gold** and select the **Coin_Gold_BaseColor** texture asset so it is highlighted in the content drawer.
3. Press and hold T and then click on the material graph, this will add the highlighted texture as a **Texture Sample** node to the graph.
4. Drag from the **RGB** pin on the **Texture Sample** node and connect it to the **Base Color** pin on the result node (labeled **M_Coins**).

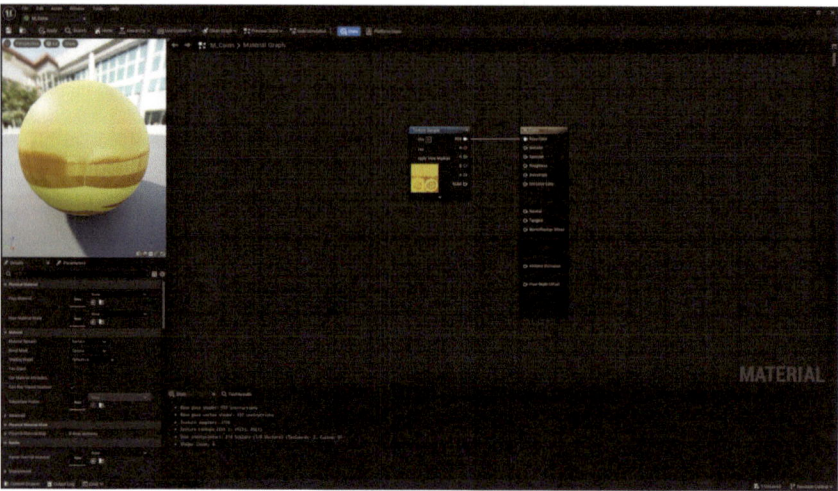

FIGURE 4.6   The M_Coins material with the base color texture added to the graph.

5. Your material should now look like the example in Figure 4.6, Save the material by clicking the Save icon in the top left corner of the material editor.

We still have a lot to add to this material, but before we add any more, let's go and test it on a mesh.

1. With the level viewport active, press 2 on the keyboard, this will jump the viewport to one of the many bookmarks we have added to the level.
2. On the right side of the desk, you will find a collection of coins next to the book, select them in the viewport, this should result in them being outlined in orange.
3. In the **Details** panel, find the **Element 0** variable in the **Materials** rollout and click the dropdown which currently says **MI_ProcGrid1**.
4. Begin typing the name of the material *M_Coins,* this should filter the list and leave you with just one material, **M_Coins**, select it.

You should see that all of the coins you selected now have the M_Coins material applied and should appear with a gold runic texture on them as shown in Figure 4.7.

With the material now applied to the meshes in the scene and confirmed to be working, we can now add the other two textures and connect them up to the material. We will start by adding the normal map and then use our merged ORM map.

Normal Map Texture

As we learned in Chapter 3, normal maps add extra lighting detail to our materials. For our coin material, we are using a normal map to enhance the design on the face of the coin, giving the visual impression of changes in height. When we use normal maps in our materials, they use a different sampler type, thankfully, because Unreal

FIGURE 4.7   The M_Coins material applied to the collection of coins on the desk.

automatically recognizes a normal map on import (typically based on file name), we don't need to change anything, but note when you do bring the texture in that the sampler type dropdown of the texture sample node, that it changes to Normal instead of Color (as used for the base color texture).

So, let's add the normal map texture to the material:

1. From the **Content Draw** (CTRL + space), drag **Coin_Gold_Normal** texture asset from the **Textures | Coins | Gold** folder into the material graph, dragging and dropping texture assets is another way to create a **Texture Sample** node.
2. Drag from the **RGB** pin on the new **Texture Sample** node and connect it to the **Normal** pin on the **M_Coins** result node.
3. Save the material.

Initially, with the normal map texture connected, you may not see much change however, if you click and drag the viewport, you should be able to rotate the view of the sphere. If you push the view upwards, you should see that the texture now appears to have depth around the runic patterns, this is the visual result of applying the normal map into the material.

USEFUL TIP

If you hold down L on your keyboard while you click and drag in the viewport, you can move the light source in the viewport, allowing you to see the effect further.

Merged (ORM) Map Texture

We also learned about merged maps in Chapter 3, discussing how they appear and what they are used for. When we add these textures to our material, we use them differently to other textures, we use the individual red (**R**), green (**G**) and blue (**B**) pins instead of the **RGB** pin. Because each texture is held in a single channel, this approach can only be used in slots which expect a grayscale image, such as roughness, metallic, occlusion, opacity, emissive power etc. The sample type for this type of texture should also change to Linear Color as opposed to Color used for the base color texture.

For the materials we are building in this book, we have decided to use three channels in the merged map textures. They are Red for Occlusion, Green for Roughness and Blue for Metallic, which is why we have labeled them with the ORM suffix, as a reminder of which channels should be connected to which input pins on the result node when building materials using these texture assets.

Let's explore how we make use of the merged map in our material:

1. Add the **Coin_Gold_ORM** texture asset to the graph as a texture sample (you can use either approach here).
2. Connect the **G** pin of the new **Texture Sample** node to the **Roughness** pin of the **M_Coins** result node.
3. Connect the **B** pin on the **Texture Sample** node to the **Metallic** pin on the result node.
4. Save the material.

With both textures now applied, head back to the viewport and look at how the coins now appear quite different to how they originally looked with just the Base Color texture, they should now have a much glossier and more metallic look to them along with the added depth to the texture caused by the normal map, as shown in Figure 4.8.

FIGURE 4.8   The coin models on the desk with the normal and ORM maps applied to the material.

Conclusion

With the merged map added to the material, we have concluded this first process. In this chapter we have added a range of different textures to a new material asset, connected the textures into the result node and applied the material to static mesh actors in the world. You should now have your first material which you have applied to the coins on the wizard's desk.

You could at this point repeat this process for lots of other texture sets and objects; however, in the next few chapters we are going to expand this material and set up more efficient ways of creating the vast number of materials we need for the wizard's desk.

Before we move on, let's check your material knowledge so far with a short quiz.

Chapter 4 Quiz

Question 1: What does a Texture Sample node do?

    a.   Provide a small section of a texture asset to use in a material.

    b.   Provide a reference to a texture asset from our projects content directory to be used in the material graph.

    c.   Provide an image of a texture to be used for reference to compare to when making a material.

Question 2: How do we add a texture to a material graph?

    a.   Dragging a texture from the Content Browser directly onto the material graph.

    b.   Adding a Texture Sample node to the graph and selecting the required texture in the Texture dropdown in the Details panel.

    c.   Selecting the texture in the Content Browser, holding down T on the keyboard and clicking in the graph.

    d.   All of the above.

Question 3: What does a normal map do?

    a.   Add additional geometry to a model to make it look better.

    b.   Add per pixel lighting information to make a model appear more detailed than it is.

    c.   Normalize the texture values to provide a better to light material.

Question 4: What textures does our merged ORM map provide?

    a.   Opacity, Roughness, Metallic

    b.   Occlusion, Roughness, Metallic

    c.   Occlusion, Redness, Metallic

    d.   Curvature, Roughness, Metallic

Answers

Question 1: b
Question 2: d
Question 3: b
Question 4: b

5

Material Instances

In this chapter, we are going to explore Material Instances, a type of asset that allows us to create variations of materials without the need to create the whole graph again. You will learn about:

- What material instances are and how we use them.
- The difference between constants and parameters.
- Material math and how we can apply it to our coin material.
- Setting up color tints and controls for roughness values.
- How to keep our material graphs tidy.

We are going to continue building on top of the coin material we produced in Chapter 4 to add features suitable for using with material instances.

What Are Material Instances?

When we build materials in Unreal Engine, we have the option to create Material Instances, this type of asset allows you to take an existing material and create versions that contain all of the same elements as the original material with the ability to change parameters such as colors, floats, Boolean values and textures which can be used as inputs into any of the material editor's nodes.

Material instances use inheritance, where a parent material passes all its properties (including all nodes, their inputs and settings) to the child material. In order to be able to change elements of the child material (or material instance) to make it look different from the parent, the parent needs to feature parameters. We can convert any node which has an input into a parameter (such as a texture in the texture sample nodes we created earlier or vector/float values in constant nodes we are going to create later in this chapter). Once converted the values become exposed in the material instance editor like those shown in Figure 5.1 where (from top to bottom) five scalar (float) parameters, a static switch (bool) parameter, three texture parameters and a vector (color) parameter are available for the user to modify, allowing them to adjust the visual result of the material instance.

Constants vs Parameters

When building materials in Unreal Engine, we need to decide what control we need to (or would benefit from) giving to artists in the team, what elements of the material

DOI: 10.1201/9781032663852-5

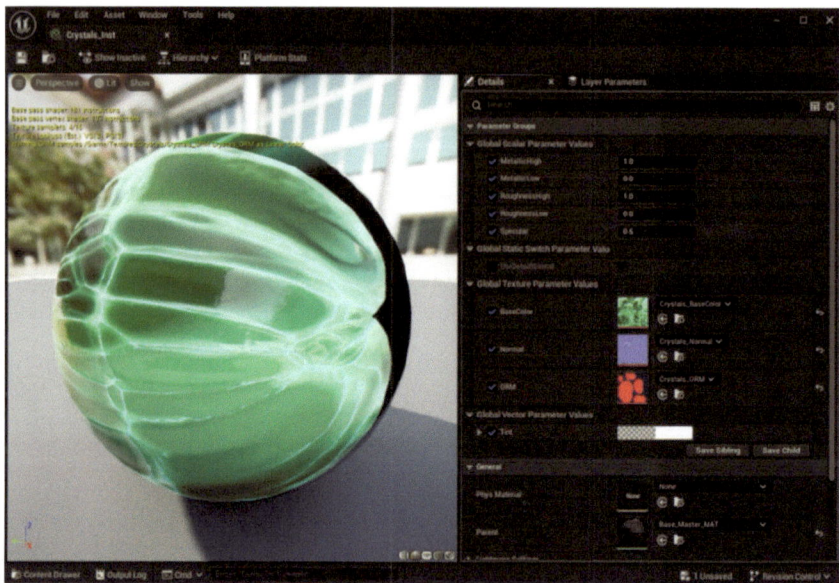

FIGURE 5.1   The Material Instance Editor showing a series of parameters which can be changed.

we want to give them access to modify, and then build these into the material graph accordingly.

Normal values in a material graph are called Constants, this is because, once created in the material, these values are set and remain the same unless you return to the graph to modify it. They are not changeable in material instances or at run time, and they don't have a name assigned to them, they are, as the name suggests, constant.

For a constant to become editable (either in a material instance or at run time), it must be converted into a parameter. Any value in a material graph, which can be set when we create materials, can be exposed to the user in a material instance. To do this, we right click on the node and choose **Convert to Parameter**.

Figure 5.2 shows each of the main node types we will be using as both constants and parameters. Note how the parameter nodes (the nodes on the bottom row) don't show their value in the top of the node, instead showing a name. This name is set when we convert the constant to a parameter but can be changed in the **Details** panel or by pressing F2 on the keyboard with the node selected.

Also in the **Details** panel of a parameter are some properties that can help us to sort the parameters when they appear in the material instance editor. The three properties we are interested in are:

- **Group** – This is a dropdown where we can select an existing group from or type into to create a new group; this allows us to separate the parameters into groups which display under different headings in the material instance editor. If this is left blank, the parameters will be sorted into type groups such as "Global Scalar Parameter Values".

FIGURE 5.2 Different constant nodes (top row) and their parameter equivalent (bottom row).

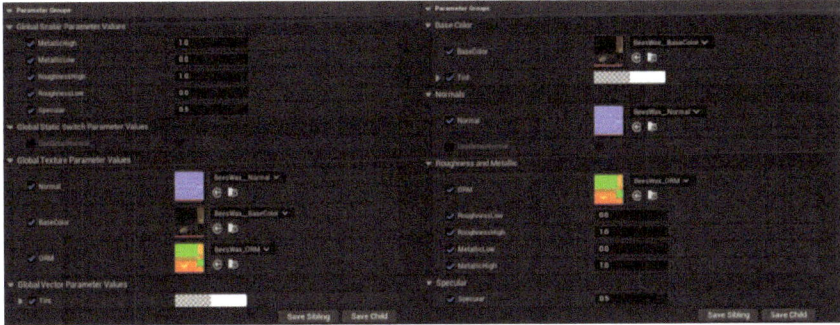

FIGURE 5.3 Automatically grouped and ordered parameters (left) and manually grouped and ordered parameters (right).

- **Sort Priority** – This integer value allows us to sort which order the parameters are listed in. The default value is 32. Parameters with higher values will appear lower in their grouped lists.
- **Desc** – This can be used to provide a tooltip to the user when they hover over the parameter name in the material instance editor. Some parameters will be obvious as to what they do, others may benefit from a little bit of explanation to ensure anyone using your materials can understand what the parameters do.

Making use of these can significantly improve the user experience of our materials. Figure 5.3 shows an automatically grouped and ordered list of parameters side by side with a manually configured list of parameters. The right side shows the effect of using the **Group** and **Sort Priority** properties.

Now that you have an idea of how material instances work, and how we can create parameters, we can modify the coin material we created in Chapter 4 to use parameters, making it possible to use the other coin textures in the **Textures** folder.

Setting up Texture Parameters

Texture Parameters enable the option for the end user of a material instance to swap out a selected texture in a material for a new texture suitable for their particular use case. This means that we can apply the same material base, via the use of material instances to objects with different UV layouts (thus requiring different textures) or simply replace the textures with a texture set with different colors or a different pattern included. To do this, we need to change our **Texture Sample** nodes into **Texture Parameters**.

1. Open the M_Coins material that we created in Chapter 4.
2. Right click the **Texture Sample** connected to the **Base Color** pin and click **Convert to Parameter**.
3. Set the parameter name as *Base Color Texture*.
4. Repeat this process for each of the other **Texture Sample** nodes, naming them *ORM Texture* and *Normal Map Texture*.
5. Click Apply and Save the material.

With the texture parameters now set up, we can check how they appear in a material instance.

1. Navigate to the **Materials** folder in the **Content Browser** where you saved the **M_Coins** material asset.
2. Right click the **M_Coins** asset and select **Create Material Instance**.
3. This should have created a new asset called **M_Coins_Inst**, rename it *MI_Coins*.

The resulting asset should look very similar to the **M_Coins** asset however while the thumbnail preview of the **MI_Coins** asset will look the same, there are a few differences within the rest of the asset icon. Note that the green line underneath the thumbnail is now slightly darker and that the asset type is shown as **Material Instance** instead of **Material** on the **M_Coins** asset.

With the asset created we can now take a look at how the parameters look within a material instance. Double click the **MI_Coins** asset and take a look, you should see the three texture parameters listed under a **Global Texture Parameter Values** section of the **Parameter Groups** rollout in the **Details** panel. This is typically on the right side of the window with a large viewport with a material ball taking up most of the window.

We have included textures for different color versions of the coin which we can use to test the material instance out.

When we create material instances, typically we would name them to make clear what the material is to be used for, for this example, we just changed the prefix from **M** for material to **MI** for material instance, now we are going to set the material instance up with a different texture, so we should first rename it before doing anything else.

1. Select the **MI_Coins** asset and rename it *MI_Coin_Silver*.
2. Open the **MI_Coin_Silver** asset.
3. Turn **ON** the check box next to **Base Color Texture.**
4. Change the texture to *Coin_Silver_BaseColor*.
5. Repeat steps 3 and 4 for the **Normal Map Texture** and **ORM Texture** selecting the *Coin_Silver_Normal* and *Coin_Silver_ORM* respectively.

You may not see much of a difference in the normal map (they are fundamentally the same texture) but you should see the preview material change significantly when swapping the ORM texture, this is because the values in the Roughness and Metallic channels of the texture are different from those in the textures for the gold coin.

The **MI_Coin_Silver** material instance can now be used in the scene. Try applying it to one of the coins on the desk…

We've also included textures for a copper coin, test your understanding and create a material instance for the copper coin, using the copper coin textures. If you are unsure, follow the last two sets of instructions but change the names and selected textures. When complete, add it to one of the coins on the desk to see the different materials you've created.

With these set up, tested and used in the scene we can now move on to more complex elements of the material, but before we do, let's go and modify the groupings for the textures so they appear in appropriately named groups in the material instance editor.

1. Open the **M_Coins** material.
2. Click on the **Base Color Texture** node and, in the **Details** panel, click in the **Group** dropdown and type *Base Color* to create a new group.
3. Repeat this for the **ORM Texture** node, creating a *Roughness and Metallic* group.
4. Repeat again for the **Normal Map Texture** node, creating a *Normals* group.

If you now check back in the material instance editor by opening either of the material instances we've created (silver and copper), you should now see each texture in its own group.

Material Math

One of the key strengths of materials in Unreal Engine is the ability to perform math operations within the materials themselves. These operations are controlled by values in the graph which, often, we expose to the end user in a material instance. These mathematical operations get applied to each pixel of a texture on a model, unless masking is used, but we won't over complicate matters with masks at this stage.

There are a lot of different math nodes which we can utilize in our materials, but we are going to focus on three of the more common approaches we might use when creating materials in this project; Add and Multiply and Linear Interpolation (Lerp).

Before we get into the depths of material math, it's important to understand how Unreal represents color values. In image editing software such as Photoshop or even Microsoft Office applications such as Word, colors are presented using RGB notation where the 256 possible values of Red, Green and Blue in a color are represented by a value between 0 and 255. Unreal also provides colors as values of RGB; however, it represents each of the channels (Red, Green and Blue) with values between 0 and 1 where the values between 0 and 1 map directly onto the 0 to 255 range normally provided in other applications. Here are some colors as represented by Photoshop and Unreal:

- Red – RGB: 255, 0, 0 | Unreal RGB: 1, 0, 0
- White – RGB: 255, 255, 255 | Unreal RGB: 1, 1, 1
- Black – RGB: 0, 0, 0 | Unreal RGB: 0, 0, 0
- Mid Gray – RGB: 128, 128, 128 | Unreal RGB: 0.5, 0.5, 0.5
- Dark Green – RGB: 7, 31, 5 | Unreal RGB: 0.027321, 0.122139, 0.019382

As you can see from the examples, some of the mappings are very easy to interpret whereas others (such as the dark green examples) can be a bit less obvious, thankfully, we don't have to work with colors in Unreal by manually typing in float values.

Now we've covered how the color values are represented in Unreal, we can start exploring the first math function, add.

Add Operations

When we do an add operation, we add the value of each channel together. The resulting color of each pixel is simply the result of adding two numbers together. Throughout this section we will include both sets of values for ease as well as hoping it will further cement the idea of how the two sets of values map onto each other.

Figure 5.4 shows a simple addition example of adding pure red (255, 0, 0 in RGB or 1, 0, 0 in Unreal RGB), pure green (0, 255, 0 or 0, 1, 0) and pure blue (0, 0, 255 or 0, 0, 1) resulting in White (255, 255, 255 or 1, 1, 1). You can see from this that each channel gets added together so for example, for the red channel, the add operation is $1+0+0=1$.

When working with addition, it is possible to exceed a value of 1 in a single channel, for example if you were to add pure red (255, 0, 0 or 1, 0, 0) to yellow (255, 255, 0 or 1, 1, 0) you would get a mathematical result of (510, 255, 0 or 2, 1, 0). We know from our understanding of color channels that each channel contains only 256 possible values (0 to 255) so what happens when we have a value which exceeds 255? Well, in Unreal Engine, the answer depends on what pin you are connecting the result to. If you are plugging this into the Base Color pin on a material, the result will simply appear as yellow as the 2 in the red channel will be automatically reduced to the limited range of 0 to 1. If, however, you choose to connect the result to the Emissive Color pin, this will accept values greater than 1 so you will get a slightly glowing yellow (a value of 1 in emissive color just results in an unlit result where that pixel doesn't respond to light or shadow).

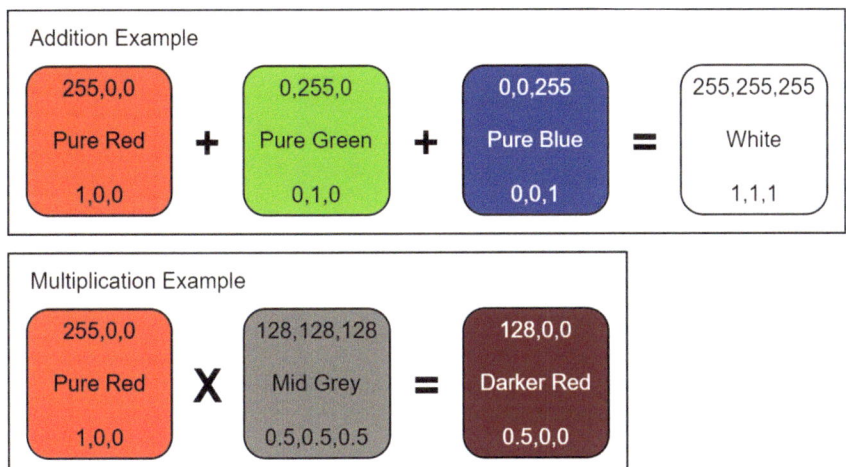

FIGURE 5.4 Material Math examples for both Add and Multiply operations.

It's best practice in situations where we are doing material math to control the output and be sure there is no risk of overpowering the values, unless we intend to. In situations such as emissive color where we need to ramp up those values to get the glow effect from the emissive, we would want to allow the values to exceed 1. In most situations however, we should consider using a Clamp node which allows us to set a maximum and minimum for the values of the result.

Multiply Operations

When multiplying two textures, or a texture and a parameter, it's important to understand what is happening. For this section, we will include both sets of values (RGB and Unreal RGB) but the multiplication is significantly easier to understand using Unreal RGB values of 0 to 1 as these are much more representative of what is actually happening because when you multiply white (255, 255, 255 or 1, 1, 1) by itself you still get the same white, not some extremely large valued result with 62025 (255 * 255) in each channel. Figure 5.4 also contains an example of a multiplication operation, showing the multiplication of pure red (255, 0, 0 in RGB or 1, 0, 0 in Unreal RGB) with a mid-gray (128, 128, 128 or 0.5, 0.5, 0.5). The resulting color is a darker red color (128, 0, 0 or 0.5, 0, 0). If you look at the Unreal values, you can see that 1 * 0.5=0.5 for the Red channel and 0 * 0.5=0 for both the Green and Blue channels.

Linear Interpolation (Lerp) Operations

Linear interpolation is the process of selecting the color of each pixel based on a weighted value, which determines how much influence each of the inputs has on the output result. Often used with a grayscale texture as a mask to provide the weighting, lerp nodes allow us to blend two textures or colors together. Like the multiply operation, for this section, we will again include both types of RGB notation; however, this is easier to consider using Unreal RGB values of 0 to 1.

Lerp nodes require three inputs (A, B and Alpha), to help explain the process, we will first consider a lerp between pure red (255, 0, 0 or 1, 0, 0) and pure green (0, 255, 0 or 0, 1, 0) with an alpha (or blend) value of 0.5. This means that for each channel of each input (pure red and pure green) is multiplied by 0.5 and then added together. So, we get a result of a greenish, yellow color (128, 128, 0 or 0.5, 0.5, 0).

If we change the alpha value to 0.75 using the same two inputs, the pure red will be multiplied by 0.25 and the pure green will be multiplied by 0.75 and the results added together. This gives an output result of a green color (64, 191, 0 or 0.25, 0.75, 0).

So far, these examples have been straight forward to see as we have been using inputs where we are always adding the multiplication result to a zero. But what about when there are multiple values in a channel to consider? For this example, we will just include the Unreal RGB to make things easier to read.

Let's consider two inputs as cyan (1, 0, 1) and yellow (1, 1, 0) with an alpha of 0.75. The alpha weighting means that the cyan channel values will be multiplied by 0.25 giving us (0.25, 0, 0.25) and the yellow channel values will be multiplied by 0.75 giving us (0.75, 0.75, 0). Adding these two results together will give us the output (1, 0.75, 0.25), a sort of beige color.

With a lerp operation, there is no risk of the values exceeding 1, assuming the input values are within the 0 to 1 range.

Now that we've explained some material math and how multiply works, we can look at implementing it into the M_Coins material.

Adding a Color Tint to the Material

With the textures all available as parameters, next we are going to build in a color tint setup to allow us to tweak the visual result provided of the Base Color texture. This approach provides the artist with a color parameter which can be used to tweak the color of the texture, in this case, the coin. When combined with a gray-scale Base Color texture, this would allow us to have any color variation of the texture we desired. As we currently have a very yellow and brown texture for our gold coin, we are going to use this approach to tone down the texture a little with a shade of gray.

We are going to be adding two nodes; a Multiply node, which performs the mathematical process on each pixel of the texture with the secondary input that will begin as a Constant 3 Vector node, which allows us to select a color value to use in the multiplication.

So, let's go back to the **M_Coins** material and add a color tint:

1. Detach the **Base Color Texture** node from the **Base Color** pin by holding down ALT and left clicking the connection line.
2. Hold down M on the keyboard and left click on the graph, this should create a **Multiply(0,1)** node, you can also do this by right clicking and typing *Multiply* or by expanding the Palette tab on the right side of the Material Editor, finding **Multiply** and dragging it onto the graph.
3. Connect the output pin from the **Multiply(0,1)** node to the **Base Color** pin on the output node.

4. Move the now disconnected **Base Color Texture** node upwards to make space below and then plug the **RGB** pin into the **A** pin on the **Multiply(0,1)** node. You should see the node's title change when you do this, to now read **Multiply(,1)**. This is because the node name represents the calculation the node is doing, where there is no number included in the name, this indicates an input has been provided via the corresponding pin.

5. Hold down 3 on the keyboard and left click on the graph, this should create a Constant 3 Vector node (which is what you would need to search for). The node will have its value in the title instead of its name, so should appear as **0,0,0** at this point.

6. Connect the white pin (RGB) of the Constant 3 Vector node into the **B** pin of the **Multiply(,1)** node. This should now change the node title to just **Multiply** now that both input pins are being utilized.

7. Double click on the Constant 3 Vector node and change the color to a mid-gray value (0.5, 0.5, 0.5). Note how when you change the value, the texture reappears on the preview sphere in the preview viewport.

8. Convert the Constant 3 Vector node to a parameter by right clicking the node and choosing **Convert to Parameter**, name it *Tint Color*. Note that this adds a fifth, gray pin to the node, this is the alpha pin. Any constant that has more than one channel will be converted to a vector parameter node with four channels.

9. Lastly, set the **Group** property of the **Tint Color** node in the **Details** panel to **Base Color** to ensure it appears in the right place in the material instance editor.

With this now added, your material graph should look like the graph shown in Figure 5.5 and the coins on the desk should appear as a darker shade of gold.

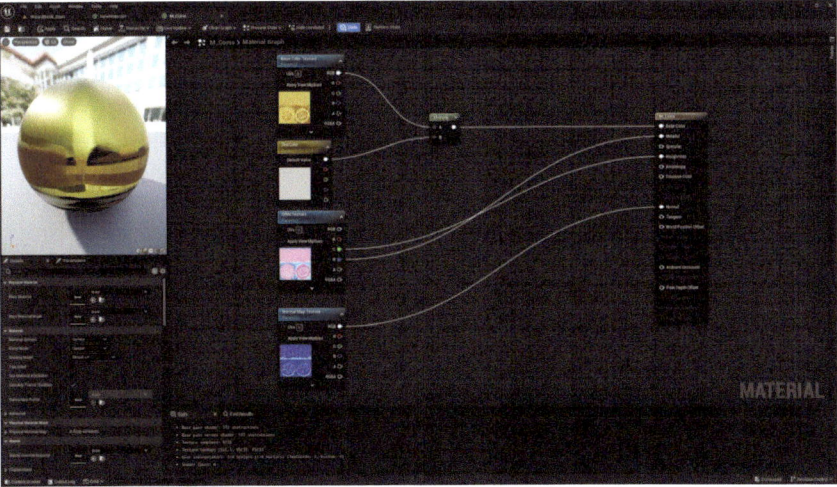

FIGURE 5.5 The M_Coins material graph with color tint added.

Take a moment to create a new material instance from the **M_Coins** material and have a play around with different values in the **Tint Color** variable, see what happens when you select something with a color, such as blue or orange, observing the effect in the viewport. You can also try swapping the **Base Color Texture** for the silver or copper versions and explore what effect the tint has on those textures. See if you can make some interesting-colored coins, you can always add the materials to the coins on the desk (or duplicate the coins if you'd like to have a wider range of different coin variations).

Controlling the Roughness Values

The final element we are going to add to this material is the ability to control the minimum and maximum roughness values which appear on the model. Different pieces of software display roughness values differently, so it's quite common to have artists complain that their materials don't look the same when they set them up in Unreal, for this reason, as technical artists, we look to add in control for how the roughness element of our material looks, using the channel output as an alpha mask instead of a texture.

For this addition, we are going to use two scalar values, these are single channel float variables inside the material graph which we can set to have any decimal value.

To add roughness control using a lerp node we need to:

1. Add a Lerp node to the graph, this can be done by holding down L on the keyboard and clicking or adding from either the **Palette** panel or right click popup.
2. Add two Constant nodes by either searching or holding down 1 on the keyboard and clicking.
3. Connect the two new Constant nodes, which will display on screen at this point as **0** nodes, to the **A** and **B** pins of the **Lerp(0,1,0.5)** node. Notice again how the name of the node updates with each connection we make.
4. Convert the constant which is connected to the **A** pin to a parameter by right clicking the node and choosing **Convert to Parameter**, name it *Roughness Min*.
5. Set the value of the constant, which is connected to the **B** pin, to 1.0 and convert it to a parameter. Name this parameter *Roughness Max*.
6. Connect the **G** pin of the **ORM Texture** node, into the **Alpha** pin of the **Lerp(,,0.5)** node.
7. Connect the output pin of the **Lerp** node to the **Roughness** pin on the result node.
8. Set the Group on both the **Roughness Min** and **Roughness Max** nodes to **Roughness and Metallic**.
9. To ensure the correct sorting order the material instance editor, set the following **Sort Priority** variables by selecting the node and typing a number into the property in the **Details** panel:
   - **ORM Texture** = *1*
   - **Roughness Min** = *2*
   - **Roughness Max** = *3*

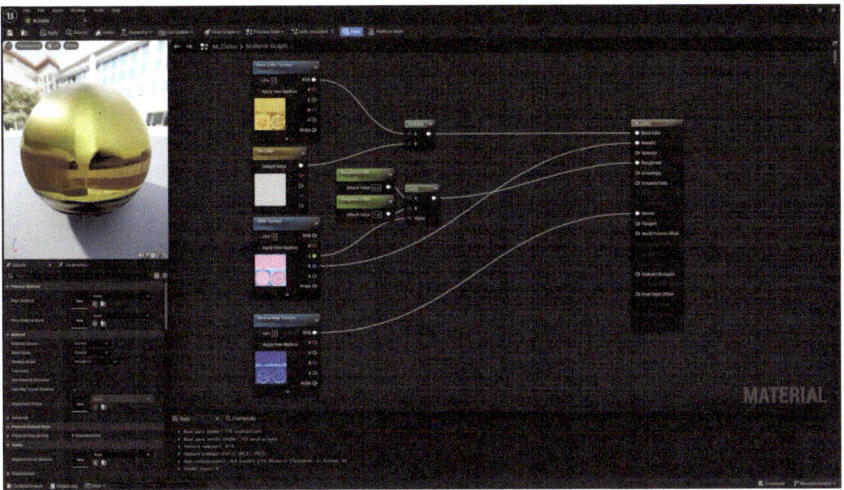

FIGURE 5.6   The coin material with the roughness controls added.

You should now have a graph which looks something like the material shown in Figure 5.6.

Now would be a good time to go and re-open some of the material instances you've created for coins so far. Play around with the **Roughness Min** and **Roughness Max** to see what effect they have on how the coins appear in the world.

As you can probably see, the material graph for our coin material is beginning to get a little messy, even with a relatively small number of nodes and connections. So, before we expand the material graph any further let's explore a few ways in which we can keep our materials tidy.

Comments and Reroute Nodes

When creating materials, it's important to try and keep them easy to read for other users and generally tidy. Two of the methods we can use to do this are comments and reroute nodes.

Comments allow us to group nodes together and label them. Reroute nodes allow us to add anchor points into a connection so that we can control its direction better, typically to prevent the connection from passing behind other nodes or to try and straighten connections out to make the graph more readable.

To add a comment box, we simply select some nodes and press C on the keyboard. Let's add some comments to the **M_Coins** graph.

1. Select the **Base Color Texture**, **Tint Color** and **Multiply** nodes by either dragging a marquee selection box with the mouse or by clicking each one while holding down CTRL.
2. Move the selected nodes to an area of their own and press C.
3. Type *Base Color, Texture and Tint* as the name of the comment.

4. Select the **Base Color, Texture and Tint** comment box and in the **Details** panel, change the **Comment Color** to *black*.
5. Turn **ON** the checkbox for **Show Bubble When Zoomed**.

You should now have a black comment box wrapped around the three nodes, clearly labeling the section of the graph. If you zoom out using the scroll wheel on your mouse, you will see a bubble popup appear as the text on the top of the comment becomes unreadable. This just helps you to navigate the larger graphs, even though our graph is quite simple, it's worth getting into the habit of turning this option on.

COMMENT BOX COLORS

Comment boxes can be created in any color you like. As default they are white, and my personal preference is to typically change them to black as I prefer how they look. In more complex materials or Blueprint graphs, color coding different sections of the graph will help to easily navigate and organize the graph, making them much easier to revisit later and find what you are looking for.

Before we add a comment around the roughness controls, let's try adding some reroute nodes to help tidy up the crossing connections. To create a reroute node, simply double click on any connection line, this will create a circle in the connection which appears the same as an output pin on a node.

Rather than explain this step by step (which could be a bit complicated to follow), take a look at Figure 5.7 and use comments and reroute nodes to lay out your material in a similar way, the aim here is to keep the graph tidy and easy to read.

FIGURE 5.7 The M_Coins material graph with comments and reroute nodes added.

Conclusion

With the material now tidied up, we have come to the end of this chapter. In this chapter, we've explored material instances and their uses as well as some aspects of material math. This has allowed us to expand our previously simple, non-reusable coin material to include parameters to allow us to choose different textures, tint the base color texture and control the maximum and minimum roughness values to adjust how the material appears using the parameters inside a range of different material instances. Let's check what you've learned.

Chapter 5 Quiz

Question 1: What is a material instance?

    a.   The state of a material at a point in time.

    b.   A duplicate of a material with all the same nodes.

    c.   A child of a material which inherits all the properties of the parent.

Question 2: What is our recommended prefix for the name of a material instance asset?

    a.   MI_

    b.   M_

    c.   MatInst_

Question 3: Which of these is the correct RGB result we will get when we multiply pure blue (0, 0, 255) and mid-gray (128, 128, 128)?

    a.   (0, 0, 128)

    b.   (128, 128, 255)

    c.   (255, 128, 128)

    d.   (128, 0, 0)

    e.   (1, 0, 0)

Question 4: What are comments used for?

    a.   Leaving fun little messages for coworkers to find.

    b.   Making a nice pattern in the material graph.

    c.   Drawing boxes around nodes to stop them escaping.

    d.   Grouping and organizing the material graph.

Answers

Question 1: c

Question 2: a

Question 3: a

Question 4: d

6

Master Materials

In Chapter 5, we built the example material for the coins to be usable with material instances by building in well labeled and sorted parameters. These parameters are the building blocks of the core ideology of Master Materials, in this chapter, we are going to be exploring that further, you will learn about:

- Additional techniques of how we design materials for others.
- Optimizing material usage by maximizing the reusability of material with instances.
- Working with tiling materials.

At the end of the chapter, you'll be all set up to create all of the material instances needed to fully texture the Wizard's Desk environment.

An Introduction to Master Materials

Master materials allow us to create a single-parent material, which can be used for lots of different materials in a scene. Master Materials are often very powerful and flexible materials with sections of their graph controlled with Boolean variables to be able to turn different sections on and off, providing control and usability but also efficiency at runtime.

When working on large projects, Master Materials are an invaluable resource to ensure a consistent art style between all materials, with materials for most objects having the same controls and functionality, and using the same inputs so assets can be produced in DCC packages, exported with their textures and new material instances can then create with ease, without the need to create new material graphs each time.

Typically, when working with Master Materials, we will create a Master Material for each of the different Blend Modes in our project. We are going to be creating Master Materials for Glass (Translucent), Subsurface and Tiling Materials as well as re-working the coin material as an Opaque, Base Master Material.

Apart from subsurface, we could build all of the possible features of these into one single master material, opting to use a translucent blend mode and setting the opacity to 1 when wanting to create an opaque material, so why don't we? Well, this approach would mean that every material we make is calculating translucency, even if the material is opaque, wasting a lot of memory and render time. It's important as a Technical Artist, to identify not only when things are good ideas and will improve things but where an idea will have a negative effect on the product, in this case, using a single master material for all those options would be a bad idea and cause a significant waste of precious resources.

DOI: 10.1201/9781032663852-6

In Chapter 4 we created the material for a coin which, in Chapter 5 we modified so it could be used with Material Instances. While we could then use it as a master material of sorts, it's not quite flexible enough to support the wide array of opaque materials in the Wizard's Desk environment. The first thing we are going to do is set up a folder for our master materials, move and rename our coin material ready to enhance it with extra features.

1. In the **Content Browser**, navigate to the folder **Content | Materials**.
2. Right click and choose **New Folder**, name the new folder: *Master*.
3. Select the **M_Coins** material, press F2, rename it: *M_BaseMaster*.
4. Drag the **M_BaseMaster** material onto the **Master** folder and on the popup, select **Move Here**.
5. Create a second new folder and call it *Instances*.
6. Move any Material Instances you might have created during Chapter 5 into the new **Instances** folder.

With our folders tidied up and our existing material renamed, let's look at adding more controls and flexibility...

Designing Materials for Others

When creating materials, we may want to work with most of the pins available on the Material Output node. So, when creating Master Materials, we need to ask ourselves a key question, "Will the materials made using instances of this material need to control this?" If the answer is yes, we need to build in control. So, we have to think about what the team may need to be able to prepare their assets in the engine using this Master Material.

Our M_BaseMaster material currently has the following:

- Texture Inputs for the following:
  - Base Color
  - ORM
  - Normal
- Minimum and Maximum Roughness

So, when we consider the materials required for the Wizard's Desk scene, we need to think about the requirements of the scene, for example, we need to be able to support metallic and non-metallic objects and, similar to the roughness, we may want to control the minimum and maximum values. We may also want to control the specular value for some objects too.

Let's begin improving the Master Material by adding in the controls for the Metallic. For this we are going to build an almost identical solution to the Roughness controls from Chapter 5 so rather than creating it all again, node by node, let's look at duplicating what we have, renaming, and setting all the parameters correctly to ensure everything works and appears in the correct place in the Material Instance editor.

Duplicating the Roughness Controls

Firstly, we need to duplicate the nodes (and the comment box) from the Roughness Controls

1. In the **Content Browser**, navigate to the folder **Content | Materials | Master**.
2. Open the M_BaseMaster Material.
3. Select the **Roughness Controls** comment box, all three nodes from within the comment, and the reroute node which is connected to the **Alpha** pin on the **Lerp** node.
4. Move your mouse to an empty area of the Material Graph and press CTRL+D, this should duplicate all of the select nodes to where you placed your mouse.

Renaming the Nodes

With everything duplicated, next we want to rename everything and update the label on the comment box.

1. Select the duplicated **Roughness Controls** comment.
2. Rename it *Metallic Controls* either by changing the **Text** property in the **Details** panel or by pressing F2.
3. Select the duplicated **Roughness Min** and **Roughness Max** nodes.
4. Rename them to *Metallic Min* and *Metallic Max* respectively either by changing the **Parameter Name** property in the **Details** panel or by pressing F2.

Sorting and Ordering the Parameters

Previously, we explored the ability to group and order the parameters we create in the Material Instance Editor and set these up for the **ORM Texture** and the **Roughness Min** and **Roughness Max** controls. Because we have duplicated the nodes, the Metallic and Roughness controls are set to the same **Sort Priority** with both Min nodes being set to 2 and both Max nodes being set to 3. This isn't going to order the value in a sensible way for other people to use, so we need to set the priorities as follows:

1. ORM Texture
2. Metallic Min
3. Metallic Max
4. Roughness Min
5. Roughness Max

To set a priority, follow these steps, using the values from the above list:

1. Click the node you wish to set the priority on.
2. In the **Details** panel, set the **Sort Priority** property to the desired position.

You should only need to modify the value on the Roughness nodes however if you didn't do this during Chapter 5, set the value on all five nodes, once complete, we can look at plugging the new Metallic Controls in.

Connecting in the Metallic Controls

With the nodes now all set up with the correct parameters set, we can plug it all in. This will result in needing to move the current nodes in the graph around a bit to make space. Because the **Metallic** pin on the Material Output Node is higher than the **Roughness** pin, it makes sense to place the new **Metallic Controls** above the **Roughness Controls.**

1. Rearrange the nodes and comment boxes so they are laid out similar to the material graph shown in Figure 6.1.
2. Connect the **B** pin of the **ORM Texture** to the reroute node inside the **Metallic Controls** comment.
3. Add some reroute nodes and resize the comment boxes to clean things up, again, use Figure 6.1 as reference.

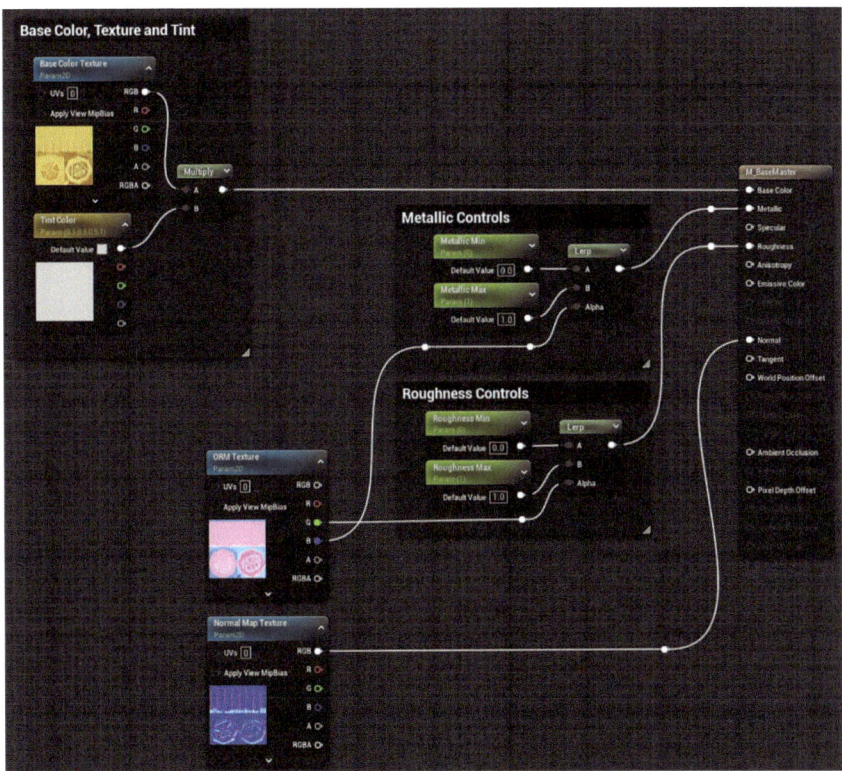

FIGURE 6.1   The M_BaseMaster material with metallic controls added.

4. Connect the output pin of the **Lerp** node inside the **Metallic Controls** comment to the **Metallic** pin on the Material Output Node.

Adding Specular Control

To control the specular input, we are simply going to use a single float parameter called Specular. Following the approach from above, we will place this between the two current sets of controls and place a comment around it for easy reading later.

1. Hold down 1 and click in the graph, this will create a float value node labeled **0**.
2. Right click the new node and choose **Convert to Parameter**.
3. Name the new node *Specular*.
4. In the **Details** panel, set the following:
   - **Default Value**=0.5
   - **Slider Min**=0
   - **Slider Max**=1
   - **Group**=*Specular* (you will need to type this in the box to create a new group)
5. Make space between the **Metallic Controls** and **Roughness Controls** comment boxes and move the Specular node in between them.
6. Connect the output pin of the **Specular** node to the **Specular** pin on the Material Output Node.
7. With the **Specular** node selected, press C to add a comment box, label it *Specular Controls*.
8. In keeping with the other comment boxes, set the **Comment Color** to Black in the **Details** panel.
9. Rearrange the graph so it is tidy, refer to Figure 6.2 as an example, you may need to add some reroute nodes.

USEFUL TIP

If you want to align nodes and reroute nodes easily, you can select multiple nodes and press Q on the keyboard, this will snap all connections on selected nodes to be straight. There are other alignment options in the **Alignment** section. Right click menu such as SHIFT+A which will align selected nodes vertically.

With the specular controls setup, we are going to move on to creating a new master material, this time for tiling materials, we will then return to this base master to add in a detail normal system which utilizes the tiling material approach.

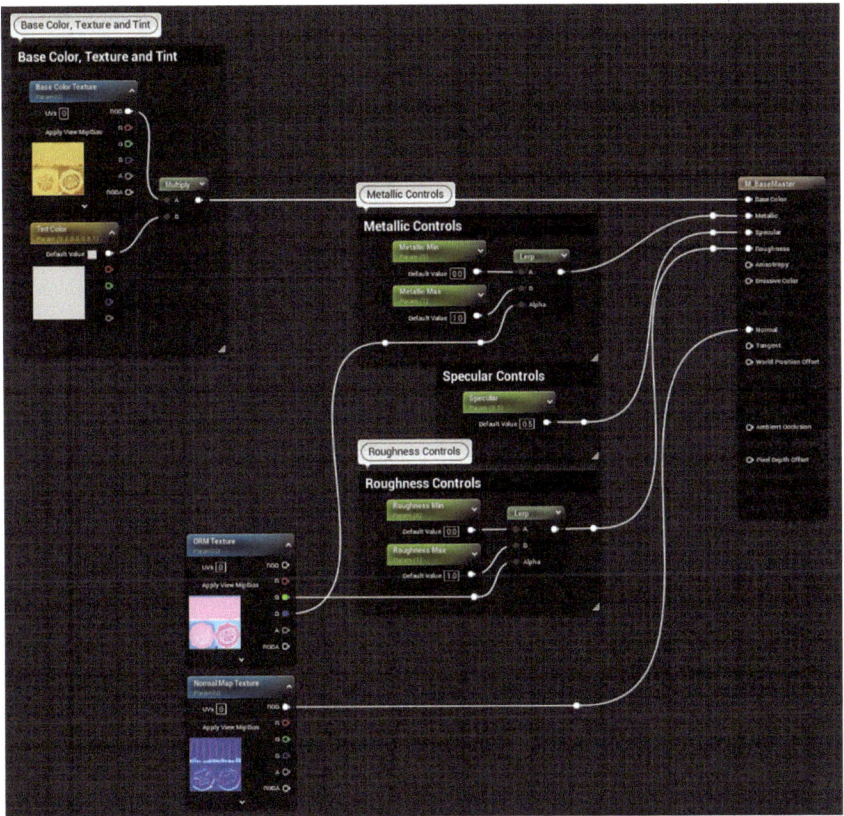

FIGURE 6.2   The M_BaseMaster material with specular controls added.

Building a Master Material for Tiling

Before extending the functionality of the Base Master Material, we are going to look at how we can control tiling in a material, and build a new master material specifically for this purpose. We are going to build the tiling material using the existing Base Master Material as a start point, so firstly, let's duplicate that and rename it.

1. In the **Content Browser**, navigate to the folder **Content | Materials | Master**.
2. Right click the **M_BaseMaster** and select **Duplicate**.
3. Name the new material *M_TilingMaster*.

With the material created, let's explore what we mean when we talk about tiling materials.

Tiling materials are used to texture large surfaces where a repeating pattern is required, such as floors or walls, or where a surface we are representing has a common pattern across multiple objects and surfaces, such as wooden items, where our textures would represent the grain of the wood.

For a material to work as a tiling material, any textures must be repeatable in both the *x* and *y* axis without any seams and anyone viewing the scene, can't identify where the edges of the texture are.

There are two significant benefits to working with tiling texture / materials. Firstly, when we unwrap objects, we don't need to worry about packing the UV into the 0–1 space of a traditional texture, we simply unwrap the object, ensuring that all of the faces have the same texel ratio and a texture appears the same size on all sections of the model. The second benefit is that we can use a library of tiling materials and they will all display correctly on the model.

When we do swap materials however, we might find that the new material is too large, or too small and that we want to scale the repeating pattern (whatever it might be) up or down, and it's that control that we look to build into our master materials, allowing an instance of a material to change the scale of a tiling texture.

We control the scale of the tiling texture using three nodes, which can be seen in Figure 6.3. The three nodes are:

- **Texture Coordinate Node** – These are labeled as TexCoord[0] where the 0 denotes which Coordinate Index we are applying the scale to, as models can have more than one unwrap applied. This is useful if you want to overlay a tiling texture on top of a normal unwrap.
- **Float Parameter** – This is used to control the size, higher numbers will increase the size of the UVs, reducing the visual size of any patterns in the texture, and inversely, numbers lower than 1 will make the visible pattern larger as the UVs are scaled down.
- **Multiply** – The multiply node is used to do the calculation, taking the UVW coordinate of each vertex on the unwrap and multiplying it by the float parameter. So a vertex on the unwrap which is positioned at 1,1 when multiplied by 2 will then be positioned at 2,2. This doubles the size of the unwrap, halving the size of the visible pattern.

We can use this approach any time we use a texture, but it's important to remember that we are doing this calculation inside the material, this does not modify the original meshes UVW unwrap, instead just manipulating it when applying the texture in the material.

Now let's move on to setting up tiling in the new material.

1. Open the new **M_TilingMaster** material.
2. To the left of all of the current nodes, create a Texture Coordinate by right clicking and searching for *Texture Coordinate*. This will create a new node labeled **TexCoord[0]**.

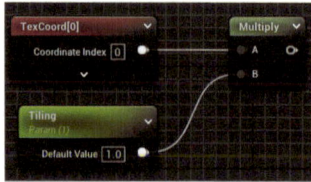

FIGURE 6.3 The tiling controls section of the M_TilingMaster material.

3. Create a new Multiply node by holding down M and clicking in the graph, to the right of the **TexCoord[0]** node.

4. Create a new float parameter by holding down 1 and clicking in the graph below the **TexCoord[0]** node and then convert it to a parameter (right click | **Convert to Parameter**) and call it *Tiling*.

5. Set the **Default Value** of the **Tiling** parameter to *1.0* in the **Details** panel.

6. In the **Group** parameter, type *Tiling* to put this control in a new group.

7. Connect the three nodes together with the **TexCoord[0]** node connected to the **A** pin of the **Multiply(0,1)** node, and the Tiling output connected to the **B** pin as shown in Figure 6.3.

8. Wrap the nodes in a comment box by pressing C, label the comment *Tiling Controls* and set the **Comment Color** to Black in the **Details** panel.

9. Connect the output pin of the **Multiply** node in the **Tiling Controls** to the **UVs** pin on each of the three textures (**Base Color Texture**, **ORM Texture** and **Normal Map Texture**).

10. Move the nodes so the connections are tidy.

With the new tiling master built, let's create a material instance which uses tiling and apply it to the floor in the scene.

1. In the **Content Browser**, navigate to the folder **Content | Materials | Master**.

2. Right click the **M_TilingMaster** and select **Create Material Instance**.

3. Name the new material *MI_StoneFloor*.

4. Drag the **MI_StoneFloor** Material Instance into the **Instances** folder and choose to **Move Here** from the popup.

5. Double click the **MI_StoneFloor** asset to open it in the Material Instance Editor.

6. Open the **Content Drawer** (CTRL+Space) and navigate to **Content | Textures | StoneFloor**.

7. Use the textures to set the texture parameters of the material instance by first clicking the checkbox next to a parameter and then dragging from the **Content Drawer** onto the texture icon. Set them as follows:

   a. **Base Color Texture=StoneFloor_BaseColor**

   b. **Normal Map Texture=StoneFloor_Normal**

   c. **ORM Texture=StoneFloor_ORM**

The settings for the material instance should now look like those shown in Figure 6.4.
Before we set the tiling, let's apply the material to the floor mesh so we can see the effect of the tiling control in the world.

1. In the viewport, click on the floor, it should be called **StoneFloor_Mesh**.

2. In the **Content Browser** navigate to **Content | Materials | Instances** and select the **MI_StoneFloor** material.

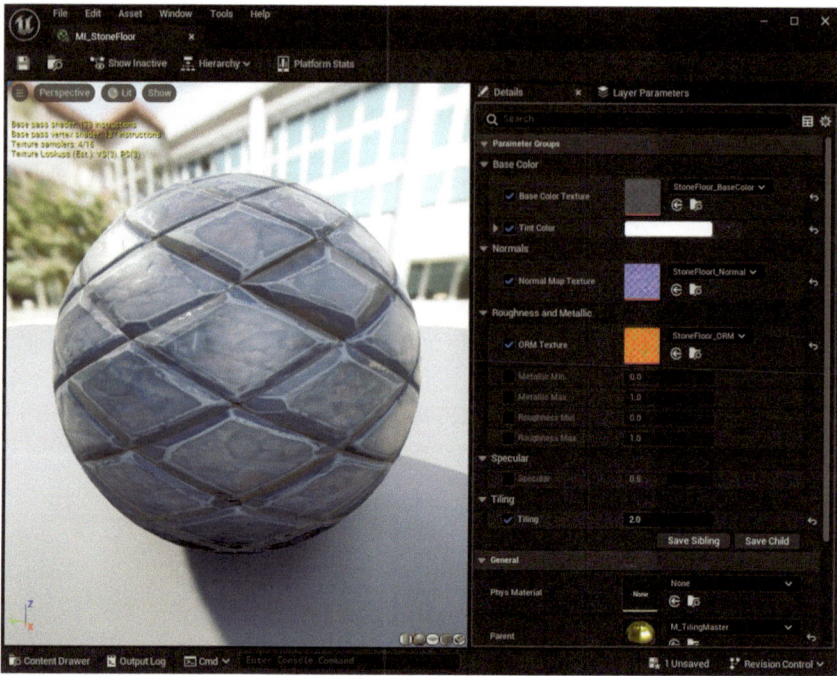

FIGURE 6.4   The tiling floor material MI_StoneFloor in the Material Instance Editor.

3. In the **Details** panel, find the **Element 0** material.
4. Click the "Use Selected Asset from Content Browser" button, the icon for this looks like an arrow in a circle. This should apply the MI_StoneFloor material to the floor mesh.

You should now see the floor looks like it is made of square stone tiles, these are a bit too big, so we can now use our tiling controls to make them smaller.

1. Open the **MI_StoneFloor** material instance again.
2. Turn on the checkbox for **Tiling**.
3. Set the **Tiling** value to *2.0*.

If you look in the viewport again now, you should now see that the stone tiles are much smaller. Feel free to explore different values and see what effect they have on how the floor feels within the room. The comparison between the two settings can be seen in Figure 6.5.

Adding in a Detail Normal Map

Detail Normal Maps, sometimes referred to as Detail Normals for short, are tiling Normal Maps which are applied to models to provide an additional level of high frequency surface detail that would be otherwise impossible to achieve using a standard

FIGURE 6.5   The tiling floor material shown with Tiling set to 1.0 (left) and 2.0 (right).

Normal Map due to restrictions with texture resolutions. The purpose of the detail we add with a detail normal is to add detail when the surface is viewed up close. A detail normal map shouldn't detract from the visual quality of the surface when it is viewed at a distance.

For the detail normal section, we are going to be replicating the tiling controls and also utilize two new nodes, these are:

- **Blend Angle Corrected Normals** – This node allows us to combine two normal maps. The top pin, labeled BaseNormal (V3) is typically used for our baked normal which matches the other textures in the material. The other pin, labeled AdditionalNormal (V3) is the normal map which we want to blend into the base normal, which in this case is our tiling, detail normal map.
- **Flatten Normal** – This node uses a float input (which we will set up as a parameter) to control the strength of the effect of a normal map. The input is labeled as Flatness (S) because the effect of lowering the value to 0 will result in a flat normal result which when combined with the blend node above, will result in no additional normal map information being added. Values below 0 (so negative values) will flip the normal map taking any raised detail and having it become a recess. High values, either positive or negative will result in an odd visual result so should be avoided. You will see some implementations of the flatten normal with a one-minus node to flip Epic's implementation when merging normal maps.

The detail normal map section of the material also gives us a good opportunity to explore how to turn sections of a material on or off when they aren't needed. To do this, we use a Switch Parameter, because that is precisely what it does, it selects from either it's True or False inputs, and any node that is connected to the unselected input then becomes inactive, removing it from the list of instructions and removing any variables from the list in the Material Instance editor ensuring only variables which have an effect on the end result are shown to the user.

We are going to add the ability to use a Detail Normal Map to both our Tiling Master and our Base Master materials, as we have just created the material for the stone floor, we will continue working on the Tiling Master...

1. If you haven't already got it open, navigate to **Materials | Master** and open the M_TilingMaster material.
2. Before we start adding new nodes, select the **Normal Map Texture** node and set the **Sort Priority** to *1* in the **Details** Panel. This is in preparation for expanding the controls in the Normals section of the Material Instance Editor.
3. Detach the **Normal Map Texture** from the Material Output Node by holding down ALT and clicking the connection line.
4. Drag back from the **Normal** pin on the Material Output Node and add a *Switch Parameter*, call it *Use Detail Normal*. The node will show an error when created, this is just because it needs both pins connecting, the error will disappear as we progress.
5. With the **Use Detail Normal** node selected, in the **Details** panel, set the **Group** to **Normals** using the dropdown and set the **Sort Priority** to *2*.
6. Connect the **False** pin of the **Use Detail Normal** node to the **RGB** pin of the **Normal Map Texture** node.
7. From the **True** pin on the **Use Detail Normal**, drag out and add a *Blend Angle Corrected Normals* node by searching for it in the popup.
8. Connect the **BaseNormal(V3)** pin on the **BlendAngleCorrectedNormals** node to the **RGB** pin on the **Normal Map Texture** node.
9. Add some reroute nodes to tidy up the appearance of the additional nodes.

Now that we've added in the switch and the node to be able to blend two normal maps together, we can now add in the detail normal texture and connect it up. We will also add the ability to adjust the strength of the Detail Normal Map using a Flatten Normal node.

1. Add a new *Texture Sample Parameter 2D* node and call it *Detail Normal*.
2. Select the **Detail Normal** node and in the **Details** panel, set the **Detail Normal** parameter to *Landscape_Mud_Normal* by clicking on the dropdown and typing in the search box.
3. Set the **Sort Priority** to 3.
4. Place the **Detail Normal** node directly below the **Normal Map Texture** node.
5. Duplicate the **Tiling Controls** section of the material, rename the comment *Detail Normal Tiling Controls*.
6. Rename the **Tiling** parameter to *DetailNormalTiling*.
7. Set the **Group** to **Normals** and set the **Sort Priority** to *4*.
8. Connect the output pin of the **Multiply** node to the **UVs** pin of the **Detail Normal** node.

9. Drag from the **RGB** pin of the **Detail Normal** node and add a *Flatten Normal* node.

10. Hold down 1 and Click on the graph to add a Float node, right click it and select **Convert to Parameter**, name it *Detail Normal Flatness*.

11. Set the **Group** of the **Detail Normal Flatness** to **Normals** using the drop-down in the **Details** panel and set the **Sort Priority** to *5*.

12. Connect the output pin of the **Detail Normal Flatness** node to the **Flatness (S)** pin of the **FlattenNormal** node.

13. Connect the **Result** pin of the **FlattenNormal** node to the **AdditionalNormal (V3)** pin of the **BlendAngleCorrectedNormals** node.

14. Wrap all of the Normal Map elements in a new comment box, label it *Normal Map and Detail Normals* and set the **Comment Color** to Black in the **Details** panel.

With the final step complete, you should have a comment box which looks something like Figure 6.6. If you need to rearrange things to tidy the graph up, do so before moving on.

Now that we've built a detail normal section of a material graph in the Tiling Master, we can reuse it on our Base Master, there are some technical approaches to reusing sections of material graphs including Material Functions, we will explore this in the second book of this series, so for now, we will just use Copy and Paste to duplicate the nodes between the two master materials.

1. In the M_TilingMaster material, drag a marquee select around the entire **Normal Map and Details Normal** comment box, this should select the comment box and all of the nodes inside.

2. Press CTRL+C to copy the nodes.

3. In the M_BaseMaster material, delete the **Normal Map Texture** node.

4. Press CTRL+V to paste the nodes into the base material graph.

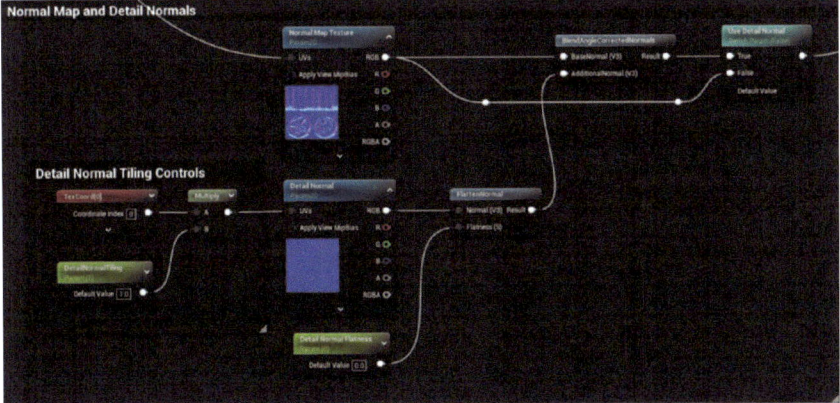

FIGURE 6.6 The Normal Map and Detail Normals section of the M_TilingMaster material.

5. Connect the output pin of the **Use Detail Normal** node to the **Normal** pin on the Material Output node.

With that complete, you should now have two master materials, both with controls for using a Tiling Detail Normal map.

Additional Master Materials

With the base master and tiling master materials completed, there are four more master materials that we need to create in order to create all of the required material instances for the Wizard's Desk scene. We need materials that work with emissive textures, subsurface scattering and translucency. This section of the chapter is going to take you through creating three master material to support those requirements, the first two (emissive and subsurface) we are going to build on the existing base master material, making some additions and changes to material parameters, for the translucent materials, we are going to create a much more parametric driven material to provide the control we need, we will then modify that for thin translucent materials using a different shading model. We are also going to create a quick bespoke material for our spiderwebs. Let's get started with the Emissive Master.

Creating the Emissive Master Material

For this master material, we are going to start with a duplicate of the base master:

1. In the **Content Browser**, navigate to the folder **Content | Materials | Master**.
2. Right click the **M_BaseMaster** and select **Duplicate**.
3. Name the new material *M_EmissiveMaster*.

With the material created, we can now go and add in the emissive setup.

1. Open the **M_EmissiveMaster** material asset.
2. Move the material output node to the right to give yourself a bit of space to add the new nodes.
3. Start by adding a new *Texture Sample Parameter 2D* node, call it *Emissive Texture*.
4. Select the **Emissive Texture** node and in the **Details** panel, set the **Emissive Texture** parameter to *Wand_Emissive* by clicking on the dropdown and typing in the search box. This is just one of the emissive textures we've included in the project.
5. Set the **Group** to *Emissive* by typing it in the box, creating a new group and then set the **Sort Priority** to 1.
6. Hold down 1 and click to create a new float node, right click it and **Convert to Parameter**, name it *Emissive Strength*.
7. In the **Details** panel, set the **Group** to **Emissive** from the dropdown and set the **Sort Priority** to 2.

8. Hold down M and click to create a new **Multiply(0,1)** node. Connect the **RGB** pin of the **Emissive Texture** node to the **A** pin of the **Multiply(0,1)** node and then connect the **Emissive Strength** node to the **B** pin.
9. Connect the output pin of the **Multiply** node to the **Emissive Color** pin of the Material Output Node.
10. Wrap the new nodes up in a comment box as before, labeling this one as *Emissive Controls.*
11. Save the Material.

This is all we need to do for the Emissive Master Material however it is worth noting that, with the current texture and Emissive Strength value, we won't see much of an emissive effect on the material preview. If you want to see the emissive effect stronger, temporarily increase the **Emissive Strength Default Value**, or create a Material Instance and test the value out there. By setting the **Emissive Strength** to really high values such as 200, you should witness a very bright section of the material. Remember to return the **Default Value** of the **Emissive Strength** node back to *1.0* if you have tested this in the Material Editor as opposed to on a Material Instance.

Creating the Subsurface Master Material

For the subsurface master, we want to create a material suitable for thin or fibrous cloth and the wax candles in the scene. For this we are going to use the Subsurface Profile shading model that we briefly mentioned in Chapter 4.

Creating this material will again use a duplicate of the Base Master and only needs us to change the Shading Model and add one additional node:

1. In the **Content Browser**, navigate to the folder **Content | Materials | Master.**
2. Right click the **M_BaseMaster** and select **Duplicate**.
3. Name the new material *M_SubsurfaceMaster.*
4. Open the new **M_SubsurfaceMaster** material in the material editor.
5. Select the Material Output Node and in the **Details** Panel, change the **Shading Model** from **Default Lit** to **Subsurface Profile**.
6. Hold down 1 and click to create a new float node, right click it and **Convert to Parameter**, name it *Subsurface Scattering Strength.*
7. In the **Details** panel, Set:
   a. **Default Value** to *1.0.*
   b. **Group** to *Subsurface Scattering* by typing it into the box.
   c. **Sort Priority** to *1.*
8. Connect the output pin of the **Subsurface Scattering Strength** node to the **Opacity** pin of the Material Output Node.

As we've only added a single node, adding a comment box is a bit unnecessary (which we have done previously for the Specular Controls), instead, we can add a comment to the node itself which will appear as a bubble.

1. Right click the **Subsurface Scattering Strength** node and in the **Node Comment** type *Subsurface*.
2. Click the Drawing Pin icon on the bubble to ensure that the bubble stays readable as we zoom in and out.

With that complete, we can now move on to our last Master Material.

Creating the Translucent Master

For the translucent master material, we are going to create a new material and rather than walk you through every step, for this material we will explore the new nodes used and the how to set the correct material parameters, but you will build the material simply by following what you see in Figure 6.7 which shows the finished M_TranslucentMaster.

For this material we are going to be using a Fresnel node. The Fresnel node allows us to represent the way light reflects off a surface at different angles by providing us with a mask which we can use to determine a falloff of reflections, transparency or other elements of our material. The Fresnel effect is why we see what appears to be a lighter almost halo-like outline on surfaces such as car paint and glass.

Before you begin building the material based on Figure 6.7, we need to create the new material and setup the correct Blend Mode:

1. In the **Content Browser**, navigate to the folder **Content | Materials | Master**.
2. Right click and choose **Material** to create a new material.
3. Name it *M_TranslucentMaster*.
4. Double click the **M_TranslucentMaster** asset to open it in the material editor.
5. In the **Details** panel, set the **Blend Mode** to **Translucent**.
6. Scroll down to the **Translucency** section of the **Details** panel and set the following parameters:
   a. **Screen Space Reflections** to True
   b. **Lighting Mode** to **Surface ForwardShading**
   c. **Apply Cloud Fogging** to True
   d. **Computer Fog Per Pixel** to True
   e. **Output Depth and Velocity** to True
7. Expand the **Advanced** section and set the following:
   a. **Responsive AA** to True
   b. **Translucency Pass** to **Before DOF**
8. Scroll down to the **Refraction** section and set **Refraction Method** to **Index of Refraction**.
9. Save the Material
10. Following the example in Figure 6.7, create the variety of nodes shown.

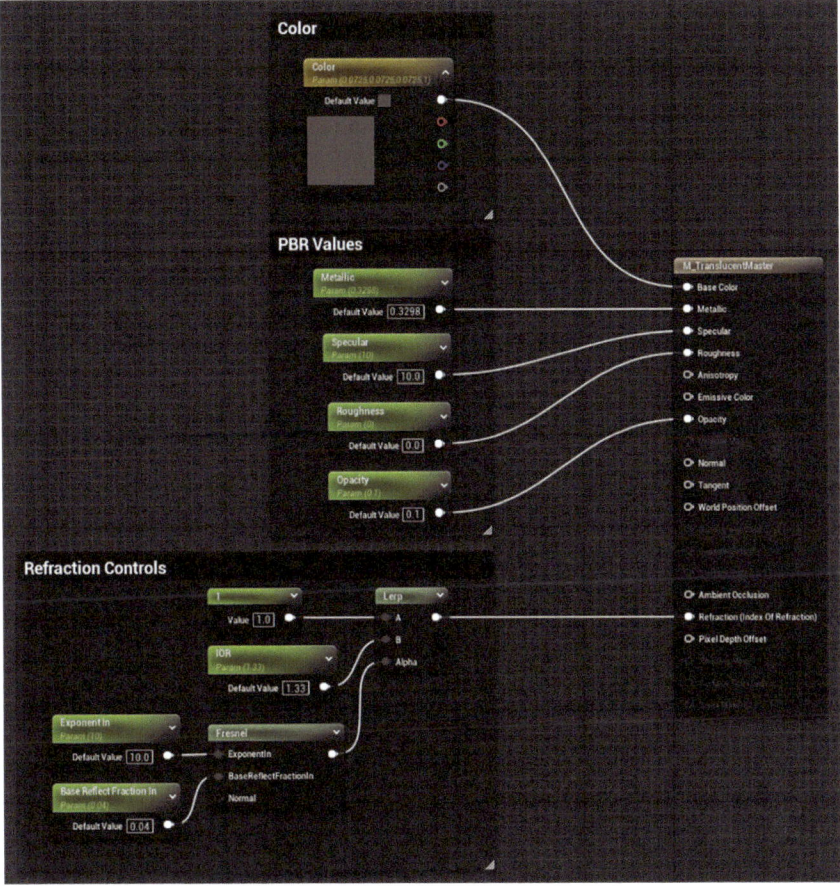

FIGURE 6.7 The finished Translucent Master Material graph.

11. Set the **Group** for the **Color** node in the **Details** panel to be *Color* and the **Sort Priority** to *1*.
12. With the nodes in the **PBR Values** comment, in the **Details** panel, set the **Group** to *PBR Values* and set the **Sort Priority** from top to bottom as *1* to *4*.
13. With the nodes in the **Refraction Controls** comment, set the **Group** to *Refraction* and set the **Sort Priority** from top to bottom as *1* to *3*.

With the Translucent Master made, we are now going to make another master material to use when creating translucent surfaces, and that is a Thin Translucent version.

Creating a Thin Translucent Master

This material will make use of the Thin Translucent Shading Model which is able to represent colored glass better than the Default Lit shading model with the Translucent

Blend Mode. This requires a small addition to the previous material which we will duplicate as a start point.

1. In the **Content Browser**, navigate to the folder **Content | Materials | Master**.
2. Right click on the **M_TransulcentMaster** material asset and choose **Duplicate**.
3. Name the new material *M_ThinTranslucentMaster*.
4. Double click on the **M_ThinTranslucentMaster** asset to open the material in the Material Editor.
5. In the **Details** panel, change the **Shading Model** to *Thin Translucent*.
6. Right click on the material graph and search for *ThinTranslucentMaterial Output*. This will give you a second output node (with a brown header) labeled **Thin Translucent Material**, this is where we give the material its color when using this shading model.
7. Duplicate the **Color** node by selecting it, placing your mouse near the **Thin Translucent Material** and press CTRL+D.
8. Now press F2 and rename the node *Translucent Color*.
9. In the **Details** panel, set the **Sort Priority** to *2*.
10. Save and **Apply** the material.

The additional nodes in the graph should look like the example shown in Figure 6.8, we've also added a comment box around the new nodes, you can choose to do this if you like.

Next up, we will create a quick, single-use material for a specific purpose in the scene.

Creating the Spider Web Material

For this material we are going to create another material which uses the Translucent Blend Mode and combine this with an Emissive Color input to allow us to make some interesting spiderwebs.

1. In the **Content Browser**, navigate to the folder **Content | Materials | Master**.
2. Right click and select **Material** to create a new material.
3. Name the new material *M_Spiderwebs*.

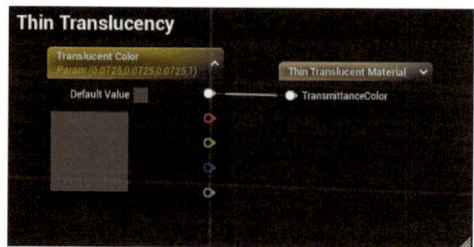

FIGURE 6.8 The additional nodes for the Thin Translucent Material.

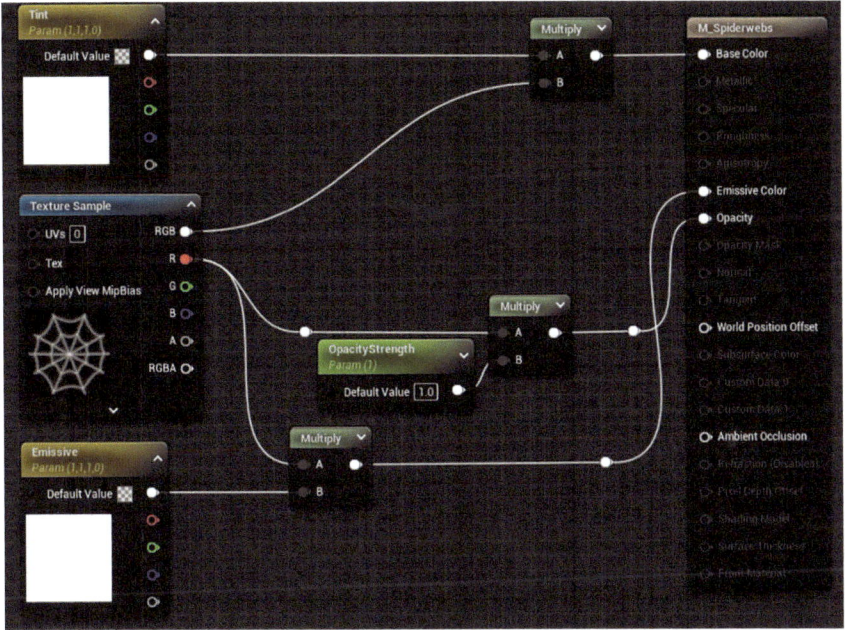

FIGURE 6.9 The M_Spiderwebs material graph.

4. Open the new **M_Spiderwebs** material in the material editor.
5. Select the Material Output Node and in the **Details** panel, change the **Blend Mode** from **Opaque** to **Translucent**.
6. Turn **ON** the **Two-Sided** option.
7. Scroll down and under **Translucency**, set the **Lighting Mode** to **Volumetric Directional**.
8. Recreate the Material Graph shown in Figure 6.9.

As we will not need a Material Instance for the spiderweb, you can apply the material directly to the **SpidersWeb_Mesh** in the scene, this should add some glowing cobwebs to the corner of the room.

Now we have all of the master materials built, we can move on to creating all of the materials for the scene using the provided textures.

Creating the Material Instances

To create all of the materials for the scene, you will need to use the information in the following tables. Each table is for a different master material and lists the name of the material instance, the folder where the textures to be used are stored, any parameters that change from the defaults and the objects in the scene that it should be applied to. When we get to making the Subsurface Material Instances, there are a couple of extra steps to make the best use of the Subsurface Profile Shading Model, but we will explain those when they are required. For now, let's make a start on authoring the rest of the materials.

M_BaseMaster

First, let's start with Material Instances which use the M_BaseMaster as a Parent Material (Table 6.1).

TABLE 6.1

List of Materials Which Use the M_BaseMaster as a Parent Material

BeesWax Material
    Instance Name: MI_BeesWax
    Textures Folder: Content | Textures | BeesWax
    Objects in Scene: BeesWax_Mesh, Cork1_Mesh, Cork2_Mesh, Cork3_Mesh, Cork4_Mesh, Cork5_Mesh, Cork6_Mesh, Cork7_Mesh, Cork8_Mesh, Cork9_Mesh

BeesWax
    Instance Name: MI_BeesWax
    Textures Folder: Content | Textures | BeesWax
    Objects in Scene: BeesWax_Mesh, Cork1_Mesh, Cork2_Mesh, Cork3_Mesh, Cork4_Mesh, Cork5_Mesh, Cork6_Mesh, Cork7_Mesh, Cork8_Mesh, Cork9_Mesh

Book
    Instance Name: MI_Book
    Textures Folder: Content | Textures | Book
    Objects in Scene: Book_Mesh, BookPages_Mesh, BookSinglePage_Mesh, Bookmark_Mesh

Book2
    Instance Name: MI_Book2
    Textures Folder: Content | Textures | Book2
    Objects in Scene: Book2_Mesh, Pile1 (Element 2)

RedBook
    Instance Name: MI_RedBook
    Textures Folder: Content | Textures | Book2 | RedBook
    Objects in Scene: BookRed_Mesh, Pile1 (Element 1)

CandleStand
    Instance Name: MI_CandleStand
    Textures Folder: Content | Textures | CandleStand
    Objects in Scene: Candle_Stand

Chair
    Instance Name: MI_Chair
    Textures Folder: Content | Textures | Chair
    Objects in Scene: Chair_Mesh

Clothbag
    Instance Name: MI_Clothbag
    Textures Folder: Content | Textures | Clothbag
    Objects in Scene: ClothBag_Mesh, Pile2 (Element 0)

Coal
    Instance Name: MI_Coal
    Textures Folder: Content | Textures | Coal
    Objects in Scene: FireBucketCoal_Mesh (Element 0 and Element 1), FireplaceCoal_Mesh

(Continued)

TABLE 6.1 (*Continued*)

List of Materials Which Use the M_BaseMaster as a Parent Material

Coin_Copper
    Instance Name: MI_Coin_Copper
    Textures Folder: Content | Textures | Coins | Copper
    Objects in Scene: BookCoin2_Mesh, Coin5_Mesh

Coin_Gold
    Instance Name: MI_Coin_Gold
    Textures Folder: Content | Textures | Coins | Gold
    Objects in Scene: BookCoin_Mesh, Coin3_Mesh, Coin4_Mesh, Coin6_Mesh, Coin7_Mesh, Coin9_Mesh, Coin_Mesh, Pile2 (Element 2)

Coin_Silver
    Instance Name: MI_Coin_Silver
    Textures Folder: Content | Textures | Coins | Silver
    Objects in Scene: Coin1_Mesh, Coin2_Mesh, Coin8_Mesh, Pile2 (Element 1)

Compass
    Instance Name: MI_Compass
    Textures Folder: Content | Textures | Compass
    Objects in Scene: Compass_Mesh, CompassPointer_Mesh

Crystals
    Instance Name: MI_Crystals
    Textures Folder: Content | Textures | Crystals
    Objects in Scene: Crystal1_Mesh, Crystal2_Mesh, Crystal3_Mesh, Crystal4_Mesh, Crystal5_Mesh, Crystal6_Mesh

DeskArch
    Instance Name: MI_DeskArch
    Textures Folder: Content | Textures | DeskArch
    Objects in Scene: DeskArch_Mesh

DeskCorner
    Instance Name: MI_DeskCorner
    Textures Folder: Content | Textures | DeskCorner
    Objects in Scene: DeskCorner_Mesh

DeskTower
    Instance Name: MI_DeskTower
    Textures Folder: Content | Textures | DeskTower
    Objects in Scene: DeskTower_Mesh, DeskTowerBanner_Mesh, DeskTowerWindows_Mesh, DeskTowerBricks_Mesh, DeskTowerBanner1_Mesh, DeskTowerBanner2_Mesh, DeskTowerSteps_Mesh, DeskTowerFlag_Mesh, DeskTowerFlagBanner_Mesh, DeskTowerShield_Mesh

DeskWalkway
    Instance Name: MI_DeskWalkway
    Textures Folder: Content | Textures | DeskWalkway
    Objects in Scene: DeskWalkway_Mesh

(Continued)

TABLE 6.1 (*Continued*)

List of Materials Which Use the M_BaseMaster as a Parent Material

DragonLeg
    Instance Name: MI_DragonLeg
    Textures Folder: Content | Textures | DragonLeg
    Objects in Scene: DragonLeg_Mesh

InkJar
    Instance Name: MI_InkJar
    Textures Folder: Content | Textures | InkJar
    Objects in Scene: InkJar_Mesh, Lid_Mesh, Lid2_Mesh

Key
    Instance Name: MI_Key
    Textures Folder: Content | Textures | Key
    Objects in Scene: Key_Mesh

Log
    Instance Name: MI_Log
    Textures Folder: Content | Textures | Log
    Objects in Scene: LogPile_Mesh

MagicGlobe
    Instance Name: MI_MagicGlobe
    Textures Folder: Content | Textures | MagicGlobe
    Objects in Scene: MagicSphereBase_Mesh, MagicSphereTop_Mesh

MagnifyingGlass
    Instance Name: MI_MagnifyingGlass
    Textures Folder: Content | Textures | MagnifyingGlass
    Objects in Scene: MagnifyingGlass_Mesh

Mortar
    Instance Name: MI_Mortar
    Textures Folder: Content | Textures | Mortar
    Objects in Scene: Mortar1_Mesh, Mortar2_Mesh

Paper
    Instance Name: MI_Paper
    Textures Folder: Content | Textures | Paper
    Objects in Scene: Paper1_Mesh

PaperPlain
    Instance Name: MI_PaperPlain
    Textures Folder: Content | Textures | Paper | Plain
    Objects in Scene: Paper2_Mesh, Paper3_Mesh, Paper4_Mesh, Pile1 (Element 0)

Pen
    Instance Name: MI_Pen
    Textures Folder: Content | Textures | Pen
    Objects in Scene: Pen_Mesh

(Continued)

TABLE 6.1 (*Continued*)

List of Materials Which Use the M_BaseMaster as a Parent Material

Pestle

> **Instance Name:** MI_Pestle
> **Textures Folder:** Content | Textures | Pestle
> **Objects in Scene:** Pestle_Mesh

Rings

> **Instance Name:** MI_Rings
> **Textures Folder:** Content | Textures | Rings
> **Objects in Scene:** Ring1_Mesh, Ring2_Mesh

Runes

> **Instance Name:** MI_Runes
> **Textures Folder:** Content | Textures | Runes
> **Objects in Scene:** Rune1_Mesh, Rune2_Mesh, Rune3_Mesh, Rune4_Mesh, Rune5_Mesh, Rune6_Mesh

Stamp

> **Instance Name:** MI_Stamp
> **Textures Folder:** Content | Textures | Stamp
> **Objects in Scene:** Stamp_Mesh

TubeStand

> **Instance Name:** MI_TubeStand
> **Textures Folder:** Content | Textures | TubeStand
> **Objects in Scene:** TubeStand_Mesh

M_EmissiveMaster

Next, we can create the two emissive materials, take note of the Emissive Strength value in Table 6.2.

TABLE 6.2

List of Materials Which Use the M_EmissiveMaster as a Parent Material

Cauldron

> **Instance Name:** MI_Cauldron
> **Textures Folder:** Content | Textures | Cauldron
> **EmissiveStrength:** 1.2
> **Objects in Scene:** CauldronHandle_Mesh, Cauldron_Mesh

Wand

> **Instance Name:** MI_Wand
> **Textures Folder:** Content | Textures | Wand
> **EmissiveStrength:** 1.1
> **Objects in Scene:** Wand_Mesh, OilContainer_Mesh

M_TilingMaster

Next, we can create the tiling materials. For these materials, be sure to set the correct Tiling value from Table 6.3.

TABLE 6.3

List of Materials Which Use the M_TilingMaster as a Parent Material

Brass
    Instance Name: MI_Brass
    Textures Folder: Content | Textures | Brass
    Tiling: 0.8
    Objects in Scene: CandleMount_Mesh (Element 1), CurtainRail_Mesh, DrawKnob1_Mesh, DrawKnob2_Mesh, DrawKnob3_Mesh, DrawKnob4_Mesh, FireBucketPoker_Mesh (Element 1), HandleKnocker_Mesh (Element 0), HandleKnocker2_Mesh (Element 0)

Iron
    Instance Name: MI_Iron
    Textures Folder: Content | Textures | Iron
    Tiling: 1.1
    Objects in Scene: Jar_Mesh, CandleMount_Mesh (Element 0), FireBucket_Mesh, FireBucketPoker_Mesh (Element 0), FireBucketShovel_Mesh (Element 0), FirePlace_Mesh, HandleKnocker_Mesh (Element 1), HandleKnocker2_Mesh (Element 1), Hinge1_Mesh, Hinge2_Mesh, Hinge3_Mesh, Hinge4_Mesh

Wood
    Instance Name: MI_Wood
    Textures Folder: Content | Textures | Wood
    Tiling: 1
    Objects in Scene: DeskUpper_Mesh, DeskCupboardDoor_Mesh, Desk_Mesh, DeskCupboardFrame_Mesh, FireBucketShovel_Mesh (Element 1)

M_TranslucentMaster

Next, we can create the glass material which uses the Default Lit Shading Model. There is only one material instance so rather than work from a table the property values are below:

- Color: 1212*12FF* (This is a Hex Linear notation which can be input into the color picker)
- **Metallic**: *0.43*
- **Specular**: *10.0*
- **Roughness**: *0.0*
- **Opacity**: *0.4*
- **IOR**: *1.41*
- **Exponent In**: *10.0*

This material instance needs to be applied to the following meshes in the scene:

- CompassBodyGlass_Mesh
- MagicSphere_Mesh
- MagnifyingGlassInterior_Mesh

M_ThinTranslucentMaster

Next we can create the thin translucent / glass material instances. For the color inputs, we've included Linear Hex Color values which can be entered into the color picker (Table 6.4).

TABLE 6.4

List of Materials Which Use the M_ThinTranslucentMaster as a Parent Material

GlassVial
> **Instance Name:** MI_GlassVial
> **Color (Hex Linear):** 031100FF
> **Translucent Color (Hex Linear):** 03EC02FF
> **Metallic:** 0.43
> **Specular:** 10.0
> **Roughness:** 0.0
> **Opacity:** 0.1
> **IOR:** 1.41
> **Exponent In:** 8.66
> **Base Reflect Fraction In:** 0.04
> **Objects in Scene:** GlassVial_Mesh

TubeGlass
> **Instance Name:** MI_TubeGlass
> **Color (Hex Linear):** 303030FF
> **Translucent Color (Hex Linear):**ECECECFF
> **Metallic:** 0.0
> **Specular:** 1.0
> **Roughness:** 0.05
> **Opacity:** 0.14
> **IOR:** 1.57
> **Exponent In:** 4.2
> **Base Reflect Fraction In:** 0.04
> **Objects in Scene:** Tube1Glass_Mesh, Tube2Glass_Mesh, Tube3Glass_Mesh, Tube4Glass_Mesh, Tube5Glass_Mesh, Tube6Glass_Mesh, Tube7Glass_Mesh, Tube8Glass_Mesh

M_SubsurfaceMaster

For the Material Instances which will use the M_SubsurfaceMaster material, we need to do a few steps before we can build the material themselves. The extra step here is to create two Subsurface Profiles which will allow us to use the full power of the Subsurface Profile Shading Model we selected when we built the Master Material.

To create the Subsurface profiles:

1. Navigate to **Materials | Instances**.
2. Right click and create a **New Folder**.
3. Call the folder *SubsurfaceProfiles*.
4. Open the **SubsurfaceProfiles** Folder.
5. Right click and navigate to **Material | Subsurface Profile**.
6. Name the profile and set the parameters based on Table 6.5.

Once you have the Subsurface Profiles created, you can go ahead and create the Material Instances and apply them to the meshes based on Table 6.6. To add the listed Subsurface Profile:

1. Open the Material Instance which is using the M_SubsurfaceMaster material as a parent.
2. Expand the **Material Property Overrides** rollout.

TABLE 6.5

List of Materials Which Use the M_TranslucentMaster as a Parent Material

Candle Subsurface Profile
    Subsurface Profile Name: SSP_Candle
    Surface Albedo: E86556FF
    Mean Free Path Color: FF2E2BFF
    Mean Free Path Distance: 2.75

Curtain Subsurface Profile
    Subsurface Profile Name: SSP_Curtain
    Surface Albedo: E82232FF
    Mean Free Path Color: 700A08FF
    Mean Free Path Distance: 2.65

TABLE 6.6

List of Materials Which Use the M_TranslucentMaster as a Parent Material

Candle
    Instance Name: MI_Candle
    Textures Folder: Content | Textures | Candle
    Metallic Min: 0.0
    Metallic Max: 1.0
    Roughness Min: 0.0
    Roughness Max: 1.0
    Specular: 0.5
    Subsurface Scattering Strength: 0.63
    Subsurface Profile: SSP_Candle
    Objects in Scene: Candle1_Mesh, Candle2_Mesh, CandleWall_Mesh
Curtain
    Instance Name: MI_Curtain
    Textures Folder: Content | Textures | Curtain
    Metallic Min: 0.0
    Metallic Max: 1.0
    Roughness Min: 0.0
    Roughness Max: 1.0
    Specular: 0.5
    Subsurface Scattering Strength: 1.0
    Subsurface Profile: SSP_Curtain
    Objects in Scene: CurtainLeft_Mesh, CurtainRight_Mesh

3. Activate the **Subsurface Profile** by clicking the checkbox.

4. Select the Subsurface Profile from the dropdown, which is currently labeled as **None**.

With the subsurface materials created, feel free to revisit the candle profile and experiment with the color values to see what other candles you can make.

You should now have a scene which is full of materials with textures applied to all of the objects on and around the Wizards Desk, removing all trace of the scene grid texture.

Conclusion

With the materials created, we come to the end of the chapter. We've explored and created a range of different master materials, making significant improvements on the material created in Chapter 5. Using those materials, you have been able to create the plethora of materials required for the scene, experiencing first hand the speed and versatility of the instanced material approach to building environments.

So, now let's check your understanding of master materials with a quiz.

Chapter 6 Quiz

Question 1: What does the Sort Priority property do?

    a.   Determine which order textures get applied to the model.

    b.   Arrange the textures in a material in memory.

    c.   Set which order parameters appear in the material instance editor.

Question 2: Which of the following is NOT a considered development benefit of adding comments to a material?

    a.   Comments allow us to leave amusing notes for colleagues.

    b.   They label which part of the graph controls what part of the material.

    c.   They make it easier to understand the graph when we come back to it later.

    d.   They help keeps the graph tidy.

Question 3: What does a Blend Angle Corrected Normals node allow us to do?

    a.   Correct the direction of a normal map.

    b.   Combine two different normal map textures together.

    c.   Fix normal map baking errors.

    d.   Flip a normal map for use on a different model.

Question 4: Which of these features are useful in a master material?

    a.   Texture Parameters

    b.   Float Parameters

    c.   Switch Parameters

    d.   All of the Above

Answers

Question 1: c

Question 2: a

Question 3: b

Question 4: d

7

Mesh Painting and Materials

In Chapter 6, we created our first tiled materials including adding the stone tiles to the floor in the room. In this chapter we are going to explore two ways to break up the repetition of the tiling material, adding visual variation and potentially narrative aspects to an otherwise predictable texture. To do this we are going to explore:

- Mesh Painting using Vertex Colors to blend textures in the Material Editor
- Decal Materials

What Is Mesh Painting?

Mesh Painting is the process of allocating vertex color values to a model. In Unreal, Static Meshes support this feature through interactive painting in the viewport. These meshes can store values in four channels (Red, Green, Blue and Alpha) for each vertex. These values can be exploited in our Materials in a number of ways, for example Blending Materials, storing light values, limiting foliage movement and much more. Figure 7.1 shows an example of a static mesh in the Static Mesh Editor with Show Vert Colors enabled.

As Technical Artists, we like to leverage Vertex Colors due to their small overheads and simplicity of creation. In older eras of games development, such as the original PlayStation and Nintendo 64 console eras, vertex color was utilized extensively to store lighting information.

Many DCC's like 3ds Max provide tools to transfer lighting to vertex colors. Often referred to as baked lighting or precomputed lighting, this approach has since been replaced by baked lighting in a games engine, which essentially does the same thing, saving the lighting onto a model but using a lightmap texture as opposed to vertex colors. In the modern era of games development, Vertex Colors are still exploited on lower end devices as a highly efficient way of providing lighting information.

In the current generation of consoles, including the PlayStation 5, Xbox Series X and modern PC graphics cards such as the Nvidia 4090 GTX we most commonly use Vertex Color to control the blending of complex materials to combat the repetition in tiling materials.

Figure 7.2 shows a tiling Stone Floor texture. When a Material is used frequently or applied on a large area with nothing dissecting it, it may become obviously repetitive. If you look closely at Figure 7.2 you will see there is one stone which is very different to the others, its repetition is quite noticeable. To break up this repetition we can use Mesh Painting to blend in another Material across certain vertices. This blending approach can be quite simple having just one blend or make use of all four material

DOI: 10.1201/9781032663852-7

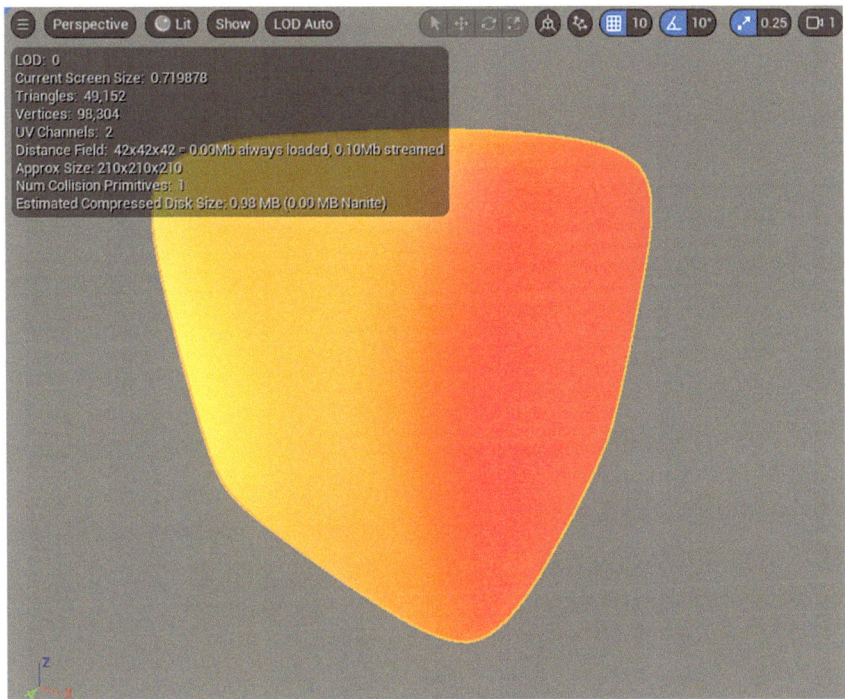

FIGURE 7.1   A static mesh of a subdivided cube with vertex colors assigned.

FIGURE 7.2   The Stone Floor in the scene in Unlit mode showing repetition.

channels (R, G, B, A) and have four blends. It's key when deciding to work with vertex colors, that you and your team keep processes consistent across different levels and materials. It's often sensible to create a ruleset in Technical Art Documentation that explains what each Vertex Channel might be used for, for example

- **Red** = Aging Variant (e.g. dust and paint chipping)
- **Green** = Damage Variant (e.g. plaster removed to reveal brickwork)
- **Blue** = Natural Blend (e.g. sand, water, and snow)

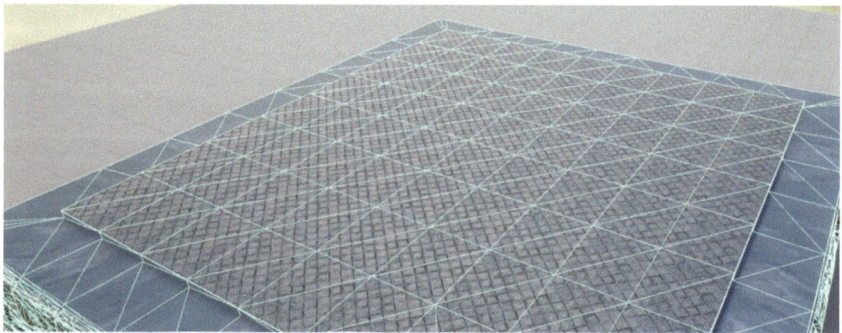

FIGURE 7.3   The StoneFloor_Mesh object with wireframe.

You may not necessarily use all of the channels on a single material but keeping the ruleset in place would allow for such circumstances.

To use vertex colors to control material blending, we need three things:

1. A mesh with enough geometry to be able to apply vertex colors effectively.
2. A material with blending setup based on vertex color data.
3. Vertex color data on the mesh.

We've already provided a suitable mesh to explore this approach with, the StoneFloor_ Mesh object (the floor in the scene) is subdivided already as shown in Figure 7.3.

With the mesh already prepared for us, let's look at building our material.

Materials and Vertex Color

When building materials to utilize Vertex Colors we rely on the Vertex Color node. The Vertex Color node is a special type of node which accesses data from the model, similar to the Texcoord node we used when making tiling materials. These node types are displayed as Red nodes in the material graph. The Vertex Color node has five unlabeled output pins. These pins are the same as a texture node in that they are (RGB, R, G, B, A), allowing us to access the combined channels or each individual channel. A Vertex Color node can be seen on the left of Figure 7.4.

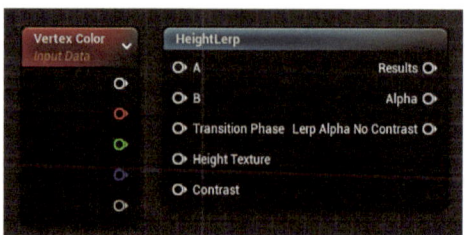

FIGURE 7.4   The additional nodes used for blending materials using vertex colors.

For the example in this chapter, we are going to blend the tiling floor material with a dirty coal material, first adding the coal dirt into the grout between the floor tiles and, on stronger sections, piling it on top of the tiles. In order to do this we are going to use the Vertex Color to control a height based blend using a HeightLerp node. An alternative approach to blending two materials would be to just use a Lerp node for this similar to how we have controlled the Roughness and Metallic elements, but the HeightLerp node allows us to use a Height Map to get the effect of the dirt building up in between the tiles. The HeightLerp node uses two material (or color) inputs and three float values that can be driven by a numerical value, or the output of a single channel from a texture, or in our case, the Vertex Color of the mesh.

Now we've explored the nodes, let's look at how we build those into a material.

Building the Material

For this example, we are going to build upon the M_TilingMaster from Chapter 6, adding the ability to blend a second set of textures into our material based on the green channel of an object's vertex colors.

The first thing we need to do is duplicate the tiling master material and make a few changes to reduce the complexity of the material. To do this we are going to remove the Detail Normal section of the material and swap the default textures we previously used to the ones for the tiling floor.

1. Navigate to **Content | Materials | Master**.
2. Right click the **M_TilingMaster** and select **Duplicate**.
3. Name the new material *M_VertexPaintMaster*.
4. Click **Save All** to ensure the new material has been saved.
5. Double click the **M_VertexPaintMaster** material to open it in the Material Editor.
6. Select all of the nodes in the **Normal Map and Detail Normals** comment box EXCEPT for the **Normal Map Texture** and delete them.
7. For now, reconnect the **RGB** pin from the **Normal Map Texture** to the **Normal** pin on the Material Output node. You can add a reroute node to tidy this up if you like.
8. Rename the **Normal Map and Detail Normals** comment box to *Normal Map*.
9. Swap all of the texture defaults on each of the Texture Parameter nodes (**Base Color Texture, ORM Texture, Normal Map Texture**) for textures form the **Content | Textures | StoneFloor** directory.

Now we have a simplified version of the material we can look at adding the Vertex Color based blending. We are going to start by adding in all of the additional textures we need to use.

1. Select the three existing Texture Parameter nodes (**Base Color Texture, ORM Texture, Normal Map Texture**) and duplicate them with CTRL + D.
2. Move the new nodes somewhere tidy so you can work on them.

3. Rename each of the Texture Parameter nodes by adding *Blend* as a prefix:
   a. *Blend Base Color Texture*
   b. *Blend ORM Texture*
   c. *Blend Normal Map Texture*
4. Set the **Sort Priority** value of those new Texture Parameter nodes as shown below:
   a. Blend Base Color Texture = 3
   b. Blend ORM Texture = 2
   c. Blend Normal Map Texture = 2
5. Right click and add a new *Texture Parameter* node, name it *Height Map Texture*.
6. In the **Details** Panel set the **Height Map Texture** to **StoneFloor_Height** which can be found in **Content | Textures | StoneFloor**.
7. Set the **Group** to *Blend* and the **Sort Priority** to 1.

With the new Texture Parameters setup, the next steps are to construct our Vertex Color driven Blend system using the Vertex Color and HeightLerp nodes we discussed earlier, we can then duplicate this for each of the sections of the material:

1. Right click on an empty part of the graph and add a *HeightLerp* node.
2. Now create a *Vertex Color* node, also by using the right click search.
3. Connect the Red output pin from the **Vertex Color** to the **Transition Phase (S)** pin on the **HeightLerp** node.
4. Connect the **R** pin of the **Height Map Texture** to the **Height Texture (S)** pin of the **HeightLerp** node.

These nodes form the reusable element which we will copy into each section of the material.

MATERIAL EDITOR FEATURE

We are going to be duplicating the **Height Map Texture** node, because this is a Texture Parameter node, each instance that we create remain connected to each other, with matching properties and parameters as long as the node names remain the same. This feature allows us to keep the graph tidy and easy to read when needing the same parameter to be used in multiple parts of the graph.

Let's set up the Base Color first.

1. Break the connection between the **Multiply** node in the **Base Color, Texture and Tint** comment box and the **Base Color** pin on the Material Output Node by holding down ALT and clicking the connection.
2. Select the nodes we previously created and duplicate them using CTRL+D.

3. Move the nodes so they are to the right of the **Multiply** node we just disconnected. You may need to shuffle things around to make space.

4. Move the **Blend Base Color Texture** to just above and left of the **HeightLerp** node.

5. Connect the **RGB** pin of the **Blend Base Color Texture** to the **A (V3)** pin on the **HeightLerp** node.

6. Connect the **Multiply** node we disconnected in step 1 to the **B (V3)** pin of the **HeightLerp** node.

7. Connect the **Results** pin of the **HeightLerp** node to the **Base Color** of the Material Output Node.

8. Arrange the nodes so everything is nicely aligned in a tidy layout.

9. Apply and Save the material.

With that connected up, we have set up the Vertex Color based blending for the Base Color, you can see an example of how we laid it out in Figure 7.5.

Next, we can repeat those steps for the Normal Map, swapping out the appropriate textures:

1. Break the connection between the **Normal Map Texture** node and the **Normal** pin on the Material Output Node by holding down ALT and clicking the connection.

2. Select the **Vertex Color** and **HeightLerp** nodes once again and duplicate them using CTRL+D.

3. Move the nodes so they are to the right of the **Normal Map Texture** node, making space as required.

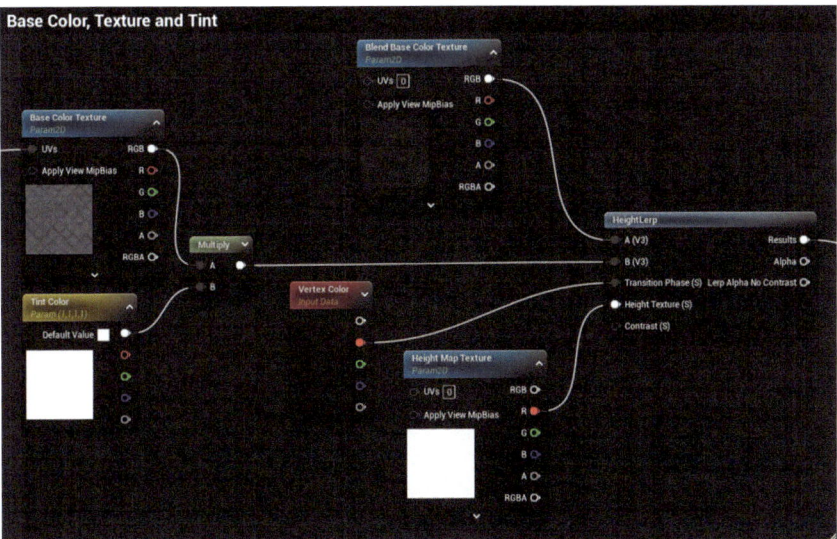

FIGURE 7.5 The base color section of the M_VertexPaintMaster material.

4. Place the **Blend Normal Map Texture** to just above and left of the **HeightLerp** node.

5. Connect the **RGB** pin of the **Blend Normal Map Texture** to the **A (V3)** pin on the **HeightLerp** node.

6. Connect the **RGB** pin of the **Normal Map Texture** to the **B (V3)** pin of the **HeightLerp** node.

7. Connect the **Results** pin of the **HeightLerp** node to the **Normal** of the Material Output Node.

8. As before, tidy things up and resize the comment box as required.

9. Apply and Save the material.

With that saved, we now have two of the three uses of the blend system; Figure 7.6 shows the Normal Map section of the graph.

The final use of the nodes we created is to control the blending of the ORM textures. For this, because we want to only use one channel of the blend for each element (Green for Roughness, Blue for Metallic), we are going to use a BreakOutFloat3Component to split the Results pin into the R, G and B component pins we need. Let's build the last blend.

1. Break the connection between the **G** and **B** pins of the **ORM Texture** node and the reroute nodes connected to the **Alpha** pins on the **Lerp** nodes in the **Roughness Controls and Metallic Controls** comment boxes respectively, by holding down ALT and clicking the connections.

2. Select the **Vertex Color** and **HeightLerp** nodes once again and this time, move them so they are to the right of the **ORM Texture** node, one again making space as required.

3. Place the **Blend ORM Texture** to just above and left of the **HeightLerp** node.

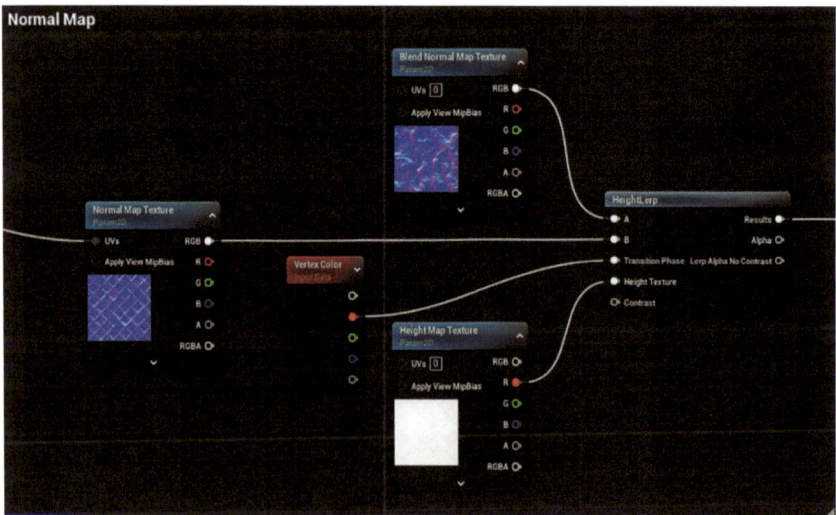

FIGURE 7.6   The normal section of the M_VertexPaintMaster material.

4. Connect the **RGB** pin of the **Blend ORM Texture** to the **A (V3)** pin on the **HeightLerp** node.

5. Connect the **RGB** pin of the **ORM Texture** to the **B (V3)** pin of the **HeightLerp** node.

6. Drag from the **Results** pin of the **HeightLerp** node and create a *BreakOutFloat3Components* node.

7. Connect the **G** pin of the **BreakOutFloat3Components** node to the **Alpha** pin of the **Lerp** node in the **Roughness Controls** comment box.

8. Connect the **B** pin of the **BreakOutFloat3Components** node to the **Alpha** pin of the **Lerp** node in the **Metallic Controls** comment box.

9. Add a comment box around the various nodes involved in the blend of the ORM textures, label it *ORM Blend*.

10. Apply and Save the material.

All of the three blends should now be setup and ready to go. You can see how we laid the ORM blend out in Figure 7.7.

With the three blends added, there is just one more control to consider: the tiling of the textures we are blending in. When we created the initial M_TilingMaster material we used as a base, we added the ability to adjust the tiling of the textures, allowing us to resize the floor texture and make the stone tiles smaller. To provide the best control over the blended result, we should also add this functionality to the new textures. Because the two collections of textures we are blending could be completely different (as is the case here), we should provide separate controls to the end user so they can scale the tiling independently for each set of textures.

1. Select the **Tiling Controls** comment box and all of the nodes inside.

2. Move the mouse below the comment box and press CTRL + D to duplicate them.

3. Select the duplicated comment box and press F2, relabel the comment box *Blend Tiling Controls*.

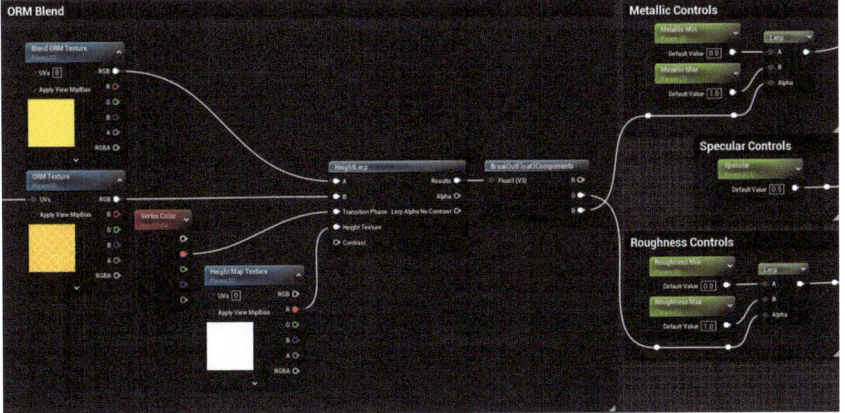

FIGURE 7.7 The ORM blend section of the M_VertexPaintMaster material.

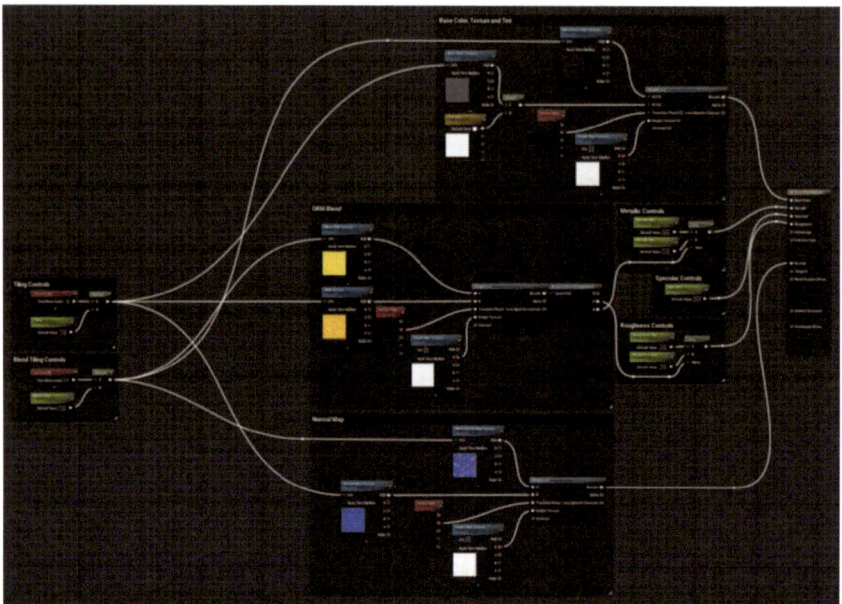

FIGURE 7.8   The completed M_VertexPaintMaster.

4. Select the **Tiling** node in the new **Blend Tiling Controls** comment box and press F2 again, rename the node (and as a result the parameter), *Blend Tiling*.

5. Set the **Sort Priority** of both the **Tiling** and **Blend Tiling** parameter nodes so they are arranged sensibly in a Material Instance.

6. Connect the output of the new **Multiply** node to the **UVs** pin of the **Blend Base Color Texture**, **Blend ORM Texture** and **Blend Normal Map Texture** nodes.

This concludes our work on making the Vertex Paint Master material, Figure 7.8 shows the completed material graph, while the nodes won't be visible in print, this image has been included so you can see the general shape and layout of the graph.

With the material setup, now we can apply it to the floor and explore the process of painting vertex colors onto a mesh in the Unreal Engine Editor.

Mesh Paint Workflow

In order to use the material we have just created, we need to have a mesh with vertex colors. The example shown at the start of the chapter in Figure 7.1 was a mesh that was imported with vertex colors already setup and baked in a DCC; however, all of the meshes used to build the Wizards Desk environment don't have vertex color baked into them. This is my design as we want to paint the vertex colors ourselves, in the scene, to ensure the result visually supports the overall scene.

To add vertex colors to a mesh in Unreal Engine, we use the Mesh Paint editor mode, so let's turn that on:

1. From the top menu bar in the main editor window, click the dropdown labeled **Selection Mode**.
2. Select **Mesh Paint**.

You should now see the editor layout change and a new part of the user interface appear, typically on the left side of the screen, this is the **Mesh Paint** tab which by default has the **Select** tool enabled, which allows you to select which mesh you wish to paint on.

The Mesh Paint toolset has three different modes, for now we are just going to focus on the **Colors** mode. If you'd like to learn more about the other modes, you can find more information in Epic Games' documentation. The **Colors** mode has a selection of tools which are visible at the top of the **Mesh Paint** tab, the key ones to be aware of for now are:

- **Select** – Allows you to select which mesh in the scene to paint on.
- **Paint** – Activates the paintbrush to directly paint vertex colors onto the mesh.
- **Swap** – Swaps the current **Paint Color** and **Erase Color.**
- **Fill** – Sets all vertices to have the **Paint Color** applied to the selected **Channels**.
- **Apply** – Saves the vertex colors of this instance mesh (in the world) to the source asset, applying these colors to all instances of the mesh.
- **Copy** – Allows you to copy the vertex colors from the selected mesh.
- **Paste** – Allows you to paste any copied vertex colors onto a selected mesh, provided the mesh is the same as the one they have been copied from.
- **Remove** – Removes all vertex colors from the selected mesh.

Before we can begin painting, we need to apply a material which supports vertex painting. At the moment, the material on the floor is the MI_StoneFloor we created in Chapter 6, we need to swap this for a new material instance based on the M_VertexPaintMaster.

1. Navigate to **Content | Materials | Master**.
2. Right click on the **M_VertexPaintMaster** material and choose **Create Material Instance**.
3. Name the new material instance asset **MI_StoneFloor_VertexPaint**.
4. Drag the **MI_StoneFloor_VertexPaint** asset onto the Instances folder and choose **Move Here**.
5. Navigate to **Content | Materials | Instances** and open the **MI_StoneFloor_VertexPaint** material in the Material Instance Editor.
6. Set the **Tiling** parameter to *2.0* the same as we did for the nonvertex paint version **MI_StoneFloor**.
7. Select the **StoneFloor_Mesh** in the viewport.
8. Drag the **MI_StoneFloor_VertexPaint** material onto **Element 0** in the **Details** panel to apply the new vertex paint version to the floor mesh.

With the material applied, we can now paint some vertex colors onto the mesh and explore the result. To begin with, this will be easier to see happening in Unlit mode so we will first swap the viewport over to Unlit and then paint the vertex colors on the mesh.

1. To swap to Unlit Mode, click the **Lit** button in the top left of the viewport and select **Unlit**. Alternatively, you can press ALT + 3 on your keyboard.
2. Ensure you have StoneFloor_Mesh selected in the viewport.
3. Click the **Paint** tool in the **Mesh Paint** panel, you should be presented with a list of options as shown in Figure 7.9.

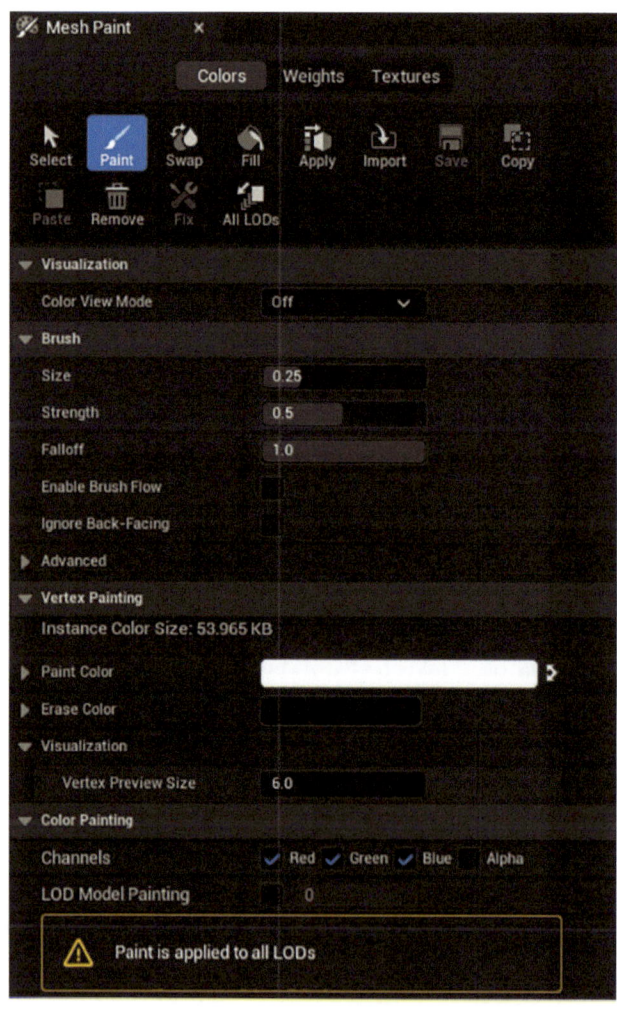

FIGURE 7.9 The brush options of Mesh Paint with the Paint tool selected.

4. Because our material was set up to just use the Red channel of the vertex color, uncheck both the **Green** and **Blue** checkboxes in the **Channels** parameter.

5. To view the current vertex colors, change the **Color View Mode** to **RGB Channels**. You should see that the mesh is completely White, so we know we need to remove color in order to blend in our alternate textures. As shown on the left side of Figure 7.10.

6. As we are only working with the Red Channel, swap the **Color View Mode** to **Red Channel**.

7. Swap the **Paint Color** and **Erase Color**, either by clicking the two headed arrow to the side of the **Paint Color** box, by pressing the **Swap** button at the top of the **Mesh Paint** panel, or by pressing X on your keyboard. The **Paint Color** should now be Black.

8. Click on and drag over the mesh in the viewport, you should see the color change and some Black shading appear. Note that this requires you to click on vertices (denoted by green squares) to have an effect.

9. Once you have some Black on the mesh, swap the **Color View Mode** to **Off** to show the textures once again. You should now see a dark gray section of the floor where you painted. This is the vertex paint working to modify the material result. As shown on the right side of Figure 7.10.

10. Swap back to Lit mode by clicking the **Unlit** button and selecting **Lit** or by pressing ALT + 4. You should now see the other elements of the material and get a better sense of the effect.

Now that you've seen how mesh paint mode works, experiment with painting bits of the floor. We'd intended for this effect to be used under the fireplace, but you could also use it in other places. Try a few different things to explore the process further:

- Try changing the **Size** and **Strength** of the brush to see how that changes the painting experience.
- Try changing the **Paint Color** to a Gray instead of Black and see how that changes things (Figure 7.11).

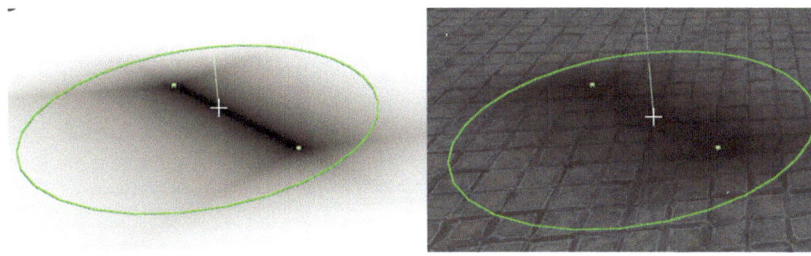

FIGURE 7.10 The floor mesh with vertex paint values shown with Color View Mode of RGB Channels and Off.

FIGURE 7.11   The fireplace with the vertex colors resulting in a blended floor material.

With that complete, we've reached the end of our exploration of Vertex Colors and Mesh Painting. What we've setup is a relatively simple material to achieve a good visual result but this technique and toolset can be pushed much further.

Improving the Material

In building the example material in this chapter, we've made a few decisions in order to keep it simple so we can successfully explore the contents of Material Blending using Vertex Colors without over complicating the material. There are a few different approaches we could take to further expand and improve the material we created, let's explore two of them:

Additional Blends

We have only blended two materials (or two sets of textures) using a single channel of Vertex Color (the Red Channel). We could repeat the process, adding in a second, third or even fourth blend to provide more flexibility to the material. The number of blends, and complexity of the material will depend on the needs of the project. As discussed earlier in the chapter, setting rules for which channels do what type of blends will help maintain consistency across a project so it's wise to consider if the blends would ever be combined. From the example earlier, we might want to combine aging and damage but perhaps would be unlikely to blend in natural elements. If this was the case, we could expand this material with a second blend and then create another Master Material for using the Blue channel for materials which would be blended with natural elements.

Separate PBR Controls per Layer

Another decision we made was to blend the ORM textures before we set the minimum and maximum values that would be used on the metallic and roughness inputs. This actually prevents us from providing full control to the appearance of each part of the blend. The solution here would be to duplicate the controls for each of the ORM textures and set up two separate HeightLerp blends. Have a go at setting this up on your own.

Bonus: Decals

In this chapter we've focused on using Vertex Colors to break up the repetition of a patterned surface, there is another approach we can use to do this too, and that is, Decal Actors.

Decal Actors are a simple actor which projects a material onto surfaces in the scene. We use decals to add detail where we are otherwise unable to due to using traditional texturing process and having either a tiling texture (where the detail would obviously repeat) or a low texel density (where the detail would be too blurry due to the low resolution). Some examples of decal use include details like Signage, both Text and Iconography, Damage and Staining. In order to use Decal Actors, we need to create materials which use the Deferred Decal Material Domain.

We've included a selection of mask textures to use with Decal Actors in the scene, allowing us to set the color of the decal in a Material Instance. To use them we need to create a new master material, as we did in Chapter 6. This process is fairly straightforward and uses a lot of the techniques we've already covered so, let's get going:

1. Navigate to **Content | Materials | Master** and create a new material, call it *M_DecalMaster*.
2. Save the asset and then double click it to open it in the Material Editor.
3. In the **Details** panel, change the **Material Domain** to **Deferred Decal** using the dropdown.
4. Change the **Blend Mode** to **Translucent**.
5. Drag out from the **Base Color** pin on the Material Output Node and add a *Vector Parameter*. Name it *Decal Color*.
6. Set the default of the **Decal Color** to be a greenish brown, we used a **Hex Linear** value of *080805FF*.
7. Hold down 1 on the keyboard and click on the graph, adding a Float node which will be labeled **0**.
8. Right click on the new Float node and choose **Convert to Parameter**. Name it *Specular*.
9. Repeat the process to create two more Float parameters, name them *Roughness* and *Opacity Strength*.
10. Set the **Default Value** of the **Opacity Strength** node to *1.0*.
11. Connect the **Specular** node to the **Specular** pin on the Material Output Node.

12. Connect the **Roughness** node to the **Roughness** pin on the Material Output Node.

13. Press SPACE to open the **Content Drawer** and navigate to **Content | Textures | Decals**.

14. Drag in the **Splat** texture.

15. Right click the resulting **Texture Sample** node and choose **Convert to Parameter**. Name it *Decal Texture*.

16. Add a Multiply node by holding down M and clicking on the graph.

17. Connect the **RGB** pin of the **Decal Texture** to the **A** pin of the **Multiply** node.

18. Connect the **Opacity Strength** node to the **B** pin of the **Multiply** node.

19. Connect the output pin of the **Multiply** node to the **Opacity** pin on the Material Output Node.

20. Set the **Group** of the various parameters to *Decal*, when setting this on the first parameter, you will need to create it by typing it into the dropdown.

21. Set the **Sort Priority** of the various parameters so they show in the following order; Decal Parameter, Decal Color, Specular, Roughness, Opacity Strength.

The resulting material should look similar to the material shown in Figure 7.12. Because this is a simple material, there isn't much need to add comment boxes.

Dirt Decals

With the material created, we can now create Material Instances to use three of the provided decal textures.

1. Navigate to **Content | Materials | Master**.

2. Right click the **M_DecalMaster** and select **Create Material Instance**.

3. Name the new material *MI_SplatDecal*.

4. Drag the **MI_SplatDecal** asset onto the **Content | Materials | Instances** folder and choose **Move Here**.

   • You could make the decals easier to find by adding a new folder in the Instances folder called *Decals*.

5. Open the **MI_SplatDecal** material in the Material Instance Editor by double clicking it.

6. Set the following parameters:

   • **Decal Color**: Hex Linear (*0B0705FF*)

   • **Specular**: *0*

   • **Roughness**: *1.0*

   • **Opacity Strength**: *0.54*

With all of the parameters set, the decal is now ready to use in the scene.

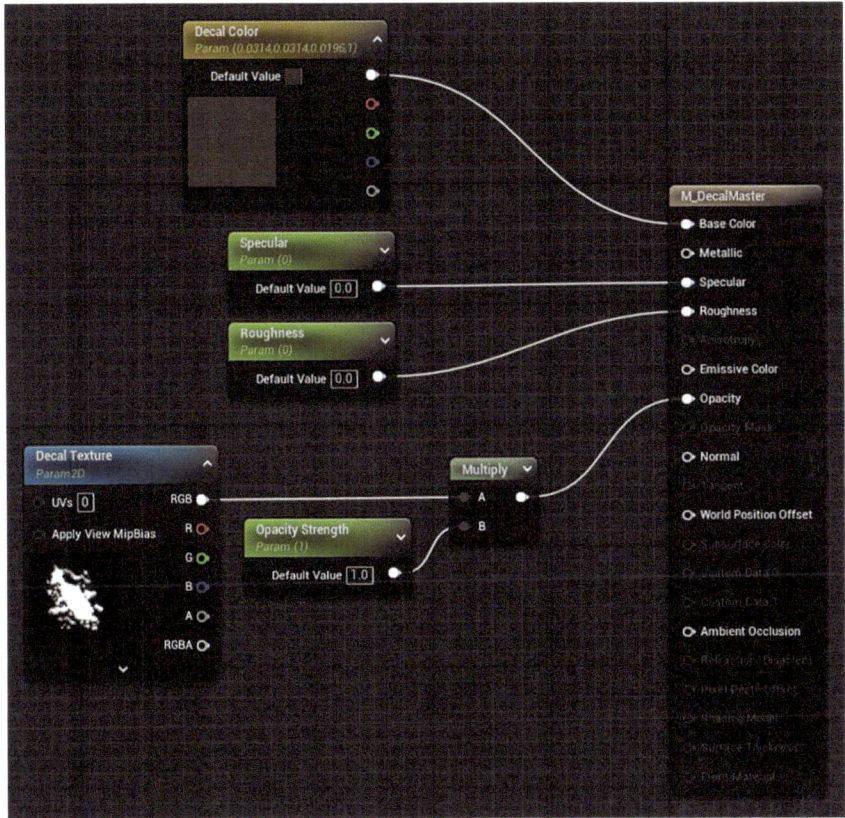

FIGURE 7.12 The finished M_DecalMaster material.

All we have to do to use a decal material in the scene as a decal actor is to drag the decal material from the Content Browser into the scene, this will automatically create a DecalActor for us.

1. Select the **MI_SplatDecal** in the **Content Browser**.
2. Drag the **MI_SplatDecal** asset from the **Content Browser** into the scene.
3. With the new DecalActor selected, rotate and scale the actor, observing the effect this has on the decal.

Figure 7.13 shows the MI_SplatDecal in the scene on the floor in front of the fireplace in Unlit mode (to make seeing the result easier). Use the **Splat2** and **Dust** textures to create two new Material Instances of the **M_DecalMaster** material. Change the values as you like to make some interesting effects. Try applying decals to other areas of the scene, for example, you could add some different color splats to the desk around the cauldron.

FIGURE 7.13   The MI_SplatDecal applied to the floor in the scene.

Book Text Decal

We have also included a decal to use to add writing to the book on the desk. For this decal however, we don't want to use our normal M_DecalMaster because, for writing, we want to represent a more ink-like behavior to the decal, so to do this we are going to make use of the Modulate Blend Mode. You will also notice that, unlike the splats, the part of the texture we want to keep is black, not white, so we also need to invert this texture in our material. So let's create a new modulate decal master.

1. Navigate to **Content | Materials | Master**.
2. Right click the **M_DecalMaster** material and choose **Duplicate**, name the new material *M_ModDecalMaster*.
   - For consistency, you could rename the original to *M_TransDecalMaster* but this is optional.
3. Open the **M_ModDecalMaster** material in the Material Editor by double clicking it.
4. With the Material Output Node selected (or no nodes at all), change the **Blend Mode** parameter in the **Details** panel to **Modulate**.
5. Change the default **Decal Texture** to be the **SpellBook** texture.
6. To invert the mask, add a *1-x* node in between the **RGB** pin of the **Decal Texture** and the **A** pin of the **Multiply** node.
7. Change the **Default Value** of the **Decal Color** to a Purple color, we used the **Hex Linear** value of 1C1331FF.
8. Apply and Save the Material.

The finished material can be seen in Figure 7.14 with the new texture and the 1-x node. With the master created you can now create a Material Instance for the text, try this on your own, give the text a little bit of transparency and a nice inky color and then drag the material into the world, onto the book. You will need to scale it down a lot (and/or change the **Decal Size** in the **Details** panel to be quite small) to get it to fit on the book. Once finished, it should look something like the example in Figure 7.15.

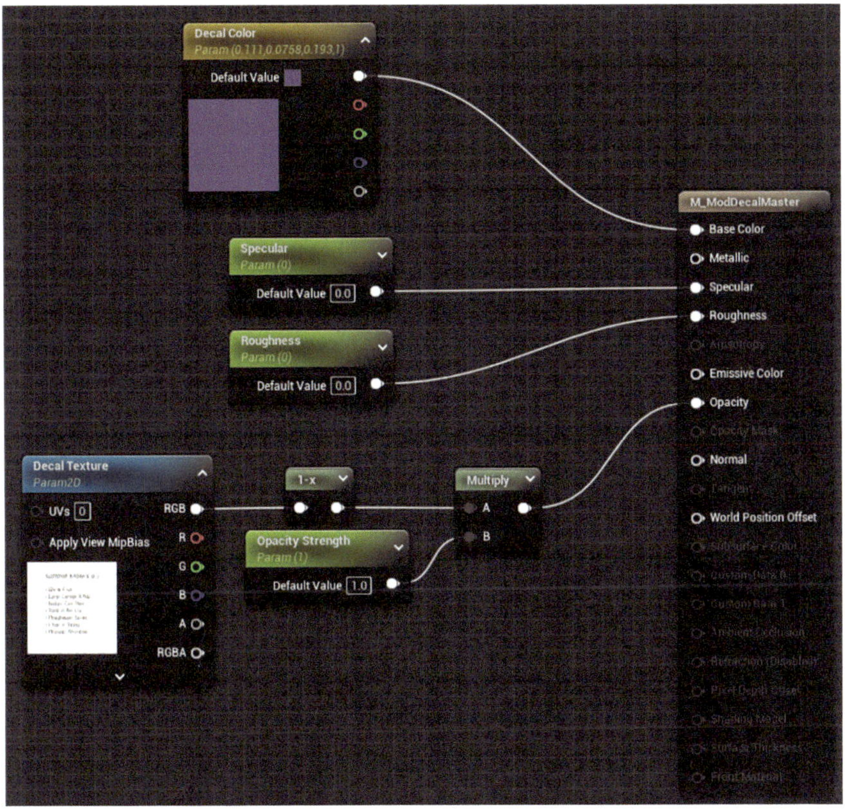

FIGURE 7.14   The finished M_ModDecalMaster material.

FIGURE 7.15   The spell book decal added to the spell book showing text on the page.

Conclusion

With the decals added to the scene, we've come to the end of this chapter. In this chapter we've explored two key ways to add variation to surfaces in Unreal Engine to help break up repetitive patterns or un-interesting parts of a scene. Using Vertex Paint data, we've built a material to blend two different sets of textures together using a Height Map and we've also explored decals. Let's check what you've learned with another quick quiz!

Chapter 7 Quiz

Question 1: Why do we use vertex paint data in modern games engines

    a.   Because it allows us to make the model extra pretty when we view it in vertex color mode

    b.   Because it's an efficient way to add information to a model which we can use in a material to improve our final result

    c.   Because we can load scene lighting data from a model to illuminate a scene

    d.   All of the above

Question 2: What is a Height Map

    a.   A grayscale texture which represents the height of a material

    b.   A map of the scene which shows us how far off the floor meshes are

    c.   A full color texture which represents the height of a material

    d.   A grayscale texture which adds extra lighting information to a material

Question 3: What does a 1-x node do?

    a.   Adds a delay of 1 second to a material

    b.   Flips a texture upside down

    c.   Inverts a texture or values

    d.   Moves a texture 1 pixel on the x-axis

Question 4: How many channels can we use for Mesh Painting?

    a.   1

    b.   2

    c.   3

    d.   4

Answers

Question 1: b

Question 2: a

Question 3: c

Question 4: d

8

Introductory Materials for VFX

Introduction

This chapter introduces you to the Material ingredients for your VFX systems, you'll learn about:

- Working with Material Blend Modes.
- Using the Particle Color node.
- Linking Material Parameters to Particle Systems.

Unreal Materials are an important ingredient that are leveraged in Unreal's VFX Editor, Niagara. In order to get the most out of Materials in Niagara we need to be aware of several features. We will create two materials in this chapter building on our Master and Instance workflow. Our VFX Master Materials will set up initial parameters that we can then leverage inside of Niagara.

But where do we begin?

Blend Modes

Our first consideration is the Material Blend Mode, we explored these in Chapter 3 when we introduced materials, for this section, we are going to create two VFX Master Materials using the Translucent and Additive Blend Modes. Let's get started and create our Materials.

Creating Our Translucent VFX Master Material

1. In the **Content Browser**, navigate to the folder **Content | Materials | Master**.
2. Right click in the **Master** folder and select Material from the menu.
3. Call the Material *M_VFXTrans*.
4. Double click the new Material to open the Material Editor.
5. In the **Details** panel, locate the **Blend Mode** Parameter, select **Translucent** from the dropdown menu, as shown in Figure 8.1.
6. Click the **Save** Button in the Material Editor.

DOI: 10.1201/9781032663852-8

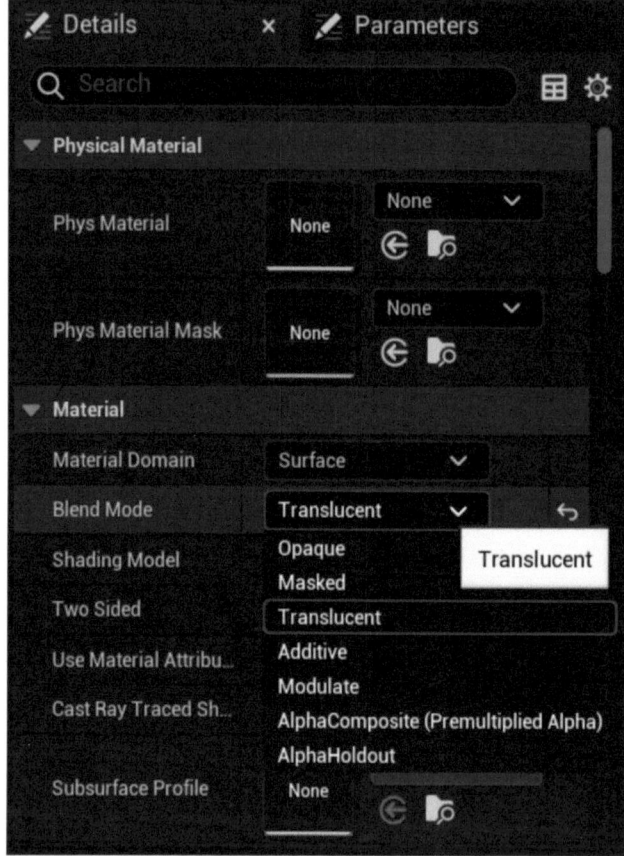

FIGURE 8.1 Unreal blend mode translucent material.

Creating Our Additive VFX Master Material

1. In the **Content Browser**, navigate to the folder **Content | Materials | Master**.
2. Right click in the **Master** folder and select Material from the menu.
3. Call the Material *M_VFXAdd*.
4. Double click on the new Material to open the Material Editor.
5. In the **Details** panel, locate the **Blend Mode** Parameter, select **Additive** from the dropdown menu.
6. Click the **Save** Button in the Material Editor.

We now have two Master Materials with their Blend Modes set. We are now going to populate the Materials with nodes that will set up functionality for Unreal's VFX System.

Shading Models

Shading Models to help us create Materials that react correctly with our scene's lights, we again explored these in Chapter 3. The two most common shading models utilized in VFX Materials are:

1. **Unlit** – This Shading Model is great for visual effects which emit light/glow. It is also the fastest Shading Model to render and as such beneficial to use when possible.
2. **Default Lit** – This is the default Shading Model and affords you access to lots of Material inputs. It is more expensive to render but sometimes necessary when you want your VFX system to react accurately to scene lighting.

Now that we've explored the more commonly used Shading Models for VFX Materials, let's apply these to our two VFX Master Materials.

Setting the Shading Model on Our Translucent Master Material

1. In the **Content Browser**, navigate to the folder **Content | Materials | Master**.
2. Double click on the Material **M_VFXTrans** to open the Material Editor.
3. Using the **Details** panel, search for the property Shading Model.
4. Set the Shading Model to **Default Lit**.
5. Click the **Save** Button in the Material Editor.

Setting the Shading Model on Our Additive Master Material

1. In the **Content Browser**, navigate to the folder **Content | Materials | Master**.
2. Double click on the Material **M_VFXAdd** to open the Material Editor.
3. Using the **Details** panel, search for the property Shading Model.
4. Set the Shading Model to **Unlit**.
5. Click the **Save** Button in the Material Editor.

Particle Color

The Material Editor has a special node called Particle Color. This node allows us to read in Particle RGB color data as well as Alpha values, inside of Unreals Material Editor over a Particles Lifespan. This allows us to create effects such as changing the color of a flame effect from blue to orange or the glow strength of electrical sparks.

In order to utilize Particle Color, we have to connect the node's outputs to our Material Graph. It's commonplace for the outputs to be connected to Material channels such as **Base Color**, **Emissive** and **Opacity**. When using the node you can also add in Parameters to help balance and adjust its effects, for example, a Multiply and a Vector Parameter to create a Color Tint.

Let's explore how to connect Particle Color to our Material *M_VFXTrans*.

Utilizing Particle Color in Our Translucent Master Material

1. In the **Content Browser**, navigate to the folder **Content | Materials | Master**.
2. Double click on the Material **M_VFXTrans** to open the Material Editor.
3. Open the **Content Drawer** and navigate to **Content | Textures | VFX_Smoke**.
4. Drag and drop the Texture **MagicCloud1** into the Material **M_VFXTrans**.
5. Right click on the **MagicCloud1** Texture Sample node and Convert it to a Parameter called *ParticleTexture*.
6. Right click in the Material Editor Graph below the created Texture Sample, and search for *ParticleColor*.
7. Create a *Multiply* node to the right of the **ParticleTexture** and **Particle Color** nodes.
8. Connect the **RGB** output pins from the **ParticleTexture** and **Particle Color** nodes to the **A** and **B** inputs on the **Multiply** node. The idea is that the Particle Color will alter the color of the smoke.
9. Connect the **Output** of the **Multiply** to the **Base Color** pin on the result node.
10. Now create another *Multiply* node just underneath the first one.
11. Connect the **R** pin of the **ParticleTexture** node into the **A** input of the **Multiply**.
12. Connect the **A** pin of the **Particle Color** node into the **B** input of the **Multiply**.
13. Finally connect the **Output** pin of the **Multiply** node to our **Opacity** pin on the result node.
14. Save the material.

The four nodes shown in Figure 8.2 afford us the ability to manipulate a textures color and transparency through Unreal's VFX system. We can increase the complexity of Materials like this by manipulating the UV's of textures or by using Merged Maps to store different information in the RGBA channels of textures.

Let's now also add the Particle Color node to our Additive Master Material.

Adding Particle Color to Our Additive Master Material

1. In the **Content Browser**, navigate to the folder **Content | Materials | Master**.
2. Double click on the Material **M_VFXAdd** to open the Material Editor.
3. Open the **Content Drawer** and navigate to **Content | Textures | EnergyOrb**.
4. Drag and drop the Texture **Particle1** into the Material **M_VFXAdd**.

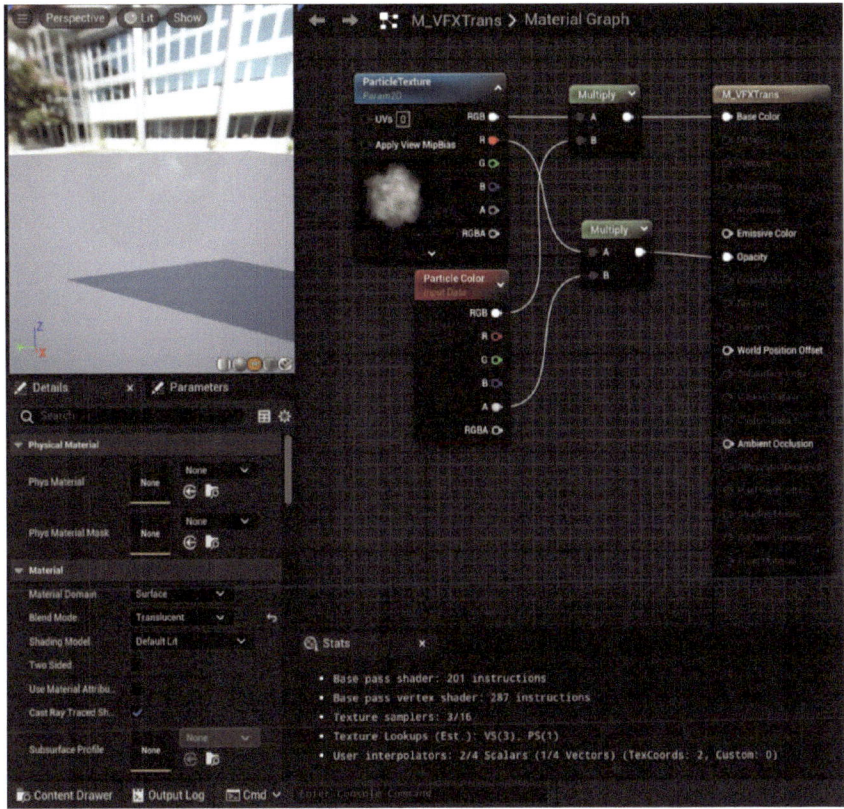

FIGURE 8.2 Unreal translucent material.

5. Right click on the **Particle1** Texture Sample and Convert it to a Parameter called *ParticleTexture*.

6. Right click on the Material Editor Graph below the created **ParticleTexture** node, and search for *Particle Color*.

7. Create a *Multiply* node to the right of the **ParticleTexture** and **Particle Color** nodes.

8. Connect the **RGB** output pins from the **ParticleTexture** and **Particle Color** nodes to **A** and **B** inputs on the **Multiply** node.

9. Connect the output pin of the **Multiply** node to the **Emissive Color** pin on the result node.

10. Create another *Multiply* Node just underneath the first one.

11. Connect the **R** pin of the **ParticleTexture** into the **A** input of the **Multiply** node.

12. Connect the **A** pin of the **Particle Color** node into the **B** input of the **Multiply** node.

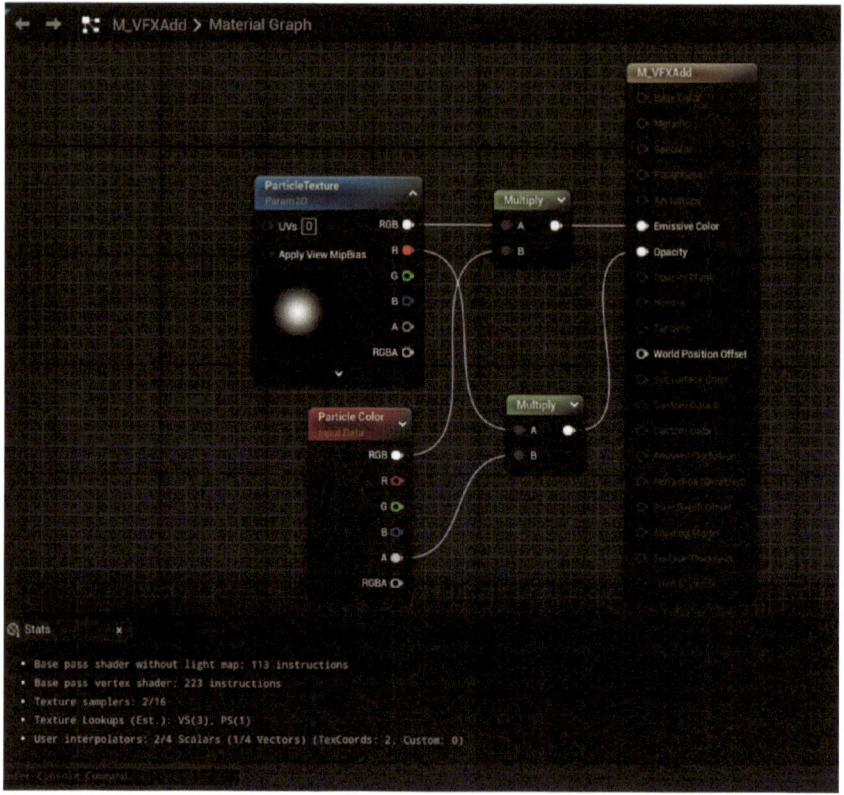

FIGURE 8.3   Unreal additive material.

13. Finally, connect the output pin of the **Multiply** node to the **Opacity** pin on the result node.
14. Save the Material. You may review your Additive Material in Figure 8.3.

We now have two basic Materials that can be used in the Niagara Editor. However, what can we do if we want to take things further? From this point we can use the Material Editor to layer up complex texture animations to help break up the repetitiveness of any Particle System. One way of doing that is to use Parameters, we are going to explore that next.

Parameters

We can leverage Parameters inside of our materials to manipulate how our Materials render within Unreal's Niagara editor. There are several ways that Parameters may help us these are:

- We can manipulate, distort and animate Texture UV's.
- We can alter the brightness or color of an effect.
- We can use Dynamic Parameters that connect Unreal's Niagara Editor to the Material Editor.

Let's explore these three approaches by modifying our existing VFX Master Materials.

Panning and UV Distortion

We are now going to distort our Texture UV's in the Material **M_VFXAdd**. To do this we are going to use a Panner node which allows us to move textures in the *X* and *Y* axis. Combining movements with masks can create quite sophisticated distortions which can make flat textures look volumetric and 3D.

Animation in the Material Editor goes alongside Animation in the Niagara Editor in Unreal. Not all Particle Systems will require distorted UV's but what we are about to do provides a way to break up the repetition of textures.

Adding Panning to Our Additive Master Material

1. In the **Content Browser**, navigate to the folder **Content | Materials | Master**.
2. Double click on the Material **M_VFXAdd** to open the Material Editor.
3. In the **Content Drawer**, navigate to **Content | Textures | EnergyOrb**.
4. Drag and drop the Texture **Particle2** into the Material **M_VFXAdd**.
5. Move this Texture Sample to the left of the **ParticleTexture** Param2D.
6. Right click in the Material Graph and Search for a *Panner* Node. Position this node to the left of the Particle2 **Texture Sample** node.
7. Connect the output pin of the **Panner** node into the **UV** input of the Particle2 **Texture Sample** node.
8. Right click in the Material Graph and Search for a *Component Mask* node. Position the **Mask (R G)** node in between the Particle2 **Texture Sample** node and the **ParticleTexture** node.
9. Connect the **RGB** output of the Particle2 **Texture Sample** into the input of the **Mask (R G)** node.
10. Connect the output of the **Mask (R G)** node to the **UV** input of the **ParticleTexture** Param 2D node. You will see our **ParticleTexture**'s node preview distort.

We are now going to add a couple of nodes to create a Mask around our Particle Texture's UVs. The Radial Mask will limit where panning and distortion can take place, you can always right click on a node and preview it if you are unsure as to its contributions to the Material Graph. When working with Masks, Panners and other functions it's nice to preview what you are doing as you build up your material to ensure everything is moving correctly. Let's now carry on building our Material.

1. Start by disconnecting the **Mask (R G)** output from the **ParticleTexture** UVs input pin by holding down ALT and clicking the connection.
2. Move the **Panner**, Particle2 **Texture Sample** and **Mask (R G)** nodes slightly to the left to create a bit of space between the **Mask (R G)** node and the **ParticleTexture** node.
3. Create a *Multiply* node in between the **Mask (R G)** and **ParticleTexture** Param2D nodes.
4. Connect the output pin of the **Mask (R G)** to the input **B** slot of the **Multiply** node and connect the output of the **Multiply** Node to the **ParticleTexture** Param2D node's **UV** input.
5. Right click and search for a node called *RadialGradientExponential*. Place this node above the **Multiply** node and connect it to the **Multiply** node's **A** input.
6. Right click on the **Multiply** Node and select **Start Previewing Node** and change the preview to show on a plane using the icons in the bottom right corner of the preview viewport. You should now see that the Particle2 Texture Sample has been masked around the edges.
7. Right click on the **Multiply** Node and select **Stop Previewing Node.**
8. Navigate to our Panner node.
9. Right click and Search for a *Time* node, connect the output of the **Time** node to the **Time** input on the **Panner** node.
10. Set the **Speed** Value on the **Panner** node to *X=0.1* and *Y=−0.1*.

You should now see our Texture move in the **Viewport**. If you don't, double check that realtime is activated by pressing CTRL+R on the keyboard. Figure 8.4 shows the finished Material in the material graph.

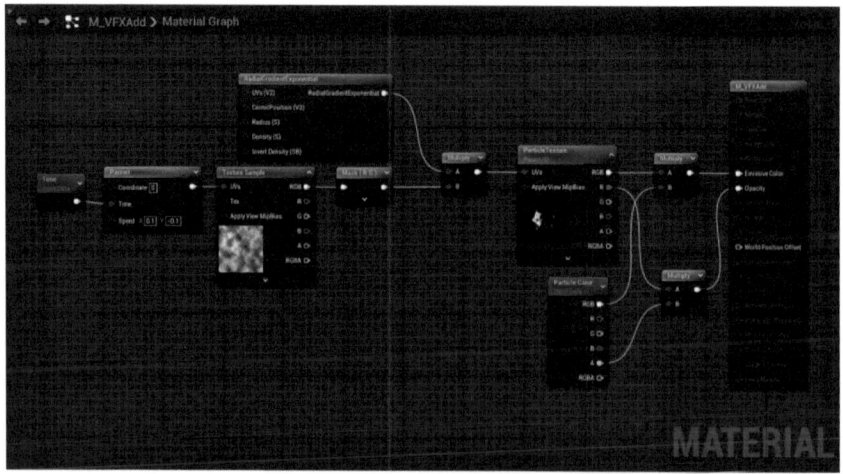

FIGURE 8.4   Unreal panning smoke UV's.

This panning approach can be layered with tiled texture coordinates fed into the **Panner** node. Try to duplicate the **Panner** section of the graph and experiment with different values fed into the **ParticleTexture** UV input. You may also observe a more complex version of this material in the following folder: **Content | Completed | Materials | Master | EnergyOrb_Master_MAT**.

Tinting VFX Materials with Scalar and Vector Parameters

The following exercise can be applied to both of our VFX Materials; however, we'll continue with the additive Master. The instructions will provide you with color and opacity overrides at the Material level. The goal is that with a couple of nodes you can tweak an entire Niagara Effect's look from a Material Instance if you wish to.

Let's begin:

1. In the **Content Browser**, navigate to the folder **Content | Materials | Master**.
2. Double click on the Material **M_VFXAdd** to open the Material Editor.
3. Select all of the Nodes inside the Material and move them to the left to make some space between our instruction nodes and the output node.
4. Above the **ParticleTexture** node, hold V and click in the Material Graph to Create a Vector Parameter node. Call this *ColorTint*.
5. Select the **ColorTint** Node and use the Detail Panel to set its Default Value to White (R = 1, G = 1, and B = 1).
6. Now hold M and click in the Material Graph to place a **Multiply** Node.
7. Connect the RGBA output (white pin) of the **ColorTint** node into the **A** input of the new **Multiply** Node.
8. Connect the **Multiply** output that is connected to our **ParticleTexture** node into the **B** input of the new **Multiply** Node.
9. Connect the new **Multiply** node's output pin to the **Emissive Color** input pin on the material output node.
10. Create another new **Multiply** below, and connect its output into the **Opacity** input pin of the material output node.
11. Connect the output of the **Multiply** node which is connected to the **Particle Color** node's **A** pin to the recently created **Multiply** node's **A** input.
12. Next Hold S and left click in the Material Graph. This will create a Scalar Parameter, label this node *OpacityStrength*.
13. Select the **Opacity Strength** node and using the **Details** panel set the Default Value of **Opacity Strength** to 1.
14. Connect the output of **Opacity Strength** to the B input of our recently connected **Multiply** Node.

The completed Material can be seen in Figure 8.5 which shows the additive material master with four nodes added to provide controls for color tinting and opacity. Simple tweaks like this allow us to easily control the look of a Material, sometimes we need these overrides to make very quick adjustments.

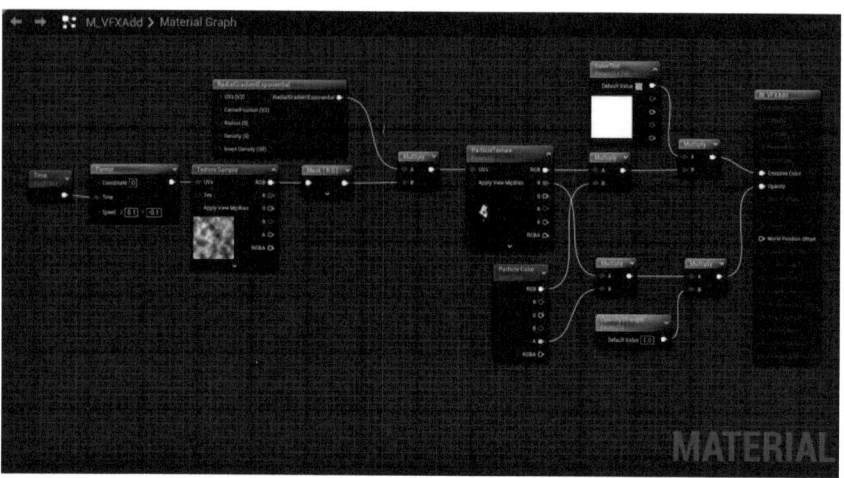

FIGURE 8.5   Tinting VFX materials.

Eroding Opacity with Dynamic Parameters

The Dynamic Parameter Node allows us to pass float data between the Material Editor and Niagara. We can create up to four Parameters that can be animated inside of Niagara that will then adjust our material. These additional parameters can be used for things like UV adjustment, Opacity Control, Emissive Glows and Erosion.

We are going to explore adding Erosion to our **M_VFXTrans** Material. Before we do, let's explore what Erosion is and why we might want to use it. In VFX, Erosion is a technique that helps us remove opaque/visible parts of a texture over time until all pixels are transparent. It can be quite helpful for dissolving a texture or reducing the visibility of an effect for smoke particles etc.

In Figures 8.6 and 8.7, the BaseColor input has been redirected to the Emissive input with an additional Multiply. This is so you can visually see the result in the book, you do not need to make this change to your materials. Thus, the instructions we provide below only modify the Opacity Input.

Eroding Our Translucent VFX Master – Value Step

This first Erosion exercise will create a material with a harder edge and remove the softness of our texture as it dissolves. It can be useful for liquids or dissolve effects, you might find on Sci Fi characters. Let's begin:

1. In the **Content Browser**, navigate to the folder **Content | Materials | Master**.
2. Check your Material **M_VFXTrans** looks like the example shown in Figure 8.2.
3. With the Material **M_VFXTrans** selected in the Content Browser, press Ctrl+D to create a Duplicate. Name this *M_VFXTrans_ValueStep*.
4. Open our newly created Material **M_VFXTrans_ValueStep**.

5. Under the **ParticleColor** node in the Material Graph right click and Search for *DynamicParameter.*

6. Select the **DynamicParameter** node and using the **DetailsPanel** type the name *Erode* into the **Param Names Index** [0] and set its **Default Value** for **R** to *0.75.*

7. Next to the **DynamicParameter** node, right click and Search for the node *Value Step.*

8. Connect the **R** pin from our **ParticleTexture** node to the **Gradient (S)** pin of the **ValueStep** node.

9. Connect the **Erode** output from our **DynamicParameter** node to the **Mask Offset Value (S)** of the **ValueStep** node.

10. Move all of our created nodes a bit to the left to make some more space between the instruction nodes and the material output node.

11. To the right of our **ValueStep** node, hold M and left click to create a *Multiply* Node.

12. Connect the **R** output from our **ParticleTexture** node to the **A** input of the **Multiply** node.

13. Connect the output from the **ValueStep** node to the **B** input of the **Multiply** node.

14. To the right of the **Multiply** node, right click and search for a *Saturate* node.

15. Connect the output of the **Multiply** node into the **Saturate** node. This will ensure values are clamped between 0 and 1.

16. Connect the output pin of the **Saturate** node into the **Opacity** input pin on the material output node.

The completed material can be seen in Figure 8.6, if you'd like to preview the erosion more clearly in the Material Editor try redirecting the BaseColor input into the

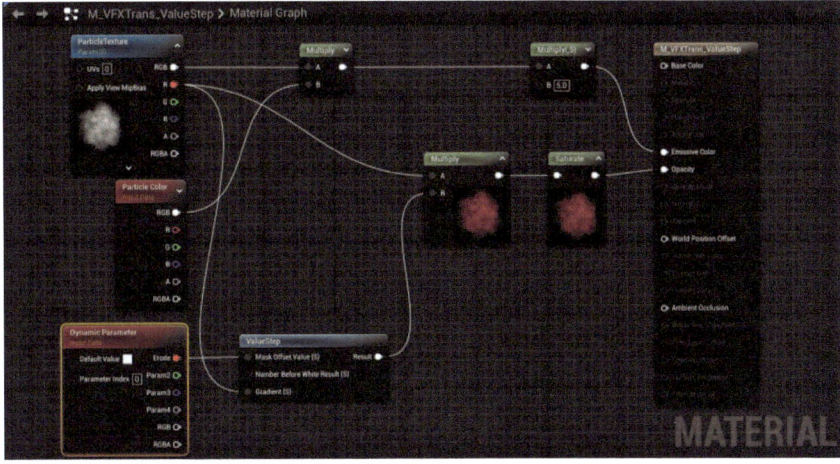

FIGURE 8.6 Eroding opacity with dynamic material parameters – value step.

Emissive input with a Multiply Node to boost the visibility. Just remember to put it back after testing. Lowering the Erode value subtly below one will show your texture dissolving while maintaining a hard edge. Different textures will Erode at different values depending on their grayscale values, a bit of testing in Niagara later on is super helpful.

Eroding Our Translucent VFX Master – Smooth Step

1. In the **Content Browser**, navigate to the folder **Content | Materials | Master**.
2. With the Material **M_VFXTrans** selected in the Content Browser, press Ctrl+D to create a Duplicate. Name this *M_VFXTrans_SmoothStep*.
3. Double click on the Material **M_VFXTrans_SmoothStep** to open the Material Editor.
4. Under the **ParticleColor** node in the Material Graph right click and Search for *DynamicParameter*.
5. Select the **DynamicParameter** node and using the **DetailsPanel** type the name *Erode* into the **Param Names Index [0]** and set its **Default Value** for **R** to *0.75*.
6. Next to our **DynamicParameter** node, right click and Search for the node *SmoothStep*.
7. Drag out from the **R** output from our **ParticleTexture** node and search for a *OneMinus* node. This should create a node labeled **1-x.**
8. Place the **1-x** node just before our **SmoothStep** Node. Connect the **1-x** output pin to the **SmoothStep Min** Input.
9. Connect the **Erode** output from our **DynamicParameter** node to the **Value** input of the **SmoothStep** node.
10. To the right of our **SmoothStep** node, hold M and left click to create a *Multiply* Node.
11. Connect the **R** output from our **ParticleTexture** to the **A** input of the **Multiply** Node.
12. Connect the output from the **SmoothStep** node to the **B** input of the Node.
13. To the right of the **Multiply** node, right click and search for a *Saturate* node.
14. Connect the output of the **Multiply** node into the **Saturate** node. This will ensure values are clamped between 0 and 1.
15. Connect the output pin of the **Saturate** node into the **Opacity** input pin on the material output node.

The completed Material can be seen in Figure 8.7.

As per our previous erosion material, if you wish to preview the effect clearly in the Material Editor try redirecting the BaseColor input into the Emissive input with a multiply to boost the visibility. Just remember to put it back after testing. By lowering the Erode value less than one gently you should the texture dissolve with a soft edge. This approach while similar is better suited to softer effects such as smoke, where fades need to be more subtle.

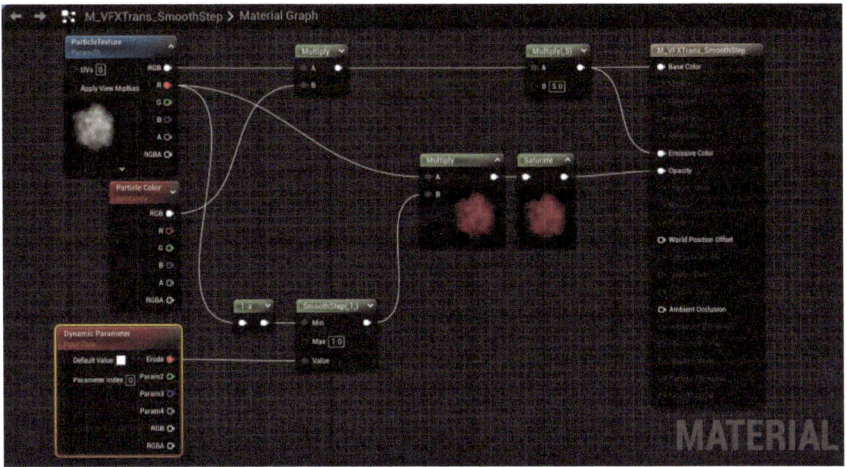

FIGURE 8.7   Eroding opacity with dynamic material parameters – smooth step.

Conclusion

In this chapter we initially created two VFX Master Materials and learned about nodes that help link Niagara and the Material. We then created two additional Materials to explore Material Erosion and Dynamic Parameters.

Over the coming Chapters we will begin to expand on these Materials and use them in the Niagara Editor. To develop the Translucent Master Material further you could explore combining the different Erosion Step Nodes with Switch Parameters. Switches can help us create less Master Materials by allowing artists to turn features on and off when required.

Before we move on, let's check your VFX Material knowledge so far with a short quiz.

Chapter 8 Quiz

Question 1: What are Blend Modes?

    a. Blend Modes allow us to turn on different parts of the landscape system.

    b. Blend Modes are responsible for drawing all the decals in a scene.

    c. Blend Modes describe how our Materials will be rendered on top of other objects in our scene.

Question 2: What are Shading Models?

    a. A textured Static Mesh

    b. An algorithm that defines how a material interacts with light

    c. A type of renderer for Particles.

Question 3: What features can we add to our Materials to break up repetition in VFX?

    a. Panners and UV Distortion

    b. Tints

    c. Dynamic Parameters

    d. All of the Above

Question 4: What is the name of the node that passes Color and Alpha values between the Material Editor and Niagara?

    a. ParticleData

    b. ParticleColor

    c. ParticleMaster

Answers

Question 1: c

Question 2: b

Question 3: d

Question 4: b

9

Introduction to Niagara and VFX in Unreal Engine

Introduction

This chapter introduces you to the Niagara Editor in Unreal Engine, you'll learn about:

- Key ingredients for Niagara Effects.
- How to work with Niagara Emitters and Systems.
- Placing and Viewing Niagara Systems in a Level.

What Is Niagara?

Niagara is a suite of tools that allows Technical Artists to create next generation Particle and Visual Effect Systems. There are four main elements in Niagara which are:

- Niagara Systems
- Niagara Emitters
- Niagara Modules
- Niagara Parameters

As a Technical Artist you have a lot of flexibility and power within these tools to create many unique and detailed effects. But why? Visual Effects add flair, motion and excitement to our Games and Scenes. The Niagara suite of tools provides a great deal of power to us as developers to create beautiful Visual Effects for our projects.

To use Niagara, we need art assets, the Niagara toolset animates and adjusts art assets over time. But what assets do we need? Most Particle Effects are made up of textures, materials, meshes and ribbons. As Technical Artists, we may be requested to generate these assets, to support your learning we have provided textures in the example project which we will use in combination with materials over the next few chapters. It's helpful to build up a library of textures as well as generating your own within DCC's like Photoshop, Houdini and Substance Designer.

Let's now move on to creating some very simple systems and explore the UI within the Niagara Editor.

DOI: 10.1201/9781032663852-9

Introduction to Niagara Systems

A Niagara System asset can contain one or more Niagara Emitters which combine to create an overall Particle Effect. For example a Plasma Weapon may have an initial Muzzle Effect, a Plasma Effect and a Smoke Effect. A Niagara System asset can control all of these separate Effects/Emitters over a singular timeline. This also means that Systems give us a powerful way to debug when things don't quite work as planned. Systems do this by providing a very handy timeline where we can see precisely when different Emitters are triggered making it quite clear which ones are working properly.

The System asset is also the part of the Niagara pipeline that is placed in Unreal Levels. As with other Unreal Actors, we can manipulate Transforms of Niagara Systems and place them throughout our worlds.

USEFUL TIP

Always keep Niagara Systems in their own folder in the World Outliner, this allows you to easily toggle VFX effects on and off as you build your worlds.

Let's now create our first Niagara System Asset. We will begin our journey with very limited features and build up the complexity over time.

Creating the DeskSmoke System Asset

1. In the **Content Browser**, navigate to the **Content** folder.
2. Click the **+ Add** button in the top left corner of the **Content Browser**.
3. Select **New Folder** from the popup menu.
4. Name the folder *VFX*.
5. Right click anywhere in the **VFX** folder and select **VFX** from the popup menu and then **Niagara System**.
6. From the Popup Menu Select **New system from selected emitter(s)**.
7. Select **Empty** from the list of template options and click the **Green +** button.
8. Click **Finish** to close the Menu.
9. Navigate back to the **Content Browser** and call the new Niagara System asset *DeskSmoke_System*.
10. Double click the **DeskSmoke_System**, this will launch the Niagara Editor shown in Figure 9.1.

The Niagara Editor shares many of the key workflow concepts of other areas of Unreal Engine. The central space is the System Overview. Niagara places modules vertically in an Emitter Overview Node or in the System Overview Node. Unlike Blueprints or Materials there are no node links, instead we have to edit and add modules to the stacks to create behaviors in our Particle Effects.

FIGURE 9.1   The Niagara interface.

To the left of the System Overview is our Preview Viewport, this will show particle motion in Real Time. We can disable playback using the shortcut Ctrl+R to turn off Real Time Performance or by using the Timeline playback controls which are underneath the System Overview. The Timeline is particularly helpful in a Niagara System asset as it allows us to control and toggle multiple emitters from one place.

We also have Parameters and Details options in Niagara Assets, The Details Panel is on the far right of the UI. The Details Panel is used to customize our Systems and Emitters. We will leverage this menu a lot to control the behavior of our Particle Effects. A common workflow you will see in this book is the conversion of a Parameters type. For example a Particle may have a set number of spawned particles by default, but we may wish to change it to Spawn a varied amount of particles using a Random Float Range. This manipulation of Parameter types will become second nature as you create more and more Niagara assets.

At the bottom left of the Niagara Editor is the Parameters, we use this section of the UI when we want to add in our own Parameters and Modules. Niagara let's us create and expose a great many data types to power our Particle Effects.

We are now going to build the **DeskSmoke_System** and start working with the Niagara UI. Ensure the **DeskSmoke_System** is open in the Niagara Editor by double clicking on the asset in the Content Browser and then we can begin.

Creating the Configuring System Asset

1. Click on our **DeskSmoke_System** Overview Node in the middle of the System Overview.
2. The **Details** panel on the right will now show the System Default Properties.
3. Under the sub menu **Random**, find the property **Determinism** and set the checkbox to *True*. This gives our System a "Seed". The idea behind this is that

FIGURE 9.2   The Niagara system overview node.

our Particle System can behave in a repeatable way, this is *not required* for most background VFX but if you have an important cutscene and you would like your effect to work in a predictable manner, using **Determinism** is key.

4. Under **Warmup**, find the property **Warmup Time** and set it to *10*. This will render the particle system a number of seconds prior to the game starting. It can be helpful to use this on persistent effects so players do not see the systems start from nothing, for example a spooky graveyard needs fog to look like it's been there for a long time and not vented from a small smoke machine. Be careful not to set **Warmup Time** too long; it can cause performance issues if over used.

5. Click the **Save** Button in the Niagara Editor.

Before progressing with our **DeskSmoke_System**, review your work against Figure 9.2 and we will then move onto using Niagara Emitters.

Introduction to Niagara Emitters

Niagara Systems can contain many Niagara Emitters however in our first Effect we will use only one Emitter. Emitters are responsible for creating our Particle Effect behaviors in several stages. During each stage we'll work with Niagara modules that add or edit Particle System Functionality.

Emitter Properties

The first section of our Emitter Overview Node allows us to control several important toggles for features such as Determinism, Local Space Control, CPU/GPU sim, and Persistent ID's. The Emitter Properties section is typically our first port of manipulation when we want to set up overall Emitter behavior.

Emitter Summary

The Emitter Summary is a user created collection of the most important/frequently used properties of a Niagara Emitter. You may wish to use them when your Emitters become very complex to provide one menu option instead of diving into multiple property menus. It's not vital that you use the Emitter Summary, however, you may find them helpful when revisiting older work or when sharing complex projects with team members.

Emitter Spawn

The Emitter Spawn group defines what happens to our Particles when they are first generated on the CPU. It only runs once and should be used to initialize System Defaults, the nodes are executed from top to bottom. You'll find in many example templates and simple effects that this Stage is often empty.

Emitter Update

Emitter Update allows us to configure how particles are created. For example, we can configure particles to Spawn Instantly or at a Rate over time. There is also the option to Configure the Emitter State. This provides us with the ability to set our Particles Life Cycle Mode. Our particle's Life Cycle sets up whether an Effect loops, runs once or a set number of times. It's possible for the Life Cycle setting to be configured by the Niagara System; this can be useful if you want a number of Emitters to all behave in a similar way.

Particle Spawn

This group is called per Particle once they are created. During this stage we set parameters of our Particles such as Size, Color, Location and Velocity. Most of these parameters can be found in the Initialize Particle node. It's likely that you will spend a fair bit of time at this stage; it is one of the most defining sections of an Emitter.

Particle Update

Particle Update controls what happens during a Particle's Lifetime and is called every frame per particle. This stage handles a lot of the animation and behavior of our Particle Effects. For example, we may wish to scale a Particle over its life, alter its color or add complex physics to it. This stage relies on good foundations and parameters from the Particle Spawn, be careful not to rush through to the Particle Update stage as it's quite easy to over complicate effects unnecessarily.

Render

The Render stage controls the visual appearance of a Nigara Emitter. We have several types of Particles we can render with the most common ones being Sprites, Meshes, Ribbons and Lights.

The Render Stage allows us to set up links to art assets and adjust them so that they behave correctly with in-game cameras and alignments. In later versions of Unreal further options have been added to the Render stage including Components, Decals, Geometry Caches and Volumes. While the feature set continues to expand, it's important to learn the common types to begin with as most Particle Effects systems will make use of them.

Let's now revisit our **DeskSmoke_System,** we are going to customize the look of our Smoke Particle effect. We'll make use of various stages and modules of the Emitter to help create a stylized smokey appearance. Let's get started!

Creating the Our Niagara Emitter

1. Click on our **DeskSmoke_System** Emitter Overview Node in the middle of the System Overview.
2. Select the **Emitter Update** stage, change the **Life Cycle** Mode from **System** to **Self** and set the **Loop Duration** to *3* Seconds.
3. Next click on the Plus Button Next to the **Emitter Update** Stage, from the menu, select **Spawn Rate**.
4. Set the **Spawn Rate** to *20*. You should now see a white circle appear in the Viewport.
5. It's helpful to hit the **Play** button on the **Timeline**, this will ensure you are viewing the Particle Effect over time. In addition, if Realtime playback does not appear to be working, click the **Triple Bar** Button in the top left of the viewport and **ensure** Realtime is **enabled/ticked**.
6. Next, move down to the **Particle Spawn** Stage, click on the **Initialize Particle** module. You'll use the **Initialize Particle** module on almost all Emitters, here we set many of the default properties for any Emitter.
7. Locate the **LifeMode** property, it should be set to **Direct Set**.
8. Now find the **Lifetime** property, by default this will be set to 5. Look to the right of the value and click on the down arrow. From the popup menu search for *Random Range Float*.
9. **Random Range Float**, allows us to add variety to a value, in this case how long a particle will live. Set the **Minimum** value to *10* and the **Maximum** to *15*.
10. Next, locate the **Sprite Size Mode** property, change this from **Unset** to **Random Uniform**.
11. Set the **Uniform Sprite Size Min** to *25* and the **Uniform Sprite Size Max** to *35*. Much like the earlier setting, this is all about adding variety.
12. Now let's move the particles apart, by default they spawn all in the same place. To do this, click the **green +** button next to **Particle Spawn** and search for *Shape Location*, select it from the menu.
13. The default shape location is a sphere, you'll see lots of white dots as shown in Figure 9.3.

FIGURE 9.3 Shape location spawn node.

Now that we have some particles spawning, it's time to place our Niagara Asset into our Level. This helps us check the scale and overall properties, you will need to refer to in-game/level performance regularly as setting values just inside an isolated Niagara Editor Window won't give you an understanding of the feel/appearance of the effect.

1. Click on the **WizardDesk_Start** tab just under the **File** Menu at the top left of the UI. This will swap to the Level Viewport while keeping the Niagara Editor Open.
2. In the **Content Browser**, navigate to the **Content | VFX** folder.
3. Left click on the **DeskSmoke_System** asset and drag it into the scene near the large green floor light by the desk. A value close to **X**=−320, **Y**=−820, **Z**=−130 would be fine.

An example of the asset placed can be seen in Figure 9.4, it's up to you if you want to use a version of the level with Materials applied which was created in the previous chapters. In this example, we are using the Checkerboard Scene to allow us to focus on the effects.

Upon reviewing the Particles in the world, the Sprite Sizes could be a bit bigger, but most importantly we should apply our Material **M_VFXTrans_SmoothStep** to get a better appreciation of the Particles appearance.

1. To apply the Material, navigate to the **Content | Materials | Master** folder.
2. Select the Material **M_VFXTrans_SmoothStep**.
3. Return to the **Niagara Editor**. If you docked the Niagara Editor you can return to it by clicking on the **DeskSmoke_System** name next to the Level Name at the top left of the UI, if you need to open the Editor from scratch find, the **DeskSmoke_System** using the Content Browser and double click the asset.
4. Click on the Sprite Renderer module, this should be at the bottom of the Niagara Emitter Overview Node.
5. Set the Material to be our Material *M_VFXTrans_SmoothStep*.
6. If you look in the level the Particles will look quite small but will now have our Material applied to each particle. To improve the effect, hop back to the Niagara Editor, click on the **Initialize Particle** module and set the **Uniform Sprite Size Min** to *115* and the **Uniform Sprite Size Max** to *125*.

FIGURE 9.4   Desk smoke placed in the world.

FIGURE 9.5   Desk smoke with our material and sprite size changes.

Figure 9.5 shows the results of our Material and Sprite Size Changes in the level.

Let's continue editing the Particle System and add some color, we are going to tint the HUE of the particles to be green. With any of these settings, we encourage you to have a play and customize the effect to your liking. The results are not an exact science!

1. Click the **green+** button next to **Particle Update** and select *Color* from the popup menu.
2. Select the **Color** module, we are given **R,G,B**, and **A** values by default. Changing these values will set the Particles Color value as our Material made use of the Particle Color node.
3. We are going to override the **Color** modules default behavior, to do this, click the little down arrow next to the **Alpha/A** value input. From the pop up menu select *Color from Curve*. This allows us to assign different colors to an Effect as a particle ages.
4. To assign a new Color to our **Color Gradient**, we can either double click the small white boxes on the top of the gradient (to open a **Color Picker**) or we can double click anywhere along the top of the gradient to create new boxes and then double click them to open a **Color Picker**. The white/colored boxes to the left represent the start of the particle's life whereas the particles on the right represent the particle's death.
5. Figure 9.6 shows two green hues have been added along the top of the gradient. If you'd like to achieve a similar result, use the following RGB Values.
   a. Color 1: **R=0, G=4, B=0.29**
   b. Color 2: **R= 0.48, G=1, B=0**

FIGURE 9.6 Particle color from curve.

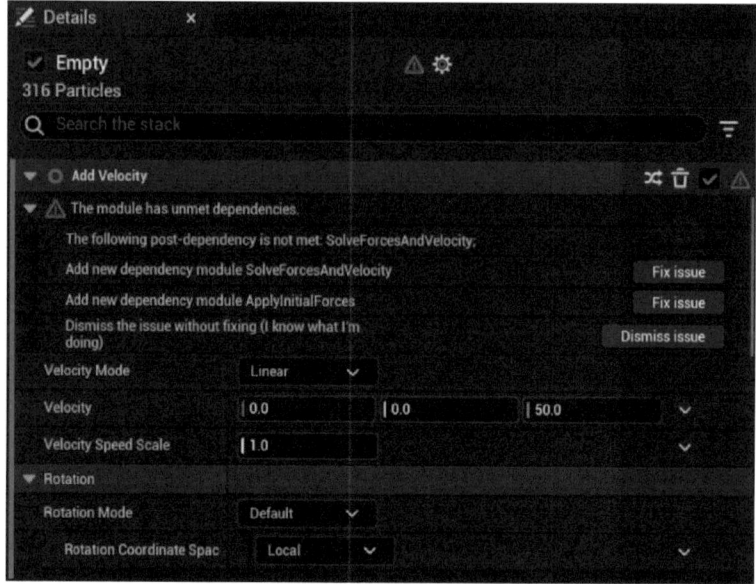

FIGURE 9.7   Modules with unmet dependencies.

6. The boxes on the underside of the gradient represent Alpha, on the left the value is set to white which represents opaque and on the right the value is black which represents transparent. We are going to leave the defaults for now but you could customize these values to create a different fading for our particles.

7. Let's now add a bit of velocity to our Particles so they enter the scene. To do this, click the green + button next to **Particle Spawn** and select *Add Velocity* from the Popup Menu.

8. When you add **Velocity** to an empty Emitter you will receive some warnings as shown in Figure 9.7, click on the **Fix Issue** button for both warnings and this will add in the necessary modules that **Add Velocity** requires.

9. Once the fix has been applied, your Particles will move in the **Z axis** by default, we'd like our Particles to move in the **X** by default so that they flow into the center of the scene.

10. Click on the down arrow to the right side of the **Velocity input** value, from the popup menu select *Random Range Vector*.

11. Set the **Velocity Minimum** *X* value to be *17* and the **Velocity Maximum** *X* value to be *20*. If you check the Level Viewport the particles should now be moving toward the center of the scene.

12. Next, click the green + button next to **Particle Update** and select *Scale Sprite Size* from the Popup Menu.

13. We can now use the graph to scale our particle size over their life. Adjust the points so that the keyframes at 0 and 1 both have values at 0. Then add a

FIGURE 9.8 Particle scale sprite size graph.

keyframe by right clicking on the graph at around 0.2 of the Particles life and set the value to 1. This will mean that the particles will grow to full size and then scale to nothing. An example of the Graph can be seen in Figure 9.8.

14. Let's now bend the particles slightly. Click the green + button next to **Particle Update** and select *Acceleration Force* from the Popup Menu.
15. Select the **Acceleration Force** module, set the value to be a **Random Range Vector** type by using the dropdown arrow. Set the Minimum Value as **X** = *0*, **Y** = *–2*, **Z** = *0* and the Maximum Value as **X** = *0*, **Y** = *0*, **Z** = *0*. This will now bend the Smoke stream around the desk.
16. You might find that a lot of the Smoke particles are intersecting with the desk, to improve this we are going to add a Collision Module. Click the green + button next to **Particle Update** and select *Collision* from the Popup Menu. If you look in the Level Viewport you should see that there are less intersections after a few seconds.

We are almost at the end of our first effect. To improve the look of the effect, you might like to try reducing the radius at which the particles are spawned. To do this;

1. Select the **Shape Location** node in the **Particle Spawn** stage.
2. Try lowering the **Sphere Radius** value to *50* or less.
3. To complete our effect we are going to incorporate the Erode parameter we created in the Material in Chapter 8. Click the green + button next to **Particle Update** and select *Dynamic Material Parameter* from the Popup Menu.
4. Our particles will now disappear as the default **Erode Value** is 0. Select the **Dynamic Material Parameter Module**, locate the **Erode Parameter** and click the down arrow icon. From the pop up menu select *Float from Curve*.
5. Our effect will now look a lot better in the Level Viewport, particles will be fading now with Particle Color Alpha and erosion making the effect look more convincing. We can customize things further by adding Keyframes to the erosion curve if we want the particles to erode sooner or later.
6. Click Save in the Niagara Editor.

Figures 9.9 and 9.10 show the result of our effect in the Level and Niagara Editor, Congratulations on building your first Effect!

FIGURE 9.9   Completed Niagara emitter for desk smoke effect.

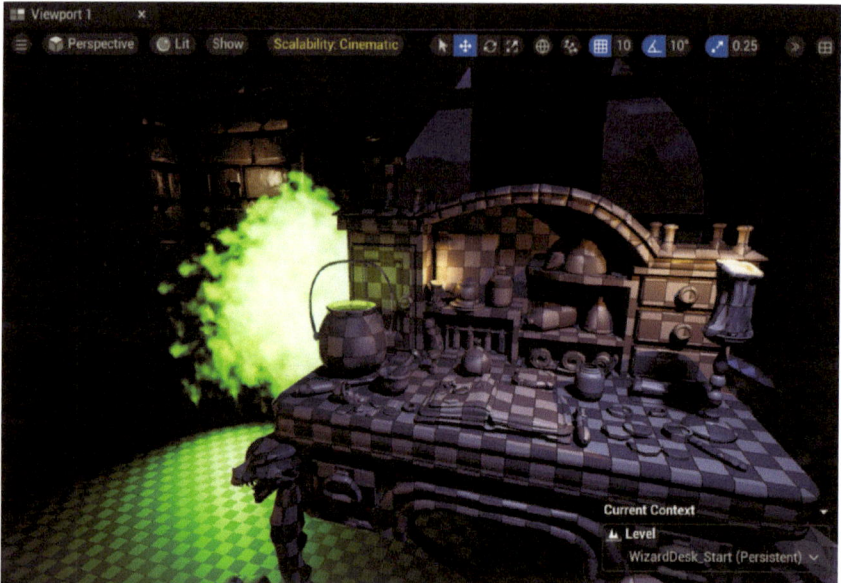

FIGURE 9.10   Level shot for completed desk smoke system.

USEFUL TIP

Try using the Show | Particle Counts option in the Niagara Viewport to learn about the number of Particles your Niagara Systems create. When Systems go over several hundred you may need to lower the Spawn Rate or Life Time to balance Game Performance.

FIGURE 9.11 Niagara templates.

Niagara Basic Templates

In our first effect we did not utilize a starting template, we did this to help us focus on creating modules from scratch. In a production environment you will find the templates very helpful, try learning about each of the example basic templates as shown in Figure 9.11. When creating your effects from scratch it's sensible to pick a template that's closest to your effect, this will help save you time and set up a lot of the required behavior.

Once you have some mastery over Niagara try to build up a library of your own templates. Having your own examples at the ready makes it much easier to focus on the visual quality of your project work and avoid technical issues.

Conclusion

In this chapter, you created your very first Niagara Particle System within the Niagara Editor. We began by learning about the different types of Niagara assets such as Systems and Emitters and then went on to fine tune our Particle Effect using modules, parameters, curves, ranges and erosion.

In the next few chapters, we will expand on this introduction to create several other effects and continue to learn the different Niagara Modules and features.

Before we move forward, let's check your Niagara Editor know how with a short quiz.

Chapter 9 Quiz

Question 1: What is a Niagara System?

    a. The Niagara System is an optimization asset in Unreal Engine.

    b. The Niagara System is a network protocol in Unreal Engine.

    c. A Niagara System is an asset that may contain one or several Emitters that build up an overall effect.

    d. It is a pre-provided replica of Niagara Falls.

Question 2: What are the most Common Render types in Niagara?

    a. Sprites, Meshes, Ribbons and Lights

    b. Sprites, Landscapes, Ribbons and Lights

    c. Decals, Brushes, Lights and Sprites

Question 3: If we want to change a Particle Systems Color over time, which Emitter Stage might we use?

    a. Particle Spawn

    b. Particle Update

    c. Emitter Update

    d. Render

Question 4: How do we use Modules in Niagara Emitters and Systems?

    a. We use modules and their parameters to implement behaviors during different Emitter stages.

    b. We use modules as a template for an entire Particle Effect.

    c. Modules can contain Several Emitters that help build up the overall effect.

Answers

Question 1: c

Question 2: a

Question 3: b

Question 4: a

10

Creating the Energy Orb

Introduction

In this chapter, we are going to build the Energy Orb System, you'll learn about:

- Creating Materials with UV Distortion Effects.
- Combining multiple Niagara Emitters in Niagara System Assets.
- Managing Different Spawn Location Types.
- Manipulating Velocities through Particle Update.

The Energy Orb Materials

To begin creating our Energy Orb, we need to make a new VFX Material, this is because we'd like a more chaotic energy and distortion in our Material. Fortunately, we can still leverage much of our existing **M_VFXTrans_SmoothStep** Material. During this next example we'll make use of nodes such as Panners and Rotators to animate texture coordinates. We will then feed this animation into our Materials UV inputs to create a chaotic energy effect.

Distorting textures is a big part of VFX Materials. The use of noise textures, tiling and animation is a great way to make an effect look more complicated than it really is. Try to keep a store of useful grayscale imagery for your VFX projects. You'll be sure to find time for random noises to make effects look more powerful and stunning. Let's now get started and build our Material!

1. To get started navigate to **Content | Materials | Master** and select **M_VFXTrans_SmoothStep**.
2. Right click on the asset in the **Content Browser** and click **Duplicate** from the popup menu. Label the duplicated Material *M_VFXTrans_EnergyOrb*.
3. Double click on the new **M_VFXTrans_EnergyOrb** Material to open it in the Material Editor.
4. Locate the **ParticleTexture** node, set the **ParticleTexture** Parameter to *Particle1* by clicking the **MagicCloud** text and using the search box. You can set this Parameter using other methods if you prefer to find the Texture in the Content Browser instead.

5. All of our new Material Nodes connect into the UV's input on the **ParticleTexture**. Make sure you have plenty of space to the left of the **ParticleTexture** node.

6. Right click in the Material Graph, search and place a *Radial Gradient Exponential Node*. This node will create a round mask that we can control the size and softness of. We are going to use this as a mask to limit the effect of a noise later on.

7. Create two Scalar Parameter nodes, hold S and left click in the Material Graph twice. Label one of the Scalar Parameters *Radius* and the other *Density*.

8. Select the **Radius** node and set its Default Value to *0.44*. Then connect the output to the input of the **Radial Gradient Exponential** node.

9. Select the **Density** node and set its Default Value to *3.45*. Then connect the output to the input of the **Radial Gradient Exponential** node.

10. Drag out from the **Radial Gradient Exponential** node and use the search popup menu to place a *Multiply* Node.

11. In the **Content Browser**, navigate to the **Content | Textures | EnergyOrb** folder.

12. Select the **TextureParticle3**, and add it to the Material underneath the **Radial Gradient Exponential** node.

13. Connect the **RGB** output of **Particle 3** texture sample to the input of **B** of the **Multiply** node we recently created.

14. To the left of the **Particle3** texture sample, right click in the graph and search for a *Rotator* Node.

15. Connect the **Output** of the **Rotator** node to the **UV** input of the **Particle 3** texture sample node.

16. Set the **Speed** value of the **Rotator** node to *3*.

17. To the left of the **Rotator** node, right click and place a *Time* node from the popup menu. Connect the output of the **Time** node into the input of the **Rotator** node.

18. Now right click in the Material Graph and create a *Texture Coordinate* node from the pop up menu.

19. Connect the output of the **Texture Coordinate** node to the **Coordinate Input** of the **Rotator** node.

20. Select the **Texture Coordinate** node and set the **U** and **V** tiling parameters to *0.7*.

The structure we've created so far masks out some of the noise from the texture Particle3, while applying a rotation over time, this can be seen in Figure 10.1. This type of node structure is used regularly to add motion to a selection of pixels, we are now going to add more complexity by adding in some panning textures. Don't worry about getting the speed and exact values of the material correct, we'll most likely revisit the material later when it's applied in our Niagara Emitters. Let's continue with the material and add in the Panning functionality which allows us to move the textures in the U and V coordinate directions.

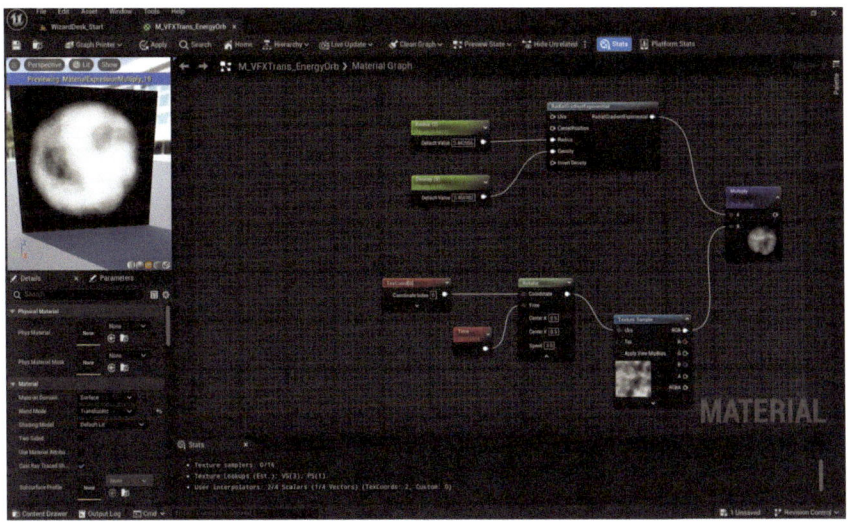

FIGURE 10.1   Rotating noise material chain.

1. In the **Content Browser**, navigate to the **Content | Materials | Master** folder.
2. Double click on our Material **M_VFXTrans_EnergyOrb** to open the Material Editor.
3. Select the **Texture Coordinate** and **Time** Nodes that connect into the **Rotator,** Copy and Paste these nodes below using Ctrl+C and then Ctrl+V.
4. Next, right click in the **Material Graph** and search and place a *Panner* node.
5. Connect the copied **Texture Coordinate** and **Time** nodes into the **Panner** node.
6. Select the **Texture Coordinate** node and set the **U** and **V** tiling to *0.5*.
7. Next, select the **Texture Sample** with the **Particle 3** texture applied and copy and paste this node below. Connect the output of the **Panner** node into the new **Texture Sample**.
8. Select the **Panner** node, set the *X* **Speed** to *0.1* and the **Y Speed** to *−0.2*.
9. If you click the **Live Update** button on the top toolbar and enable *Real Time Nodes* and *All Node Previews* you should now be able to see the **Particle 3** texture sample animate. Figure 10.2 shows the Panning Material Chain and Live Update options.
10. Select all of the nodes in the Panning Chain, copy them and paste a new chain of nodes below.
11. Select the copied **Texture Coordinate** node and set its **U** and **V** **tiling** to *0.004*, this will make the texture very large.
12. Select the copied **Panner** node and set its **X** and **Y Speed** to *0.04*. The animated texture preview should show a very subtle change in grayscale values.

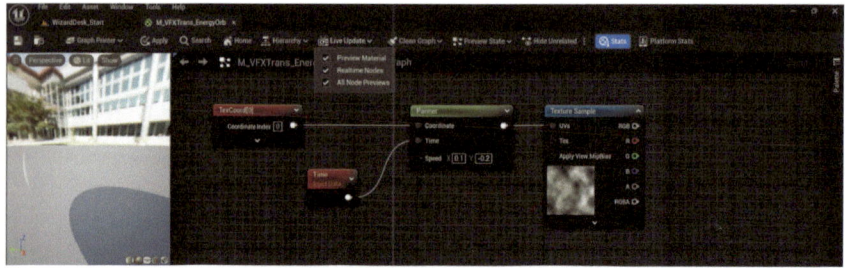

FIGURE 10.2   Panning material chain.

13. Next place a **Multiply** node in front of our animated texture sample nodes as shown in Figure 10.3 and connect the respective **RGB** output pins into the **Multiply A** and **B** inputs. In Figure 10.3, we've expanded all of the Material nodes out so you can see the values more easily, you do not have to do this, this is purely for ease of checking.

14. Next we want to combine both the Multiplies from the Panning and Rotating chains, to do this, place another *Multiply* node into the graph and connect the **A** and **B inputs** from the other multiply nodes as shown in Figure 10.4.

If you preview the result of all of this work you should see a dark smokey cloud texture that rotates and pans. We now need to connect this into the UV's of our **ParticleTexture 2D** Param node.

1. Create a *Scalar Parameter* by holding S and left clicking in the Material Graph. Label this scalar parameter *UV DistortionEXP* and set its value between *0.5* and *0.9*. A higher value will mean less distortion.

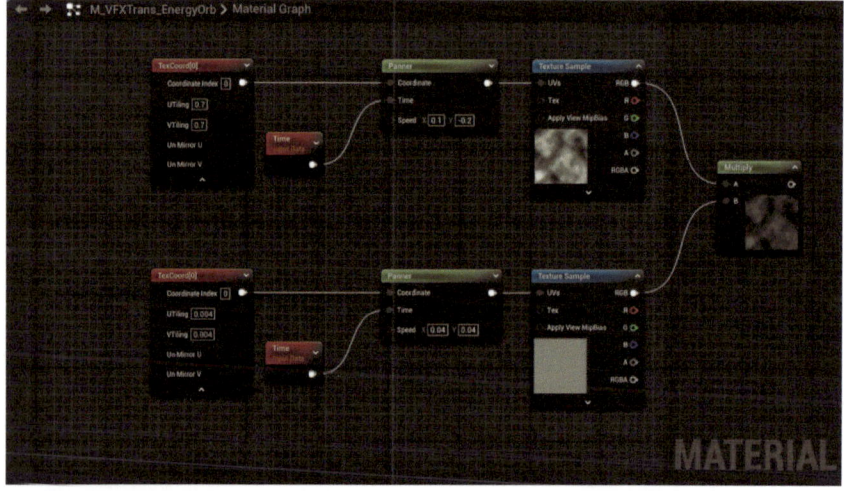

FIGURE 10.3   Combining the panning chains.

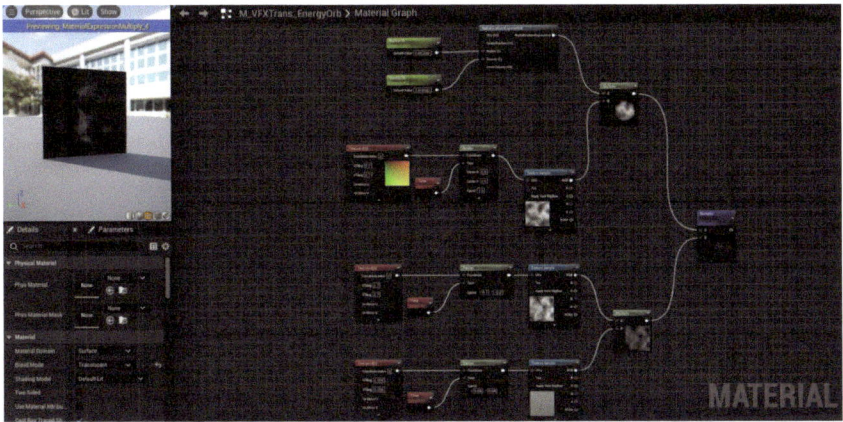

FIGURE 10.4 Combining the panners and rotation chains.

2. Next, create a *Power* node by right clicking in the Material Graph and search for the *Power*.

3. Connect the last **Multiply Output** into the **Base Input** of the **Power** node and connect the **Scalar Parameter UV Distortion EXP** node into the **Exp Input** of the **Power** node. This gives us a way to brighten up the panning and rotating effects, the Multiplies we used before can reduce the overall strength of the effect.

4. Add a *Component Mask* to the graph by right clicking in the Material Graph and searching for *Component Mask*. Ensure that only the **R** and **G channels** are active in the **Component Mask** by setting only those checkboxes as on in the **Details** panel. We do this as the texture's we added to the Panner and Rotator chains have three coordinates, which will not fit into UV space which only has 2.

5. Connect the output of the **Power** node into the input of the **Component Mask**.

6. Next create an *Add* node by holding A and left clicking in the **Material Graph**, connect the **Output** of the **Component Mask** into the **B** input of the **Add** node.

7. Just above the **Add**, create a *TextureCoordinate* node by right clicking in the **Material Graph** and searching for *Texture Coordinate*.

8. Connect the output of the **Texture Coordinate** node into the **A** input of the **Add** node.

9. Finally, connect the **output** of our **Add** node into the **UV input** of the **ParticleTexture Param 2D** node.

The final result of our Material is visible in Figure 10.5, we've now added several layers of UV distortion that adds a lot of detail and interest to the very simple Particle1 texture asset. In your own time it would be good to consider how you could make the material more animatable. You could consider parameterising values and also by

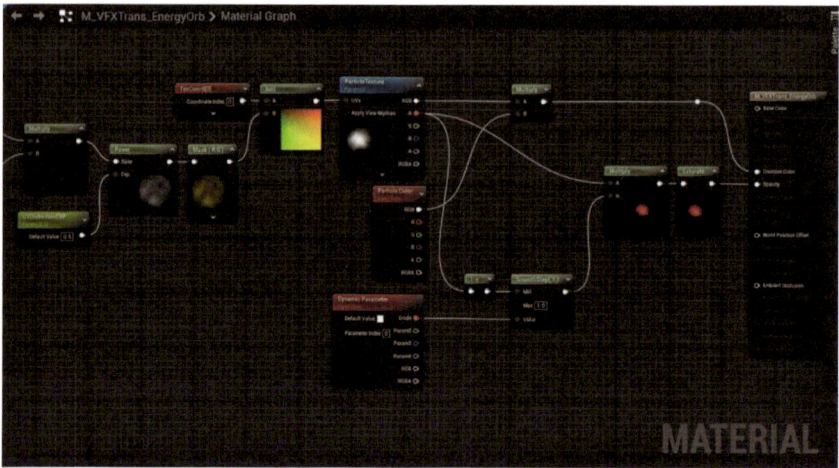

FIGURE 10.5   Combining everything into the UV input.

integrating the Dynamic Parameter node to afford further animation in Niagara. With this material created, we can now move onto Niagara to test it out!

The Energy Orb

We now need to create several Niagara Assets. When a Particle Effect has very distinctive behavior, it makes sense to create separate Emitter Asset in the Content Browser, for our Energy Orb we are going to create the following assets:

- **Energy Storm Emitter** – this will be a series of stationary particles which will feature the Material Discussed in this chapter.
- **Orbiting Particle Emitter** – this is a series of particles which move with vortex noise around the central storm.
- **A Niagara System** – this will incorporate both Emitters and allow us to place the Particle Effect into the world.

Let's get started…

The Energy Storm Emitter

1. In the **Content Browser**, navigate to the **Content | VFX** folder.
2. Right click anywhere in the **VFX** folder and create a **FX\Niagara Emitter** asset. From the pop up menu set the Template to be **Single Looping Particle** and label the asset *EnergyStorm_Emitter*.
3. Right click again in the **VFX** Folder and create a second **FX\Niagara Emitter** asset. From the pop up menu set the Template to be **Empty** and label this asset *OrbitParticle_Emitter*.

4. Open the **EnergyStorm_Emitter** asset by double clicking it in the **Content Browser**.

5. Select the **Sprite Renderer Module** and locate the **Material** parameter. Click where it says **DefaultSpriteMaterial** and using the **Search** options set the value to be *M_VFXTrans_EnergyOrb*.

6. Next, select the **Spawn Burst Instantaneous** module and remove it by pressing the Delete Key. Click the Orange + button next to **Emitter Update** and select *Spawn Rate*.

7. Select the **SpawnRate** module and set the **Spawn Rate** parameter to *3*.

8. Let's now set some visual properties of our Particles, to do this select the **InitializeParticle** module and locate the **LifeTime** Parameter, click on the dropdown arrow to the right of where it says **EmitterCurrentLoopDuration** and set the value to *Random Float in Range*.

9. Set the **Minimum** value to be *4* and the **Maximum** value to be *10*. This will add a slight variation to the particles we spawn.

10. Next, set the **Color Mode** to **Direct Set** and set the value to be *R=0.303821*, **G**=*2.0*, **B**=*3.0*, and **A**=*1*.

11. Let's now add a bit more size variation. Locate the **Sprite Size Random** parameter and set it to Random. Set the **Uniform Sprite Size Min** to *6* and **Uniform Sprite Size Max** to *16*.

12. Next, let's add a bit of rotation, Click the Green + button next to **Particle Update** and search for *SpriteRotationRate*.

13. Select the **SpriteRotationRate** module, click the dropdown arrow to the far right of the **Rotation Rate** value, and change the value to *Random Float in Range*.

14. Set the **Minimum** value to be *0* and the **Maximum** Value to be *5*.

Let's now preview the Effect so far in the Level:

1. Select the **Mesh** *MagicSphere_Mesh* in the **World Outliner**.

2. Ensure a Glass Material has been applied to **Material Element 0,** so that the **Magic Sphere** is **Transparent**. If you have not yet attempted the **Glass Material**, you can find a completed example in the folder **Content | Completed | Materials | Instances | TubeGlass_Inst.**

3. Right click anywhere in the **VFX** Folder and create a **FX\Niagara System** asset. From the pop up menu select **New System from selected emitters(s)**.

4. Set the **Asset Filtering** to **Parent Emitters**.

5. Left click on the **EnergyStorm_Emitter** before clicking the Green + button. We can then click **Finish** to create the **System Asset**. If you find this overly complex, you can always create an Empty System asset and drag and drop the Emitters into the System Asset when it's open in the Niagara Editor.

6. Label the Niagara System Asset as *EnergyOrb_System*.

7. Ensure both Niagara System Asset and Niagara Emitters are all saved, you can do this in either the Content Browser, or Niagara Editor if you have the assets open.

8. Now drag and drop the **EnergyOrb_System** asset from the **Content Browser** into the level and place it inside the **MagicSphere_Mesh**. Note that you will need to disable grid snapping (options in the top right corner of the viewport) as the effect is quite small. Figures 10.6 and 10.7 show the effect so far in game and in the Niagara Editor.

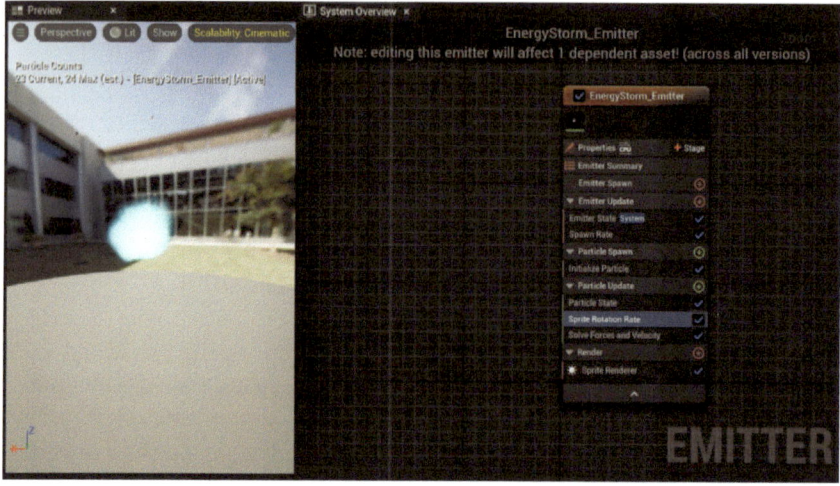

FIGURE 10.6 Previewing our energy storm emitter in the Niagara editor.

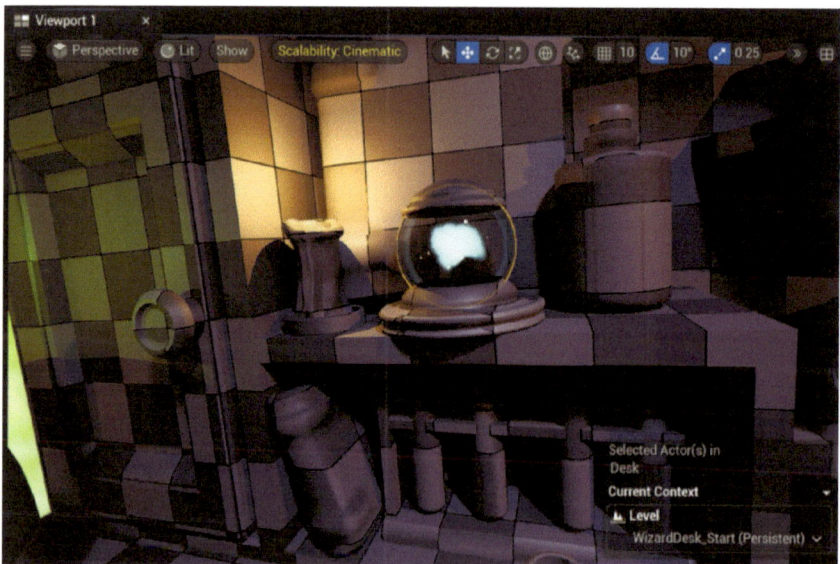

FIGURE 10.7 Previewing our EnergyOrb_System in the level.

Now that we have created our Energy Orb System and preview it in the level we can move onto further detailing the effect. We'll learn about why additional emitters are often needed and push our creativity with Niagara further.

The Orbiting Emitter

We have created the focal point of our effect, however, VFX look more impressive and cooler when layered. By this we mean that the effect either has additional emitters, meshes or materials that help to add more visual interest to our work. We'll now look at how we can do that for our cool Energy Orb.

Our next part of the process will be to create the Orbiting Particles, these particles will quickly rotate around the storm in the center to add some additional visual interest. We'll do this by using location nodes to spawn the particles differently and then add velocity to move the particles. To take the effect further you may want to experiment with some of the Dynamic Parameters or Color fading from the previous chapter.

Let's start building the Orbiting Emitter:

1. In the **Content Browser**, navigate to the **Content | VFX** folder.
2. Right click anywhere in the **VFX** Folder and create a **FX\Niagara Emitter** asset. From the pop up menu set the Template to be **Empty** and label the asset *OrbitParticle_Emitter.*
3. Select the **EmitterState** module in the **EmitterUpdate** stage, change the parameter **LeftCycle** to *Self.* Then set the **Loop Duration** to *4.*
4. Now click the Orange + Button in the **EmitterUpdate** stage and create a *Spawn Rate* module.
5. Select the **Spawn Rate** module and set the **SpawnRate** Parameter to *15.*
6. Select the **Initialize Particle** Module. Change the **LifeTime** parameter to a *Random Float in Range* using the dropdown arrow. Set the **Minimum** value to *3* and the **Maximum** Value to *4.*
7. Now set the **SpriteSizeMode** to be *Random Uniform.* Set the **Uniform Sprite Size Min** to be *0.1* and the **Uniform Sprite Size Max** to be *0.3.* These particles will be quite small so expect to zoom in a fair bit to keep track of them.
8. Click the Green + Button next to the **Particle Spawn** stage. Select *Shape Location* from the menu. The Shape Location node allows us to create particles based on a primitive shape. This can be helpful when we want to spread particles out and stop them from spawning at 0,0,0.
9. Select the **Shape Location** module. Change the **Shape Primitive** to *Ring / Disc.* Set the **Ring Radius** to *3.* You should now start to see the particles appear in a Ring formation, you will likely need to zoom into the **Niagara Viewport** to see this.

The problem with this approach so far is that the particles are spawned randomly around the ring, if we want to animate them to create a follow effect, we need them to spawn more orderly. Let's set that up!

1. Still in the **Shape Location** module, set the **Ring / Disc Distribution Mode** to *Direct.*Set the **U Position** to *Uniform AOr BFloat*. This maps half the particles to A and half to B. It will look counterproductive for now, as the sprites will be moved to 0,0,0 temporarily but when we start to apply forces later, all will be revealed.

2. Next click the Green + Button next to the **Particle Update Stage** and search for a *Color Module*.

3. Select the **Color Module**. Change the **Color Module Value** type to **Color From Curve**. Set the Left and Right most upper **Color** values to $R = 0$, $G = 0.71744$, and $B = 1$.

4. Next, click the Green + Button next to the **Particle Update Stage** and search for a *Vortex Force* Module.

5. Select the **Vortex Force** module. Set the **VortexForceAmount** to *5*. Set the **Origin Pull Amount** to *55*. You should now see several discs of particles orbiting around a Central Point. You can add more discs by adjusting the **Emitter Duration** and **Life Time** of the particles.

6. To close the gaps of the Disc without spawning further particles we could affect the particle size by their speed. To do this, select the Sprite **Renderer**, change the **Alignment Parameter** to *Velocity Aligned*.

7. Next click the Green + Button next to the **Particle Update Stage** and search for a *Scale Sprite Size by Speed* Module.

8. Select the **Scale Sprite Size by Speed** Module. Change the **Velocity Threshold** to around *200*. Experiment with **Max Scale Factor Y** value, numbers of *50* or above will stretch the particles out quite drastically. Figure 10.8 for an example shows an example with *Y* being 75.

9. Hit **Save** in the **Niagara Editor** to store our Changes.

We've now created our Orbiting Particle, as we move into the next exercise keep an eye on the speed and size of the particles. Our next task will be to merge the two Emitters together. We want the Orbiting Particle to help ground our Energy Orb. If the Orbiting Particle ends up being a bit too big or fast the effect can fall apart. It's important to think of balance when you join multiple Emitter systems, things like size, speed, color, texture can really impact the overall effect. Don't be afraid to stray from the values we include in the book, you might prefer a different look to the values we provide!

FIGURE 10.8   Previewing our OrtbitParticle_Emitter in the Niagara editor.

Energy Orb System

To bring the two Emitters together we need a System Asset. Let's now build this Asset to create our overall Energy Orb effect.

1. Navigate to the **Content | VFX** folder in the **Content Browser**, double click on the asset **EnergyOrb_System**.
2. Hop back to the Content Browser, and while still in the **VFX** folder, select the **OrbitParticle_Emitter** and drag and drop it into our **EnergyOrb_System**. This will add the Emitter alongside the **EnergyStorm_Emitter.**
3. With both Emitter's added to our System, click **Save** in the Niagara Editor.
4. Close Niagara so that you can preview the effect in the viewport.

You should now see both Emitters working in our System asset in the Level. An example of this can be seen in Figure 10.9. This effect has a relatively low Particle Count, you could take this further by adding more Orbiting Emitters and or adjusting their Vortex Axis to create different Orbits to make things more interesting and chaotic.

USEFUL TIP

Duplicating Emitters in System Assets can help create cool looking effects with only minor adjustments, Figure 10.10 shows our Orbital Particle Emitter duplicated several times with only adjustments made to the Vortex Force Axis. The resulting Orbital Effect looks much more interesting.

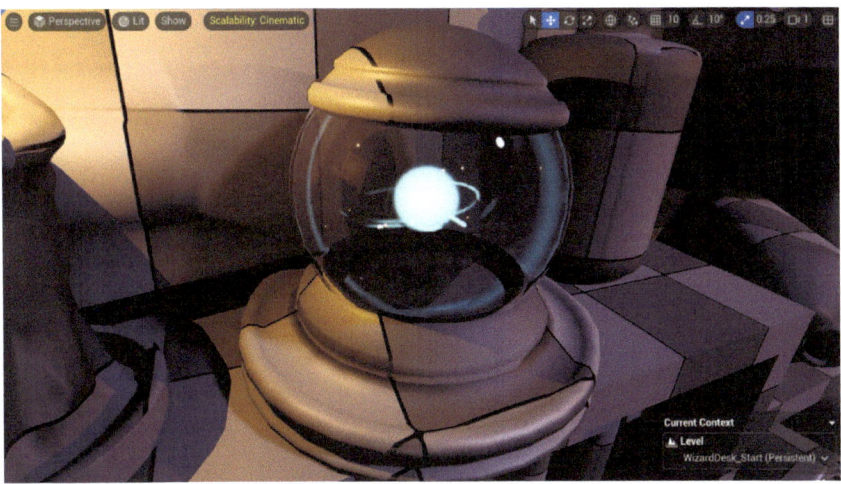

FIGURE 10.9 Previewing our final energy orb system in the level.

FIGURE 10.10   Energy orb Niagara system with extra emitters.

Conclusion

In this chapter, we started out learning about Panning and Rotating UV space to add distortions to our Materials. The new Material created the chaotic backbone for our Energy Orb Emitter. We went on to create a two stage Emitter in the Niagara Editor to help replicate stationary energy particles and orbiting high energy particles. The combined Particle Effect has allowed us to manipulate shape locations and place particles in different positions around our scene. Try experimenting with the Shape Location module to create your own interesting patterns.

In the next chapter we'll explore how we can create sparks for our cauldron effect!

Before we move forward, let's check your Material and Niagara know how with a short quiz.

Chapter 10 Quiz

Question 1: What Inputs does a Panner node have?

a.   Speed, Mass and Coordinate

b.   Coordinate, Time and Speed

c.   Acceleration, Coordinate and Time

Question 2: Which are methods to add more Emitters to a Niagara System?

a.   Drag and drop a new Emitter from the Content Browser into the Niagara Editor.

b.   Copy and paste an Existing Emitter in a Niagara Editor.

c.   Right click and select Add Emitter in the Niagara Editor.

d.   Press E while in the Niagara System Editor.

e.   All of the above.

Question 3: What shapes does the Shape Location node allow us to do in the Niagara Editor?

a. The Shape Location node allows us to draw particles on a shape at a specific location. It is commonly used in Particle Spawn to set up particles.

b. The Shape Location allows only Particles that are a certain shape to move.

c. The Shape Location node adjusts the deformation of landscapes in the Unreal Editor.

Question 4: Why do we need to use a Mask Component node when connecting Noises / Textures into UV inputs of other textures?

a. The Mask Component node makes the UV's more efficient.

b. The Mask Component node allows us to hide the UV's.

c. The UV Input only affords two channels, The Mask Component Node can reduce the amount of channels coming from a Texture/Noise to make the connection compatible.

Answers

Question 1: b

Question 2: e

Question 3: a

Question 4: c

11

Creating Our Sparking Cauldron

Introduction

In this chapter, we will create our Sparking Cauldron VFX System, you'll learn about:

- Animating swirling particles for our Cauldron's bubbles.
- Changing Particle color over time to add variation to our Cauldron's particles.
- Spawning random sparks that alter size and collide with our world.
- Manipulating velocities through Particle Update to create energy bursts and constant bubbling effects.

Our completed effect will sit just inside the Cauldron_Mesh model in the scene, which is on the left side of the desk. We are going to work with relatively simple materials in this chapter and rely on Niagara to do more heavy lifting compared to the past couple of examples. We'll work with Emitters before creating and placing the final system within the level.

To begin creating our Sparking Cauldron Effect we need to make a new VFX Material Instance. We are only going to change the texture of our Instance, this will allow us to make the effect look more like a magical particle than a smoke or a fog. To get started let's create the material.

1. Navigate to **Content | Materials | Master** and locate the **M_VFXTrans** Material.
2. Right click on the asset in the **Content Browser** and click **Create Material Instance** from the popup menu.
3. Name the new instance Material *MI_CauldronSwirl* and move the Material Instance to the **Instances** folder.
4. Double click on the **MI_CauldronSwirl** Asset.
5. In the Material Instances Editor, tick the box next to the **ParticleTexture** Parameter.
6. Then use the dropdown next to the **ParticleTexture** Parameter and search for the **MagicSparkle** Texture.
7. Now **Save** and **Close** the **Material Instance**.

The Material Instance should look like the example shown in Figure 11.1. Adding slight visual changes to VFX particles is a really fast way of creating separation

DOI: 10.1201/9781032663852-11

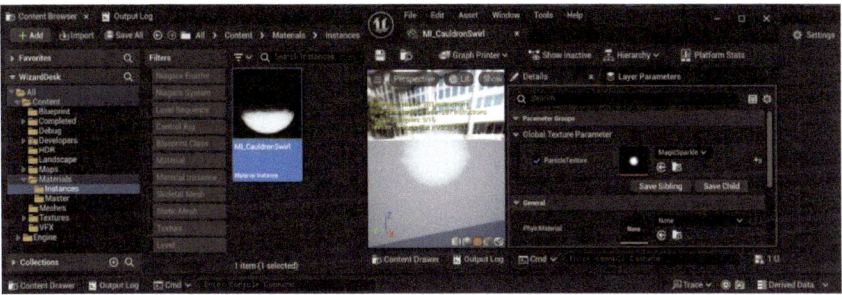

FIGURE 11.1   MI_Cauldron Swirl.

between different effects. Try to build up a library of cool alphas, textures and patterns that can help drive your Materials. Let's begin creating our Cauldron Bubbles Emitter.

The Cauldron

The Cauldron Bubbles Emitter

1. In the **Content Browser**, navigate to **Content | VFX**.
2. Right click anywhere in the **VFX** Folder and create a **FX\Niagara Emitter** asset.
3. From the pop up menu set the Template to be **Fountain** and label the asset *CauldronBubbles_Emitter.*
4. Right click again in the **VFX** Folder and create a second **FX\Niagara Emitter** asset.
5. From the pop up menu set the Template to be **OmniDirectionalBurst** and label the asset *CauldronSparks_Emitter.* We'll revisit this Emitter later on.
6. Double click on the **CauldronBubbles_Emitter** in the **Content Browser** to open up the Niagara Editor.
7. Select the **Sprite Renderer** Module, change the **Material Parameter** to our Cauldron Swirl Material (*Material | Instances | MI_CauldronSwirl*).
8. Select the **SpawnRate** Module, change the *SpawnRate* **Parameter** to *25*. The default value is 90, this can be a bit much for chunky/big particles.
9. Select the **Initialize Particle** Module, locate the **Lifetime Mode Parameter** and set the **LifetimeMin** value *6* to and the **LifetimeMax** value to *8*. Having a longer life time will allow our particles to move further, this can be helpful for a smoke like effect.
10. Now select the **Shape Location** Module, set the **Sphere Radius** to *1*. This will bring the particles closer together.
11. Let's now lessen the velocity. Select the **Add Velocity** Module. Set the **Velocity Speed Minimum** to *3* and the **Velocity Speed Maximum** to *7*.

12. Next, either delete or disable the **Gravity Module** and **Drag** Modules. The particles will now clump close together.

13. To scale the particles over time, click the Green + Button next to the **Particle Update** stage and select *Scale Sprite Size*. Use the Graph to make the first key frame a value of *1* and the second keyframe to be a value of *0*. This will start the particles as a large chunky size scaling to nothing over a particle's life. You may want to experiment with the graphs curves/linearity to control the effect of the fade.

14. Let's now spread the particles out a bit. Click the Green + Button next to the **Particle Update** stage and select **Vortex Force**. Set the **Vortex Force Amount Parameter** to *5* and set the **Origin Pull Amount Parameter** to *4*.

15. Lastly, let's add some Color variation to the Particles. Disable or Delete the ScaleColor Module. Then click the Green + Button next to the **Particle Update** stage and select **Color**. Change the **Color Parameter** type to a **Color From Curve** using the dropdown arrow. Using the Gradient options, create a fade from a warm cream color through a yellow/green hue. The following values are a rough guide, Cream: **R = *1.0*, G = *0.92*, B = *0.46*** and Green: **R = *0.24*, B = *1.0* and G = *0*.** You can add additional color or alpha slots on the gradient by left clicking on the upper or lower tracks. Feel free to experiment to create an interesting fade.

16. Click the **Save** button in the **Niagara Editor** to store our Changes.

We've now built the main body of our Cauldron effect, as shown in Figure 11.2. The Bubbles Emitter adds a continuous stream of noxious and magical particles swirling upwards. Try experimenting with their color and speed to create a really cool flume of particles exiting the Cauldron. We are now going to move the Sparks Emitter, here we are going to create particles that explode out of the Cauldron randomly.

The Cauldron Sparks Emitter

In this next activity, we will create some sparks to resemble some magic overheating and shooting out of the Cauldron. We are going to do this by spawning several particles in a burst, at a random time. This type of creation adds a bit of variety and can be useful for things like damaged mechanic parts of electrical grids.

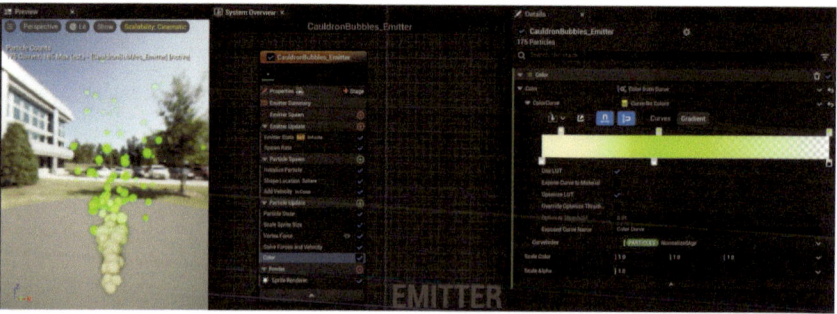

FIGURE 11.2 Cauldron bubbles.

We'll also create particles that scale by the speed, this type of motion allows us to use relatively simple textures and create elongated sparks. Scaling like this is helpful as it can add a sense of speed and direction to an effect.

Let's begin!

1. In the **Content Browser**, navigate to the **Content | VFX**.

2. Double click on our **CauldronSparks_Emitter** to open the Niagara Editor.

3. Select **Emitter State** Module. Change the **Loop Behavior Parameter** to *Infinite* and the **Loop Duration Parameter** to *4.0*.

4. Select **Spawn Burst Instantaneous** Module and change the **Spawn Time** to *Random Float Range* using the dropdown arrow to the right of the Parameter. Set the **Minimum Value** to be 0.5 and the **Maximum value** to be 2.5

5. Change the **Spawn Amount Parameter** to a *Random Int Range* using the dropdown arrow to the right of the Parameter. Set the **Minimum Value** to *25* and Set the **Maximum Value** to 45.

6. Click the **Initialize Particle** Module. Let's make the Sparks much smaller, to do this set the **Uniform Sprite Size Min** to *0.05* and **Uniform Sprite Size Max** *0.25.*

7. Select the **Shape Location** Module and set the **Sphere Radius** to *10*.

8. Select the **Add Velocity** Module. Change the **Velocity Mode** to *Cone*.

9. Set the **Cone Axis** to X = *0*, Y = *0, and* Z = *1*. This will fire the particles upwards.

10. Press the Green + Button next to **Particle Update** and select the **Scale Sprite Size** by **Speed** Module. Change the **Max Scale Factor** to X = *1 and* Y = *15*. This will elongate the particles as they move faster.

11. Let's add a bit more Drag, Select the **Drag** Module and set the **Drag Parameter** to *3*.

12. Next select the **Sprite Renderer** and change the **Alignment** to Velocity Aligned. This will make the sparks alignment now follow correctly as they speed up.

13. Select the **Scale Color** Module and delete it by pressing the Delete Key.

14. Press the Green + Button next to **Particle Update** and select the **Color** Module. Set the Color to be R = *0.23*, G = *1.0, and* B = *0*. If you'd like to scale these values to add a bit of glow see the V value to a number greater than *1*, for example *25*.

15. The particles are looking pretty good now but a bit too similar. Let's adjust the **Scale Sprite Size** by **Speed** Module a bit further. Change the **Max Scale Factor** to use *Random Range Vector 2D*, this allows us to add a bit more variety to the particles stretching as they speed up. Set the **Minimum** values to be **X** = *1* and **Y** = *4* and the **Maximum** values to be **X** = *1* and **Y** = *30*. You should notice that some of the particles now stretch and have a varied length.

16. The final module we are going to add will handle our Particles Collision. Press the Green + Button next to **Particle Update** and select the **Collision** Module. Change the **CPU Collision Trace Channel** to be *World Static*.

Most of the geometry in our world is static meshes so it makes sense to trace against this type of mesh. Feel free to adapt this as required in your own systems. For example you may create an effect that needs to collide with a moving mesh, character or a different type of geometry.

17. Click the **Save** button in the **Niagara Editor** to store our Changes.

This concludes our Sparks Emitter, we've now created particles that spawn instantaneously and explode in different directions. This type of effect is commonly used for things like sparks and embers. Varying how your particles are spawned helps create different senses of motion within your overall Visual Effect. We are now going to look to integrate the work we've done so far into a Niagara System Asset.

The Cauldron System 1

We are now going to build our Niagara System Asset that will bring in the various Emitters. This gives us the ability to further edit and access properties. Once we've created the initial System Asset we'll drop this in the level so we can preview how the effect is going.

1. Head back to the **Content Browser**, right click in anywhere in the **VFX folder** and choose to create a *Niagara System*.
2. From the pop up Menu select **New system from selected emitter(s)** and click next. Set the **Asset Filtering** type to *Parent Emitters*.
3. Hold down Ctrl and left click on both **Cauldron Bubbles Emitter** and **Cauldron Sparks Emitter** and then press the green + button and finally press the **Finish** button.
4. Label the **Niagara System** as *Cauldron_System*.
5. Drag and drop the Niagara System into the level to preview the final effect, as shown in Figure 11.3. A rough position of **X** = *−199.4*, **Y** = *−886.8*, and **Z** = *−127.2* should place the system in about the right place.

Your Emitter should look like the example shown in Figure 11.4. We could quite easily leave the Particle Effect at this point, we have some fun bubbles and some colliding sparks, but can we do something a bit more? Yes! We are going to look at Event Handlers and use our colliding sparks to generate some sizzling particles when the sparks hit objects like the desk. This last effect will be very fine and quick, but will help make the effect fit into our world.

USEFUL TIP

Use the Show Menu in the Niagara Editors Preview Viewport to help monitor Particle Counts, Memory and other Niagara Performance Concerns.

FIGURE 11.3 Level preview of cauldron sparks emitter and cauldron system.

The Cauldron Sizzle Emitter

In this exercise we are going to alter our Sparks Emitter slightly and then make a new Emitter for our new Sizzle particles. This final Emitter will exist only for a brief moment and add a little flash and swirl as the Sparks hit objects. With colliding effects like this we need to be careful not to make them over powering/too distracting. When you have completed the effect, experiment with the lifetimes and spawning of the Sparks and Sizzle Particles until you are happy that the scene doesn't feel too busy.

Let's get started!

1. In the **Content Browser**, navigate to **Content | VFX**.
2. Double click on our **CauldronSparks_Emitter** to open the Niagara Editor.
3. Select the **Properties Options** at the top of our Emitter, enable the **Requires Persistent ID's** checkbox. This must be enabled to use the Collision Events later. Fortunately, if you ever forget, Niagara will warn you through errors and logs.
4. Select the **Collision** Module and set the **Restitution** value to be *0.1*. This is shown in Figure 11.5. Restitution controls the amount of energy a particle retains after colliding. A value closer to 0 will remove energy with a value

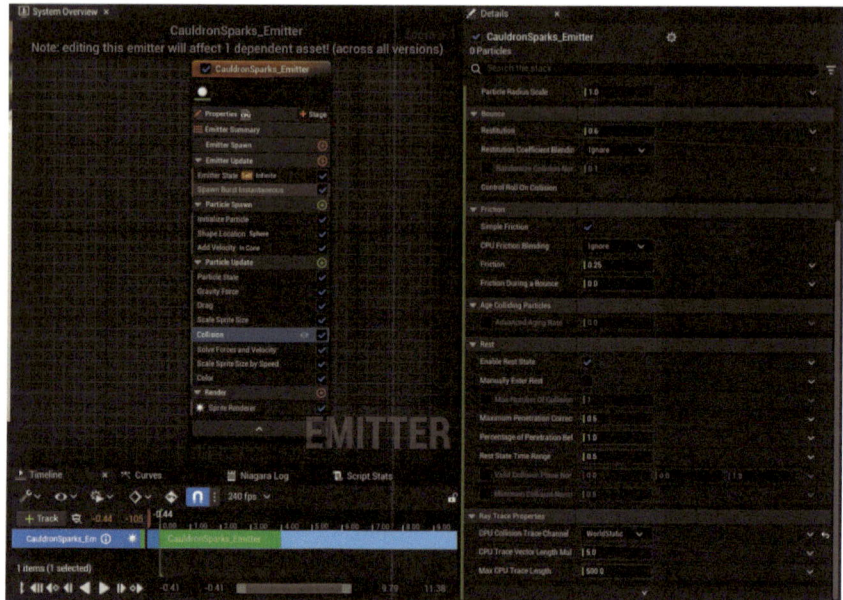

FIGURE 11.4   Niagara preview of cauldron sparks emitter.

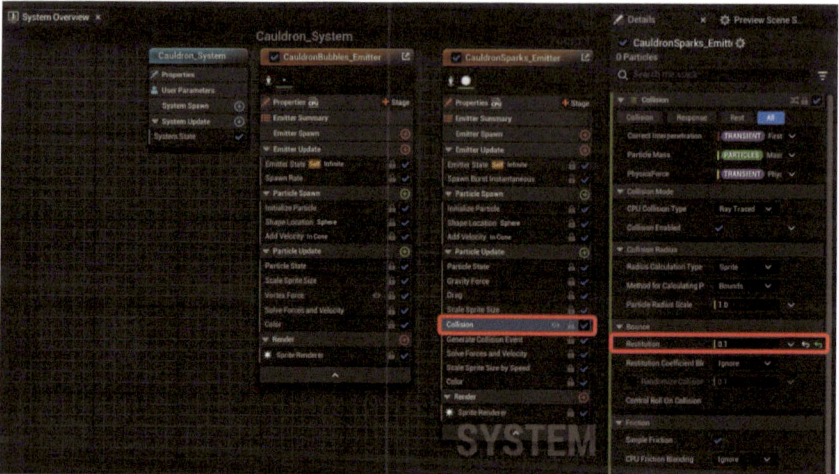

FIGURE 11.5   Collision restitution.

closer to 1 means it will maintain the same energy from before the collision. In our case we'd like our Spark particles to slow down after hitting an object.

5. Next click the Green + Button next to **Particle Update** and using the menu select the *Generate Collision Event Module.*

FIGURE 11.6 Generate collision event module.

6. Select the **Generate Collision Event** Module and set the **Delay Between Collision** value to be *0.8*. This is shown in Figure 11.6. This module allows us to broadcast that collisions are occurring to other emitters, it is one of the main event modules along with Location and Death events that help us pass along useful properties. The Delay Between Collision value allows us to control how many collisions can occur within a time period, if we have lots and lots of particles colliding within a short time performance can be really hurt. It is unlikely there is a perfect value here, so please do experiment with different values. A value too high could be boring, whereas a value too low could hurt in-game performance.

Now that we've modified our Sparks Emitter to generate collisions we can proceed to create our Sizzle Emitter. The Sizzle Emitter will make use of the collisions to help place its particles. Always try to build events prior to trying to use them, while this may sound obvious it's easy to get in a muddle and wonder why things aren't working.

1. In the **Content Browser**, navigate to **Content | VFX**.
2. Right click anywhere in the **VFX** Folder and create a **FX\Niagara Emitter** asset.
3. From the pop up menu set the Template to be **DirectionalBurst** and label the asset *CauldronSizzle_Emitter*. We are going to customize many properties about this Emitter, it doesn't really matter which template you start from.
4. Double click on the **CauldronSizzle_Emitter** asset to open up the Niagara Editor.
5. Select the **Emitter State** Module and set the **Life Cycle Mode** to *System*.
6. Remove/Disable the **Spawn Burst Instantaneous** Module. We'll control the spawning of the Sizzle Particles through events.

7. Select the **Initialize Particle** Module. Set the **Lifetime Min** to *0.4* and the **Lifetime Max** to *2*. You may wish to lower the **Lifetime Max** a bit more if the particles stay in the scene a bit too long.

8. Change the **Mass Mode** Parameter to *Unset*. We don't need to use this in the effect. Sometimes you may find some Modules or parameters can be removed or unset if variation isn't required.

9. Change the **Sprite Size** to *Random Uniform*. Set the **Uniform Sprite Size Min** to *0.1* and the **Uniform Sprite Size Max** to *0.25*.

10. A lot of the values in this emitter are very small as the particles will be very small on screen, our next task is to lower the velocities. Select the **Add Velocity** Module. Set the **Velocity Speed Minimum** to *4* and the **Velocity Speed Maximum** to *9*. Change the Cone Axis to be **X** = *0*, **Y** = *0*, and **Z** = *1*. Lastly set the **Velocity Cone Angle** to *65*.

11. Remove or disable the **Gravity** Module.

12. Select the **Drag** Module, press the *Reset Arrow* to change the default value to *1*.

13. Remove or disable the **Scale Color** Module.

14. Remove or disable the **Scale Sprite Size by Speed** Module.

15. Click the Green + Button next to **Particle Update** and select the *Vortex Force Module*.

16. Select the **Vortex Force** Module and set **Vortex Force Amount** to *35* and **Origin Pull Amount** to *55*. As these particles could spawn anywhere in the world, we also need to change the **Vortex Origin**, the default value will always put the **Vortex Origin** in the wrong place. Click the Down arrow to the right of **Simulation Position** and search for *Particles Initial Position*. This will put the Vortex wherever the Sizzle Particles spawn.

17. Click the Green + Button next to **Particle Update** and select the *Color Module*.

18. Select the **Color** Module, change the **Color** to *Color from Curve*. Then set the first color value on the gradient to be **R** = *213*, **G** = *500*, and **B** = *0*. Then add another box half-way along the upper track and set the values to be **R** = *0.47*, **G** = *1*, and **B** = *0*. This will create a very bright flash when the particles spawn.

19. Next we need to add in some functionality to read in the Collision Event from our sparks. To do this click the Orange + **Stage** button at the top of the **CauldronSizzleEmitter** and pick *Event Handler from the menu*.

20. You'll now see the **Event Handler** Stage added above our **Renderer** Stage.

21. Select the **Event Handler Source**, change the **Execution Mode** to *Spawned Particles* and Set the **Spawn Number** to *10*. You can also use the **Random Spawn Boolean** Checkbox to add variation here. This will control how many particles spawn when our Sparks particles Collide. Be careful as it's easy to spawn several thousand particles here by mistake.

22. Click the Green + Button next to the **Event Handler Stage** and select the *Receive Collision Event Module*.

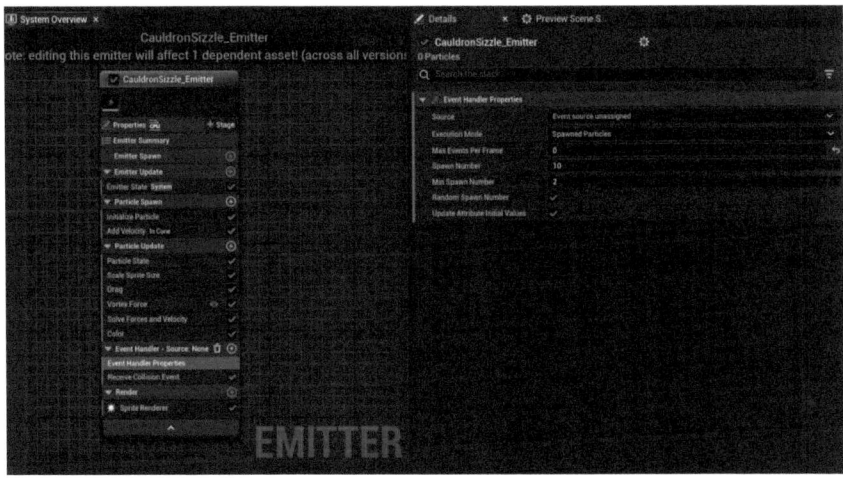

FIGURE 11.7 Cauldron sizzle emitter.

Our Emitter is now complete, please find an example in Figure 11.7. Our next task will be to ensure all of the Emitters work properly within our System Asset. Occasionally you'll design an Emitter that can only work in a level, in most cases because of collision or external parameters. Try to set up Niagara System Assets early on to help you test your work as soon as possible.

The Cauldron System 2

We have now completed the Cauldron Sizzle Emitter, to test it out we need to add it to the **Cauldron_System** asset. It's worthwhile keeping Emitters open when working with Niagara System Assets as you may find you want to go back and forth to alter some properties.

1. Go back to the **Content Browser** and open up our **Cauldron_System** by double clicking the asset in our **VFX** folder.
2. Drag and drop our **Cauldron_Sizzle_Emitter** from the **Content Browser** into the **Cauldron_System** asset. Place the Emitter to the right of the existing Emitters, we now have all 3 of our **Cauldron Emitters** in the same System Asset.
3. Select the **Event Handler Properties** Module and click on the dropdown arrow next to the **Source Parameter**. From the Menu Pick the *Collision Event* Generated from our **Sparks Emitter**. Our Emitters are now linked together and Collision data will pass from one to the other.

If you go to the level, you should now find very small twirly glows where our sparks particles collide with geometry in the world. Examples of the final System and glow in the level can be seen in Figures 11.8 and 11.9.

FIGURE 11.8   Cauldron sizzle event handler properties.

You will want to spend some time going back and forth between Emitters and the System asset to tweak the effects visual look. You can do this either by editing the Emitters and saving changes, this will pass onto the System asset or you can edit the Emitters properties directly in the System Asset. Editing the System Asset may seem easier but note that any changes you make directly in the System Asset will not be automatically passed down to any Emitters.

Conclusion

We've created several distinct systems for our Cauldron Particle effect, during the process of creation, we've explored how we can utilize more advanced features such as the Event Handler Stage to add Generate and Receive Events. This adds a layer of complexity when we want to start connecting emitters. In your own time it's worth looking at the different types of parameters that these events can pass through such as locations and velocities. In some situations, you may wish to pass through velocities unlike the Cauldron example, perhaps you may want to create Lazer reflections or bouncing balls that don't slow down.

In our next chapter, we'll be exploring Sub UV Animation in Niagara to create a Fire Particle System. Before we move on let's test our knowledge with a quick quiz!

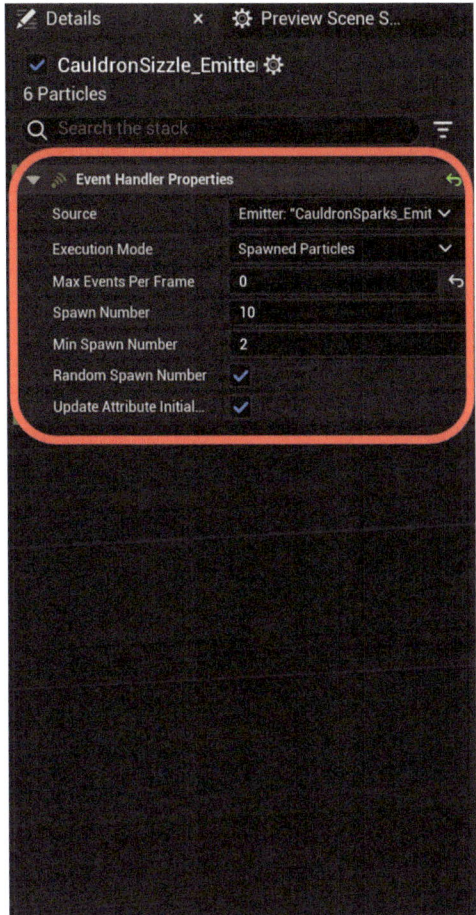

FIGURE 11.9 Cauldron sizzle particles in the level.

Chapter 11 Quiz

Question 1: What does Persistent ID do in the Niagara Editor?

    a. Persistent ID provides us with a way to identify particles over the course of effect, which can be useful for Events such as collision.

    b. Persistent ID generates a Material ID for our Particle System allowing us to change materials.

    c. Persistent ID creates a name for each Particle Stage that we can use in Blueprints.

Question 2: What Module should we use if we want to adjust a Sprite Particles Size by Speed?

    a.   Transform Sprite Size by Speed

    b.   Scale Sprite Size by Force

    c.   Scale Sprite Size by Speed

    d.   Press E while in the Niagara System Editor.

    e.   All of the above.

Question 3: When adding variation to Particle Color what option provides us with a nice Gradient to animate Color and Alpha?

    a.   Color Over Time.

    b.   Color From Curve.

    c.   Color.

Question 4: What is the Difference between Spawn Rate and Spawn Instantaneous.

    a.   Spawn Rate will create a number of particles continuously whereas Spawn Instantaneous will destroy particles.

    b.   Spawn Rate will create a number of particles at the Beginning of an Emitters Life whereas Spawn Instantaneous will create Particles at the end of an Emitters Life.

    c.   Spawn Rate will create a number of particles continuously whereas Spawn Instantaneous will create a number of particles at a precise moment.

Answers

Question 1: a

Question 2: c

Question 3: b

Question 4: c

12

The Dawn of Fire

Introduction

In this chapter we create our Fire VFX System, you'll learn about:

- Sub UV Materials Construction to support Flipbook Textures.
- Sub UV Niagara nodes to animate Smoke and Fire Emitters.
- Working in Extra Emitters to add depth and motion.

This is the first time we'll use a very special texture. In Unreal we have the option to use a texture called a Sub UV Texture, these are more commonly known as Flip Books across other programs. These textures contain frames of animations which cycle through as a game plays. Flip Books can be created in programs such as Photoshop, Blender, After Effects, 3ds Max and even in Unreal using Plugins such as Fluid Ninja. Flip Books tend to be used when an effect requires a specific type of movement, such as the fluid in flames. We try not to use Flipbooks for all effects as they can be quite large images and unnecessary; however, for fire, smoke and complex simulations they are very handy. An example of a flipbook can be seen in Figure 12.1.

Sub UV Materials

Let's now investigate how we can incorporate a Flipbook Texture into an Unreal Material and the Niagara Editor. We will start by duplicating and modifying one of our existing materials before later going into Niagara.

Let's get started!

1. In the **Content Browser**, navigate to the folder **Content | Materials |Master**.
2. Duplicate the Material **M_VFXAdd** and label the new Material *M_VFXSubUVAdd*.
3. Double click on the Material **M_VFXSubUVAdd** to open the Material Editor.
4. Select and delete the nodes that connect into the **ParticleTexture 2D Param** Node. We do not need any UV distortion for this Material.
5. Right click in the Material Graph and search for a *TextureSample ParameterSubUV* node.

DOI: 10.1201/9781032663852-12

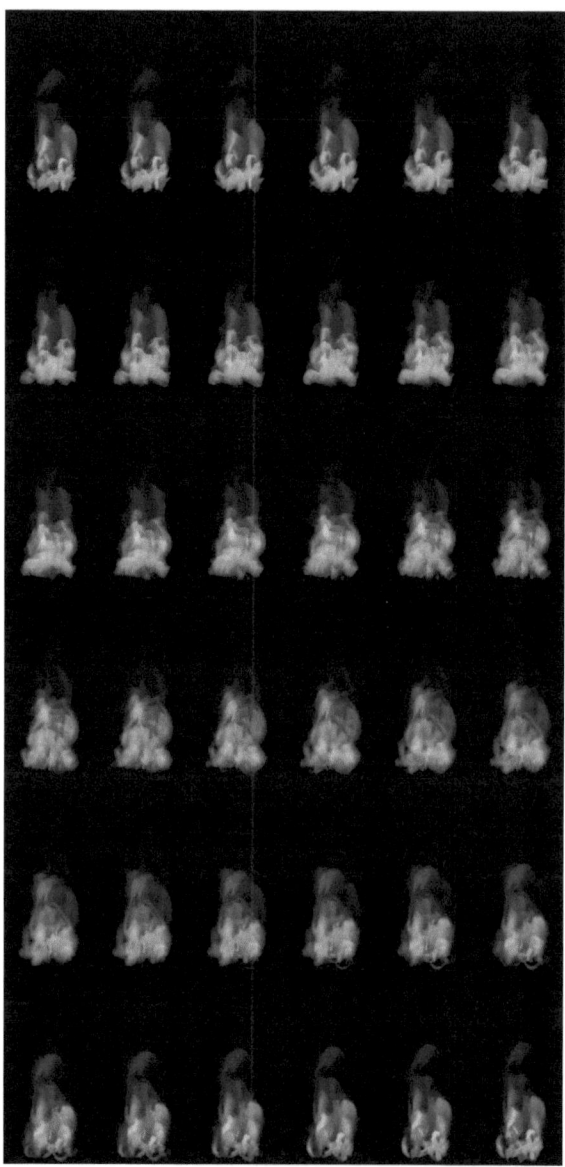

FIGURE 12.1   Fire flipbook texture.

6. Rename this node *SubUVTexture*. Using a Parameter allows us to load in different Flip Books for different effects should we need to.

7. Go to the **Content Browser**, locate the **Fire** Texture in the folder **Content | Textures | VFX_Fire** and set it as the Texture in our **SubUVTexture** Node by using the Use Selected Button in the Material Editor or another method of your choosing.

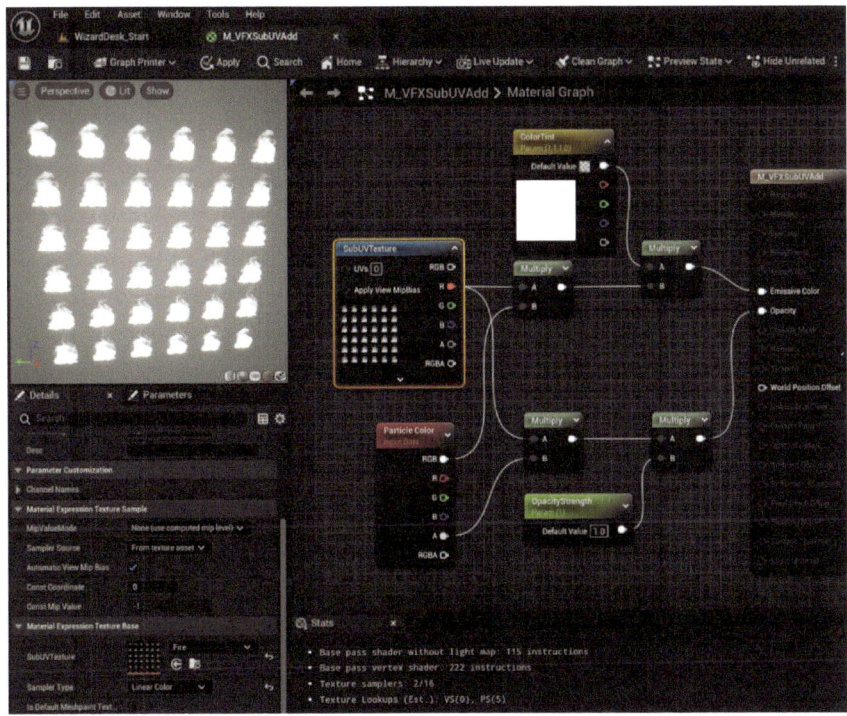

FIGURE 12.2 M_VFX Add Material connections.

8. Replace the connections that currently hook up the **ParticleTexture2D Param** Node to the **SubUVTexture** Node as shown in Figure 12.2.
9. Press the **Save Button** in the Material Editor.

In our new Sub UV Material there are two options for adjusting the color of our texture. One is through Particle Color Animation and the other is via the ColorTint Vector Parameter Node. Both of these options are fine and will work great, however there is a third option we could consider which is not currently setup in the Material. The additional option is a **BlackBody** node, this node will convert a grayscale image into fire colors automatically using the grayscale intensities. The workflow below will show you how you can implement this into your materials, however we won't use this in our effect. To try the following exercise, we recommend that you duplicate the **M_VFXSubUVAdd** Material in the Content Browser and label it **M_VFXSubUVAddBlackBody** then open up the material to try the following exercise.

1. Add a *Multiply* Node just by holding **M and left clicking** by the **Emissive Color** Input on the Material Result Node. Redirect the existing **Emissive Color** Input into the **A** Input of our **Multiply** Node and set the **B** value to a number greater than *2500*. We need large values to transform the Grayscale texture into the right range for the **BlackBody** to work. A low number will

result in a red looking result while a high number will eventually become white.

2. Then add a **BlackBody Node** by right clicking and searching for the node from the pop up menu.
3. Connect the output of the **BlackBody Node** to the **Emissive Color** input.
4. You should now see the Grayscale values have been replaced with warm fiery tones.

We won't save this addition, it's purely for you to see it working. An example of the completed effect can be seen in Figure 12.3. To adjust this further we could bring the **BlackBody** and Multiply node prior to the Color Tint or the Particle Color Multiply allowing these adjustments to stack on top of the **BlackBody** effect. We could also add a Dynamic Parameter Node with a multiply to allow us to adjust the BlackBody intensity even further. However, for now we will move onto utilizing our Sub UV Master, close the **Material Editor** and **do not** save the changes.

Let's create 2 Material Instances and then move onto Niagara.

1. In the **Content Browser**, navigate to the folder **Content | Materials | Master**.
2. Right click on our **Material M_VFXSubUVAdd** and select **Create Material Instance,** label the Instance *MI_Fire*.
3. Right click again on our **Material M_VFXSubUVAdd** and select **Duplicate,** label the *Material M_VFXSubUVTrans*.
4. Double click on the Material **M_VFXSubUVTrans**. Set the **Blend Mode** to *Translucent* and the **Shading Model** to *Default Lit*.
5. Press the **Save Button** and **Close** the **Material** Editor. We need a Translucent Sub UV as Smoke behaves differently to the flames.
6. Right click on our **Material M_VFXSubUVTrans** and select **Create Material Instance,** label the Instance *MI_Smoke***.**

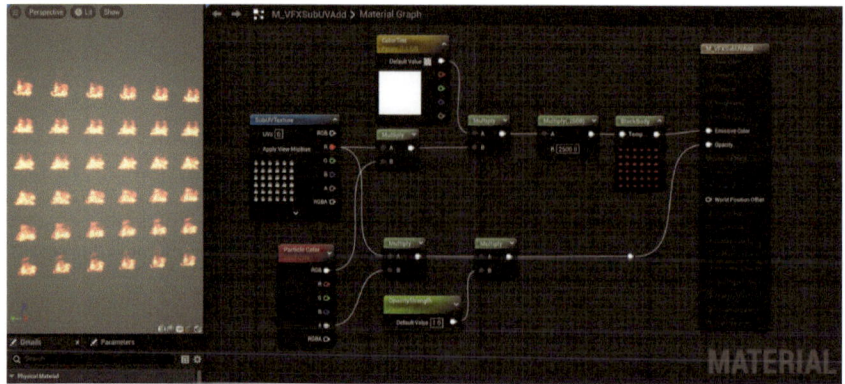

FIGURE 12.3 BlackBody demonstration.

7. Double click on our **MI_Smoke Instance** to open the Material Instance Editor.

8. Tick the box next to the **Parameter SubUVTexture**, this will allow us to change the Texture. Click the **down arrow** next to where the current Textures name is, which will be **Fire** and set this to *Smoke*. Lastly press the **Save Button**.

9. Move both **MI_Fire** and **MI_Smoke** to the **Content | Materials | Instances** folder.

We've now prepared our Material Instances so we can move on to Niagara. It's wise to separate out Material instances between Fire and Smoke due to color, shape and motion differences. Try to break up your VFX into different material assets to afford greater control of your VFX in Niagara.

Flames

Flames – Sub UV Emitter

We are now going to use these materials in our Fire Particle Systems. For the rest of this chapter, we are going to build a Flame Emitter, Smoke Emitter, Flame Embers Emitter and a Flames Background Emitter. This series of Emitters will join together to form our overall Fire System. It's important to break down the effect and build up the layers slowly. When deciding on how to separate layers in your own project look for distinctive movement, color, appearance and animation. It is however not a race to use as many Emitters as possible, make them all count and have a distinct role.

Let's get started with our Flames Emitter.

1. In the **Content Browser**, navigate to the **Content | VFX** folder.

2. Right click anywhere in the **VFX** Folder and create a **FX \ Niagara Emitter** asset. From the pop up menu choose to create a new Emitter and set the Template to be **Fountain** and Label the asset *FlamesSubUV_Emitter*. We are going to customize many properties about this Emitter, it doesn't really matter which template you start from.

3. Double click on the **FlamesSubUV_Emitter** asset to open up the Niagara Editor.

4. Click on the **Sprite Renderer Module**, replace the **Material** using the drop-down arrow and look for our Instance *MI_Fire*.

5. Next look for the Sub UV options. *Enable* the Parameter **Sub UV Blending Enabled**. Set the **Sub UV Image Size** to be $X = 6$ and $Y = 6$. These numbers relate to the numbers of rows and columns in the original Fire Flipbook texture. When creating your own systems, you will need to adapt this number to match the source texture.

6. Next select the **Spawn Rate** Module and set the **Spawn Rate** Parameter to *65*.

7. Now select **Initialize Particle** Module , Set the **Lifetime Min** to *1* and the **Lifetime Max** to *7*. This will create quite a variation in the age of the flames.

8. Set the **Color** to be **R** = *1.0*, **B** = *0.33 and* **C** = *0.29*.

9. Set the **Uniform Sprite Size Min** to *50* and the **Uniform Sprite Size Max** to *60*. These values will likely need testing later on when the Emitter is in a System Asset. Don't ever feel locked into the values we run through as we build effects.

10. Set the **Sprite Rotation Mode** to *Unset*. Most of the animation/motion we want to come from the Flip Book texture.

11. Select the **Add Velocity** Module, Set the **Velocity Minimum** to *3* and the **Velocity Maximum** to *12*. Eventually we want the flames to rise very slowly upward. For now, you'll see particles fall to the floor due to Gravity which we'll adjust shortly.

12. Next *disable* or *delete* the **Gravity** Module.

13. Next *disable* or *delete* the **Scale Color** Module.

14. Click the Green + Button next to **Particle Update** and select the Scale Sprite Size *Module*.

15. Select the **Scale Sprite Size** Module, apply a *Pulse Out Template*. This starts the Flames particles as zero, before growing to full size and then slowly fading out over time. If you don't like this look, please feel free to customize the keyframes however you wish.

16. Click the Green + Button next to **Particle Update** and select the *Color* Module.

17. Select the **Color** Module and change the **Color** Parameter to *Color from Curve* using the dropdown arrow. Along the top track of the gradient, create several boxes to animate the color changing from Yellow, to Orange, to Red. This will create a transition of our flames as they age. If you would like the flames to appear visible for longer you could also try dragging the white box on the Alpha track to the right, this will slow down the fade out of the particles. An example can be seen in Figure 12.4.

18. Now let's click the Green + Button next to **Particle Update** and select the *Sub UV Animation* Module.

19. Select the **Sub UV Animation** Module. Set the **StartFrameRangeOverride** to *0* and the **EndFrameRangeOverride** to *35*. These properties are useful if you want to specify certain sections of a Flip Book for an effect.

20. Make sure the **Sprite Renderer Parameter** points to our *Sprite Renderer* by using the dropdown arrow. If you do not set this the UV Animation won't work.

21. Lastly you may wish to experiment with the **Shape Location** Module, the Shape Primitive is set to **Sphere** by default which is fine but a lower radius of around *5* will create flames closer together. Another option is to use a **Ring** for the **Shape Primitive** with a radius of around *12*. The Ring provides a little bit more volume but both are fine to use.

22. To preview our Emitter, let's turn off the default background. To do this click **Windows** and then ensure **Preview Scene Settings** is enabled from the

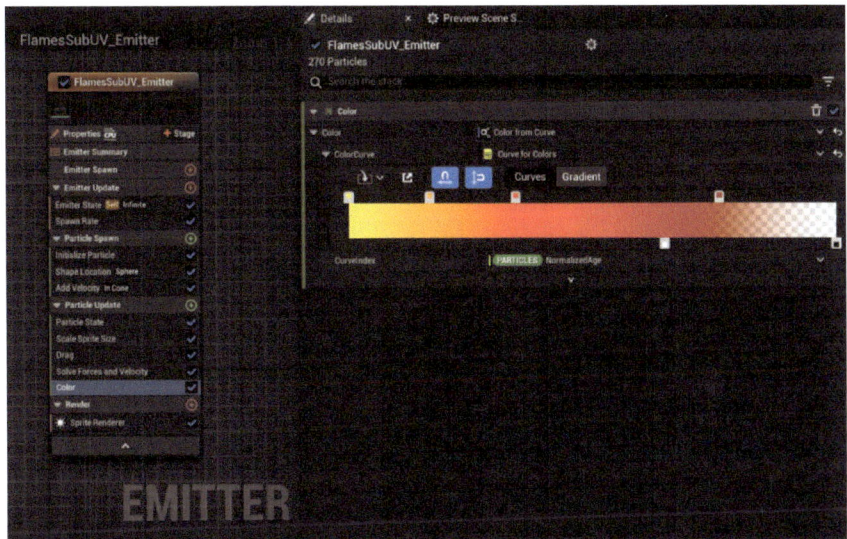

FIGURE 12.4 Flames color gradient.

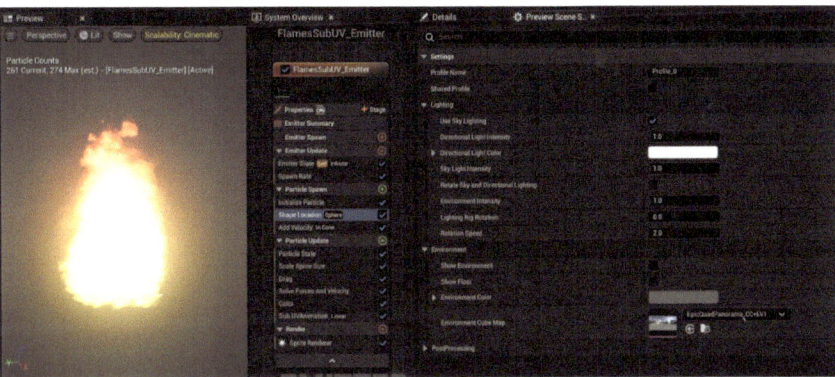

FIGURE 12.5 Flames sub UV emitter.

Popup Menu. You should now see **Preview Scene Settings** options on your screen. Using the Menu Disable *Show Environment*. We can also pick an **Environment Color** for example a *Dark Gray* to help the flames Stand out a bit more. See Figure 12.5 for an example.

This effect by itself is pretty cool, but it lacks depth. In the next activity we are going to create a very similar emitter that will add a bit more of a deeper red flame to the background. The steps we've followed so far can be useful for all kinds of Flip Book based effects, be sure to try this out with other textures you create/have access to.

Background Flames – Sub UV Emitter

Let's now start creating our Background Flames Emitter.

1. In the **Content Browser**, navigate to the **Content | VFX** folder.
2. Right click on our **FlamesSubUV_Emitter** asset and select **Duplicate**. Label the Duplicate *FlamesBackgroundSubUV_Emitter*.
3. Double click the **FlamesBackgroundSubUV_Emitter** asset to open the Niagara Editor.
4. Select the **Color** Module. On the top row, delete all the Color boxes and except the first one at the start of the upper track. Set the color to be a very deep red with values of **R** = *0.03*, **G** = *0* and **B** = *0*.
5. Select the **Initialize Particle** Module, change the **LifeTime Max** to *5*. Next set the **Uniform Sprite Size Min** to *75* and the **Uniform Sprite Size Max** to *90*.
6. Select the **Add Velocity** Module. Increase the **Velocity Minimum** to *12* and the **Velocity Maximum** to *25*.

USEFUL TIP

Try to use Emitters like Layers, avoid falling into the trap of trying to do too much with one Emitter. If a specific behavior is needed for an effect that's usually a good time to opt for an additional Emitter for a Visual Effect.

Our Background Flames Emitter is now complete, it's very similar to the original Flames Emitter. The idea here is that it's slightly larger, darker and moves just a bit quicker. It helps add a bit of extra depth to the flame coloration. The completed Emitter can be seen in Figure 12.6 it looks very similar to Figure 12.5 but darker in appearance and a bit larger.

We'll now move on to add some chaotic embers that will float upwards as our flame burns. This Emitter will follow steps similar to those found in the Cauldron Chapter.

Flames Embers – Emitter

The goal with this stage of the effect is to add a different type of movement to help break things up and give a bit of randomness to the visuals. Let's get started!

1. In the **Content Browser**, navigate to the **Content | VFX** folder.
2. Right click anywhere in the **VFX** Folder and create a **FX \ Niagara Emitter** asset. From the pop up menu choose to create a new Emitter and set the Template to be **Fountain** and Label the asset *FlamesEmbers_Emitter*. We are going to customize many properties about this Emitter, it doesn't really matter which template you start from.

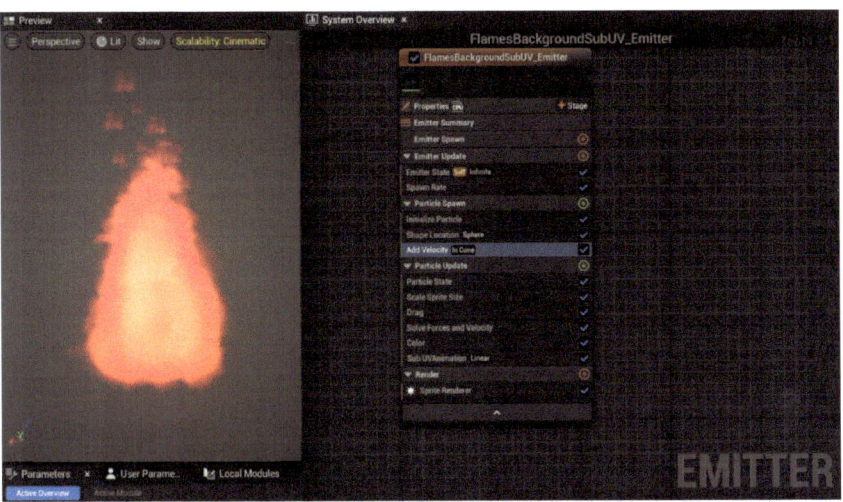

FIGURE 12.6 Flames background sub UV emitter.

3. Double click on the **FlamesEmbers_Emitter** asset to open up the Niagara Editor.

4. Select the **Emitter State Module** and set the **Loop Duration** to *5*.

5. Select the **Spawn Rate** Module and Set the **Spawn Rate Parameter** to *12*.

6. Select the **Initialize Particle** Module. Set the **Lifetime Minimum** to *2* and the **Lifetime Maximum** to *4*. You can make this a bit larger if your flame effects need to fill a larger area, for example a bonfire.

7. Set the **Color** value to **R** = *55,* **G** = *1,* **B** = *0*. This will make the embers very bright.

8. Select the **Shape Location** Module and increase the **Sphere Radius** Parameter to *22*. This will spread out the Ember spawning a little bit.

9. Select the **Add Velocity** Module. Change the **Velocity Mode** to *Linear*. Change the **Velocity** type to a *Random Range Vector*. Set the **Minimum Velocities** to be *X* = *−12,* *Y* = *−12 and Z* = *2*. Set the **Maximum Velocities** to be *X* = *12,* *Y* = *12 and Z* = *6*.

10. Delete or Disable the **Gravity** Module.

11. Set the **Uniform Sprite Size Min** to *0.1* and the **Uniform Sprite Size Max** to *1*.

12. Click the Green + Button next to **Particle Update** and select the *Scale Sprite Size* Module.

13. Select the **Scale Sprite Size** module, apply a *Linear Ramp Down* Template. This will fade the embers down to 0 over the course of their life.

14. Click the Green + Button next to **Particle Update** and select the *Curl Noise Force* Module.

15. Select the **Curl Noise Force** Module. Set the **Noise Strength** to *2* and the **Noise Frequency** to *5*. This adds a bit of variation to the Embers movement.

FIGURE 12.7   Flames ember sub UV emitter.

We've now completed our Flame Embers, you should see very small but bright particles floating quite randomly through space. You can see an example of this Emitter in Figure 12.7 When Emitters like this get added to Systems you may wish to alter life time, velocities and brightness should the effect look a little busy or too slow.

Flames Smoke – Sub UV Emitter

We are now going to move onto our final emitter which will be our Smoke Emitter. This will follow a similar creation methodology to the other Sub UV effects. We shall use our work in the FlamesSubUV_Emitter as a base before making several edits.

   Let's create some smoke!

1. In the **Content Browser**, navigate to the **Content | VFX** folder.
2. Right click on our **FlamesSubUV_Emitter** asset and select **Duplicate**. Label the Duplicate *FlamesSmokeSubUV_Emitter*.
3. Double click the **FlamesSmokeSubUV_Emitter** asset to open the Niagara Editor.
4. Select the **Sprite Renderer** Module, Set the Material Parameter to *MI_ Smoke*. This is important as we not only want a different texture for the Emitter but this Material Instance is Translucent so the smoke will be fainter than the flames.

5. Change the **Sub Image Size** *X* to *8* and the **Sub Image Size** *Y* to *4*. Ideally, we also want our Flip Book textures to be in the power of two to MIP properly, in this example the smoke is a rectangle. Keep an eye when sourcing your own Flip Books as they can come in all shapes and sizes.

6. Select **Emitter State** Module and set the **Loop Duration** to *5*.

7. Select the **Spawn Rate** Module and set the **Spawn Rate** Parameter to *25*.

8. Next, click the **Initialize Particle** Module, lower the **Lifetime Max** to *5*.

9. Set the Color to **R** = *0.11*, **G** = *0.11* and **B** = *0.11*. This is a deep gray, the colors you see in the Niagara Editor Viewport will likely be a lot brighter for the Smoke Material. Be sure to revisit some of the Color properties after building the System Asset later.

10. Set the **Position Mode** to *Simulation Position*. Add a position offset of *X* = *0, Y* = *3 and Z* = *25*. This will move the whole smoke simulation upwards and a bit behind the Fire effect.

11. Set the **Uniform Sprite Size Min** to *125* and Set the **Uniform Sprite Size Max** to *275*.

12. Select the **Shape Location** Module and set the **Sphere Radius** to *0.5*.

13. Next, select the **Add Velocity** Module, change the **Velocity Mode** to *Linear*. Change the **Velocity type** to a *Random Range Vector* using the dropdown arrow to the right. Set the **Velocity Minimum** to *X* = *−5, Y* = *−5 and Z* = *15*. Set the **Velocity Maximum** to *X* = *5, Y* = *5 and Z* = *25*.

14. Select the **Scale Sprite Size Module** and change the template to *Ease In*.

15. Select the **Color** Module, remove all of the fire colors on the upper track. Place a single Dark Gray on the Upper Track with a value of **R** = *0.08*, **G** = *0.08 and* **B** = *0.14*. This will create a very subtle blue tint to the smoke.

16. Lastly select the **Sub UV Animation** Module. Set the **End Frame Range Override** to *0*.

A completed example of the Flames Smoke Emitter can be seen in Figure 12.8.

We've now built our Emitters, feel free to adjust their properties and hone in the visuals as you wish.

Flames System

We now need to build the Niagara System asset so we can test the VFX in our level.

1. In the **Content Browser**, navigate to the **Content | VFX** folder.

2. Right click in the **VFX** Folder and create a **Niagara System Asset**. From the pop up menu, select **New system from selected emitters(s)**. Then enable **Parent Emitters** to change the filter of what templates we can select. Ctrl click on the 4 Flames Emitters and press the Green + button and then click **Finish**.

3. Label the created System Asset *Flames_System*. An example of the completed Niagara System Asset can be seen in Figure 12.9.

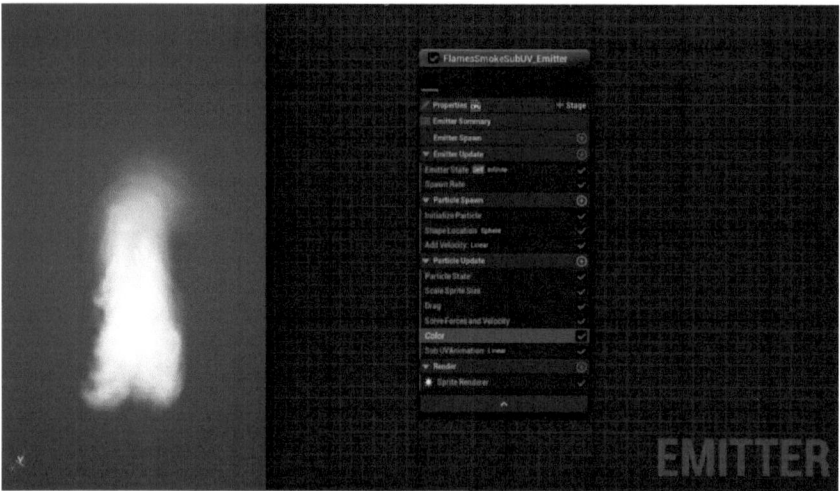

FIGURE 12.8 Completed flames smoke emitter.

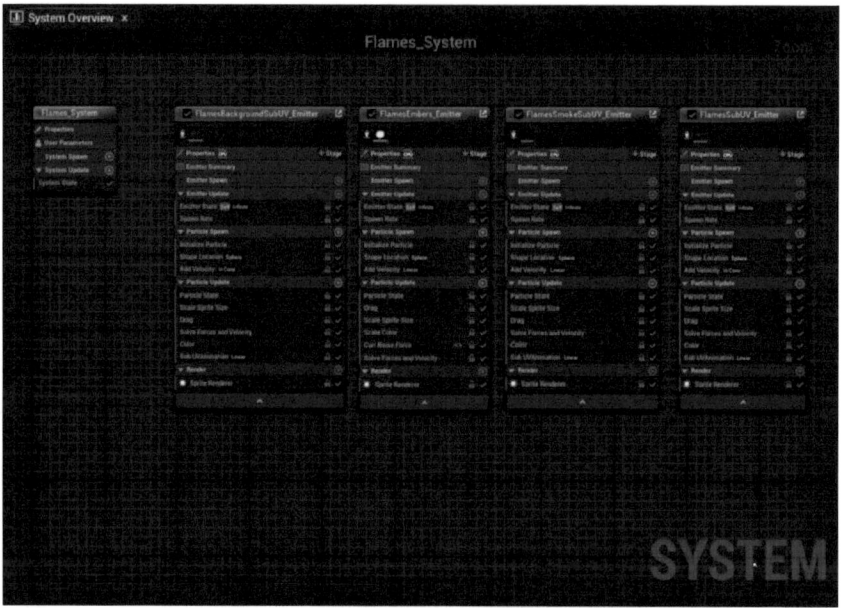

FIGURE 12.9 Completed flames system asset.

4. Drag and drop the **Flames_System** asset into the level and set the **Transform Location** Parameter to $X = 8.296107$, $Y = -531.712063$ *and* $Z = -222.383232$.

This should place the **Flames_System** asset nicely in the fireplace, Figure 12.10 shows the completed asset in the Level.

FIGURE 12.10   Completed flames system.

Conclusion

In this chapter, we've built a multi-tiered fire effect that exploited the Sub UV system. There are many ways to build these types of effects for games, in addition to what we've looked at here, you could look at UV distortion to create flames, fluid solvers in Unreal and other DCC packages as well as pyro simulations in packages such as Houdini. This system has many parameters that can be adjusted to improve performance of games. If you do explore fluid solvers and simulations, be mindful of the effects potential impact on framerate and other in game resources. Fire and Explosions can have quite performance-hungry effects.

In our next chapter, we'll be exploring Magic Missiles. Before we move on let's test our knowledge with a quick quiz!

Chapter 12 Quiz

Question 1: What does Sub UV Animation allow us to do in Niagara?

    a.   Sub UV Animation allows us to cycle through Flip Book Texture Frames in Niagara.

    b.   Sub UV Animation enables us to animate the spawning of particles in Niagara.

    c.   Sub UV Animation can be used to animate light renderers in Niagara.

Question 2: What is a Flip Book?

    a.   A Flip Book is a book that can be rotated.

    b.   A Flip Book is a multiple texture asset that can be mirrored.

    c.   A Flip Book is a single texture that contains multiple frames of animation.

    d.   All of the above.

Question 3: What does a BlackBody Node do?

    a.   A BlackBody Node controls the opacity of Fire Effects.

    b.   A BlackBody Node controls the roughness value of Fire Effects.

    c.   A BlackBody Node can convert grayscale values into Fire color values for use in the Material Editor.

Question 4: Why is it important to build a fire effect out of multiple emitters?

    a.   Using a single emitter would make the effect too bright.

    b.   Certain effects require very different behaviors and materials. It's not possible to model all particle behavior in a single Emitter.

    c.   Using multiple emitters allows us to create each flame's individual tendril.

Answers

Question 1: a

Question 2: c

Question 3: c

Question 4: b

13

Magical Spells and Fireworks

Introduction

In this chapter, we create our Magical Spells and Missile Systems, you'll learn about:

- How to create Beam effects using Ribbon Emitters.
- How to create Multi-tiered magical spells.
- Using Location and Death Events to trigger explosions and trails.

Up until now we've used Sprite Renderers and Materials to drive our Particle Emitters. We'll now utilize **Ribbon Renderers** for the first time in this chapter. Ribbon Renderers are great when you want to create a series of connected particles for example wispy smoke, beams and trails. Ribbons are created by a series of polygons that face the camera. We have several Ribbon options including multi planes, tubes and polygons that add to the overall complexity and amount of geometry within the effect.

When utilizing **Ribbon's** there are a variety of special modules that we'll use. These modules include **Spawn Beams**, **Beam Width** and **Update Beam**. Most of these modules have only a few options for customization by default; they will need to be included in the overall Emitter structure by default. The default behavior of a **Ribbon Emitter** is to create a straight trail from an origin point to an end location. This makes them great for lasers and trace type effects in addition to the effects mentioned earlier. The **Beam** itself can be composed of as few or as many particles, by adding many particles we can apply modules such as **Curl Noise Force** or **Jitter Position** to animate the position of the beam.

Magic Spell

Magic Spell – Beam Emitter

We'll begin by creating the **Beam Emitter** for our Magic Spell system, we'll define the appearance by adding more complexities to the **Beam's** animation and look. Once we've created this first emitter, we'll then begin to add some **User Parameters** and a second Emitter to control some contact sparks.

DOI: 10.1201/9781032663852-13

Let's get started!

1. In the **Content Browser**, navigate to the **Content | VFX** folder.
2. Right click anywhere in the **VFX** Folder and create a **FX \ Niagara Emitter** asset. From the pop up menu choose to create a new Emitter and set the Template to be **Dynamic Beam** and Label the asset *MagicSpellBeam_Emitter.*
3. Double click the **MagicSpellBeam_Emitter** to open the Niagara Editor.
4. Select the **Emitter State** Module. Set the **Loop Behavior** to *0.1*, eventually we'll set this behavior to be controlled by the final System asset.
5. Select the **Beam Emitter Setup** Module, set the **Absolute Beam End** checkbox to TRUE. We'll customize this asset in the System asset as well. For now though set the **Beam End** value to *X = 500, Y = 0, and Z = 0.* If we were building a Beam with a calculated target, the **Beam End** value is what we'd set in Blueprint, it's often updated by Line Trace's to simulate a weapon projectile hitting a target.
6. Next, select the **Initialize** Module and set the **Lifetime Value** to *0.1.*
7. Let's now change the color of our beam. Select the **Color** Module and set the **RGB** values to **R** = *1.3*, **G** = *25*, and **B** = *0.38*. This will make our Beam glow a very bright green hue.
8. Next, click the Green + Button next to the **Particle Update** Stage and add a *Jitter Position Module*. This will add a lot of noise to the beam. Set the **Jitter Amount** Parameter to *7.3*. The frequency of the Jitter is dependent on the amount of particles created, in our effect, 100 particles are created in the **Spawn Instantaneous** Module. If we wanted to create a smoother looking beam we could either spawn fewer particles or add less Jitter.
9. Now let's create a pulsing effect that goes down the beam. To do this click the Green + Button next to the **Particle Update** Stage and add a *Curl Noise Force* Module.
10. Select the **Curl Noise Force** Module. Change the **Noise Strength** parameter to use a *Float from Curve Noise* by using the dropdown arrow to the right. Setup the following four points on the graph as follows:
    a. Point 1, **X** = *0*, and **Y** = *0*
    b. Point 2, **X** = *0.1*, and **Y** = *7500*
    c. Point 2, **X** = *0.9*, and **Y** = *7500*
    d. Point 4, **X** = *1*, and **Y** = *0*
11. Change the **Curve Index** Parameter to *Ribbon Link Order* using the dropdown arrow on the right.
12. Set the **Scale Curve** Parameter to *5*.
13. Adjust the **Noise Frequency** Parameter to *5*.
14. Enable the **Pan Noise Field** Checkbox and see the *X* Value to *25*. Our Beam will now look like it's moving both vertically and horizontally. Lower values of 0–5 will show the movement through the noise field more clearly while a higher value will add a bit more chaos. Many of these settings will need testing in your game levels to check appearance and look.

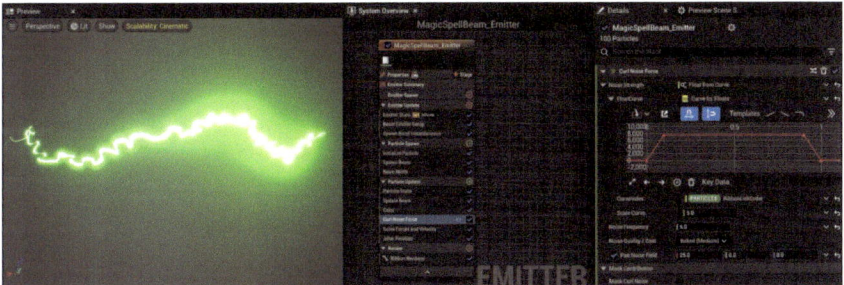

FIGURE 13.1 Magical spell beam emitter.

15. Lastly hit the Save button and close the Niagara Editor. You can see the completed Emitter thus far in Figure 13.1

We've now built the key component of this effect. The Beam we've created is really awesome, but keep an eye on the settings, it's easy for it to get out of control and become too wild. Be sure to test Modules such as Curl Noise and Jitter in Level as soon as possible to ensure you are happy with the values. We are now going to move onto the Sparkling emitter which will help create the idea of energy dissipating from the beam.

Magic Spell – Sparkling Emitter

We are now going to create a **Sparkling Emitter** that will serve as a contact effect to show that a beam has hit a surface. This effect will spawn particles quite frantically in all directions to showcase the **Magic Spells** energy. When creating this emitter feel free to experiment with the property values and make it your own unique look.

1. In the **Content Browser**, navigate to the **Content | VFX** folder.
2. Right click anywhere in the **VFX** Folder and create a **FX \ Niagara Emitter** asset. From the pop up menu choose to create a new Emitter and set the Template to be **Omni Directional Burst** and Label the asset *MagicSpellSparkling_Emitter*.
3. Double click the **MagicSpellSparkling_Emitter** to open the **Niagara Editor**.
4. Select the **Emitter State** Module. Set the **Loop Behavior** to *0.1*, eventually we'll set this behavior to be controlled by the final System asset.
5. Select the **Spawn Burst Instantaneous** Module and set the **Spawn Count** to *75*.
6. Select the **Initialize Particle** Module. Set the **Lifetime Min** to *0.1* and the **Lifetime Max** to *0.5*.
7. Set **Uniform Sprite Size Min** to *0.4* and **Uniform Sprite Size Max** to *3*.
8. Disable or Remove the **Shape Location** Module.

9. Select the **Add Velocity** Module. Change the **Velocity Speed Minimum** to *200* and the **Velocity Speed Maximum** to *355*. Also change the **Velocity Origin** to *Particles Position*, using the dropdown menu on the right. Make sure the **Origin Offset** is set to *0* for *X, Y* and *Z*.

10. Disable or Remove the **Gravity Force** Module.

11. Select the **Drag** Module and set the **Drag** Parameter to *0.5*.

12. Disable or Remove the **Scale Sprite Size** Module.

13. Disable or Remove the **Scale Color** Module.

14. Next click the Green **+** Button next to the **Particle Update** Stage and add a *Color* Module. Change the **Color** Parameter to be *Color From Curve* Using the dropdown arrow to the right. Create 4 points on the upper curve track

    a. Point 1, **V** = *0*, **R** = *0*, **G** = *550.0*, and **B** = *15*

    b. Point 2, **V** = *0.05*, **R** = *0.09*, **G** = *2*, and **B** = *0.03*

    c. Point 3, **V** = *0.4*, **R** = *0.08*, **G** = *1.0*, and **B** = *0*

    d. Point 4, **V** = *1*, **R** = *0.46*, **G** = *1.0*, and **B** = *0*

    These values will create an immediate flash when the particles spawn and then a green/yellow hue for the rest of the particles life.

15. Next, click the Green **+** Button next to the **Particle Update** Stage and add a *Curl Nosie Force Module*. Set the **Noise Strength** to 3000 and **Noise Frequency** to *70*. Lastly enable the **Pan Noise Field** and set the vector as **X** = *0,* **Y** = *0,* and **Z** = *1*.

16. Let's now stretch our fastest particles. Click the Green **+** Button next to the **Particle Update** Stage and add a *Scale Sprite Size by Speed* Module. **Set the Max Scale Factor** to **X** = *1* and **Y** = *15*.

17. Lastly select the **Sprite Renderer** Module. Change the **Alignment Parameter** to *Velocity Aligned*.

18. Click the **Save Button** and close the Niagara Editor. An example of the finished Emitter can be seen in Figure 13.2 for you to review.

The two emitters so far provide the initial beam and surface contact of our effect. The remaining three will create the impact & final blast. We are going to create an energy

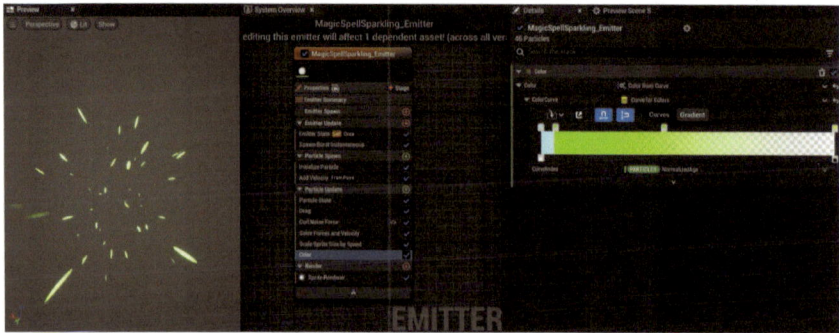

FIGURE 13.2   Magical spell sparking emitter.

charge next that will travel the length of the beam and when it hits/falls in line with the **Sparkling Emitter** it will create two additional emitters which will add a blast ring and extra explosive particles. When creating several **Emitters** like this it's important to keep note of color and speed values as you develop the **Emitters** separately, trying to keep values in line early on can help us avoid tweaking many things later.

We are generating this chapter's effects without complex materials and textures, as an additional exercise you could look to add distorted smoke trails to our beam/an additive spark material to our **Sparking Emitter**. Always try to look for ways to build further interest into what we are practicing.

Magic Spell – Energy Charge Emitter

Let's now make our Energy Charge Emitter.

1. In the **Content Browser**, navigate to the **Content | VFX** folder.
2. Right click anywhere in the **VFX** Folder and create a **FX \ Niagara Emitter** asset. From the pop up menu choose to create a new Emitter and set the Template to be **Single LoopingParticle** and Label the asset *MagicSpellEnergyCharge_Emitter*.
3. Double click the **MagicSpellEnergyCharge_Emitter** to open the **Niagara Editor**.
4. Select the **Emitter State** Module. Change the **Life the Cycle Mode** to *Self*, Set the **Loop Behavior** to *Infinite* and the **Loop Duration** to *4*.
5. Select the **Spawn Burst Instantaneous** Module, set the **Spawn Time** to *2*. This helps us emulate a warm up time of a spell charging before releasing an energy attack. In a game it's likely that parameters like this would be controlled in Code/Blueprint and the Spawn Time would be 0.
6. Select the **Initialize Particle** Module and set the **Uniform Sprite Size** to *44*.
7. Let's now add velocity to our Emitter. In a game this stage would represent the time taken for a bullet/attack to hit an object/character. Click the Green + Button next to the **Particle Spawn** Stage and select **Add Velocity** Module. Change the Velocity to *Random Range Vector* by using the dropdown arrow. Set the **Velocity Minimum** to **X** = *1250*, **Y** =*0*, and **Z** = *0* and the **Velocity Maximum** to be **X** = *1300*, **Y** = *0, and* **Z** = *0*.
8. Let's now scale this particle down over time. Click the Green + Button next to the **Particle Update** Stage and add a *Scale Sprite Size* Module. Use the Graph to add the following five points.
   a. Point 1, **X** = *0*, and **Y** = *0*
   b. Point 2, **X** = *0.03*, and **Y** = *1*
   c. Point 3, **X** = *0.08*, and **Y** = *0.33*
   d. Point 4, **X** = *0.3*, and **Y** = *0.2*
   e. Point 5, **X** = *1*, and **Y** = *0*
9. Drag a selection over the 5 points using the left mouse button, this will select the points. Next right click in the graph space and set the point **Tangents** to

User. This gives us the ability to change the tangents/speed of the size scaling. Experiment and tailor the feel of the animation to your choosing.

10. Next, let's add a flash of color to the Emitter. Click the Green + Button next to the **Particle Update** Stage and add a *Color* Module. Select the **Color** Module and Change the **Color** Parameter to *Color from Curve*. Using the Upper Gradient track, add four color values using the list below.

    a.   Point 1, **V** = *0*, **R** = *175*, **G** = *2500*, and **B** = *0*
    b.   Point 2, **V** = *0.05*, **R** = *0.32*, **G** =*5*, and **B** = *0*
    c.   Point 3, **V** = *0.25*, **R** = *2.43*, **G** = *5*, and **B** = *2.76*
    d.   Point 4, **V** = *1*, **R** = *1*, **G** = *1*, and **B** = *1*

11. Next, let's add a flash of color to the Emitter. Click the Green + Button next to the **Particle Update** Stage and add a *Kill Particles in Volume* Module. By default this will instantly kill the Charge particle. Ideally we want to expose this property with a user parameter. For now though, set the **Sphere Radius** to *50* and the Origin Offset to **X** = *500*, **Y** = *0*, and **Z** = *0*. This will place the Volume away from the particle for now.

12. Next let's add a flash of color to the Emitter. Click the Green + Button next to the **Particle Update** Stage and add a *Generate Death* Module.

13. Click the **Properties** Module at the top of the **Emitter** and Enable **Requires Persistent ID's**.

14. Click the **Save Button** and close the Niagara Editor. An example of the finished Emitter can be seen in Figure 13.3 for you to review.

Our **Charge Emitter** will now create two types of Blasts', one will be a chaotic **Omni Direction** effect and the other a ring. Each type of effect like this will need a bit of experimentation, so do not feel constrained to any properties or values we provide. When working on a pack or set of effects it's worth tracking values in a Spreadsheet or production tool like Confluence. Having access to quick color, size and velocity values across Game Attacks/Spells will make it easy for you to not only create cool effects but also help your team balance effects. It can be quite easy to get wrapped up in a particular particle effect and forget that it's a very basic weapon in a game. Try your best to always link back to team documentation and reference.

FIGURE 13.3   Magical spell energy charge emitter.

Magic Spell – Energy Charge Blast Emitter

Let's now create our first Blast…

1. In the **Content Browser**, navigate to the **Content | VFX** folder.
2. Right click anywhere in the **VFX** Folder and create a **FX \ Niagara Emitter** asset. From the pop up menu choose to create a new Emitter and set the Template to be **OmniDirectionalBurst** and Label the asset *MagicSpellEnergyChargeBlast_Emitter.*
3. Double click the **MagicSpellEnergyChargeBlast_Emitter** to open the Niagara Editor.
4. Self the **Initialize Particle** Module and set the **Lifetime Min** to *0.1* and the **Lifetime Max** to *0.6*. Then change the **Uniform Sprite Size Min** to *2.5* and the **Uniform Sprite Size Max** to *5*.
5. Delete/Disable the **Shape Location** Module.
6. Select the **Add Velocity** Module. Set the **Minimum Velocity** to *−2000.0* and the **Maximum Velocity** to *2000*. Set the **Offset Origin** to *0,0,0* and change the **Velocity Origin** to *Particles Position*.
7. Delete/Disable the **Gravity** Module.
8. Delete/Disable the **Scale Color** Module.
9. Next click the Green + Button next to the **Particle Update** Stage and add a *Curl Force Noise* Module.
10. Select the **Curl Force Noise** Module. Set the **Noise Strength** to *10000.0* and the **Noise Frequency** to *17.0*.
11. Then click the Green + Button next to the **Particle Update** Stage and add a *Scale Sprite Size by Speed* Module. Set the **Max Scale Factor** to *X = 1* and *Y = 3*.
12. Then click the Green + Button next to the **Particle Update** Stage and add a *Color* Module. Using the Upper Gradient track, add four color values using the list below.
    a. Point 1, **V** = *0*, **R** = *0*, **G** = *6000*, and **B** = *700.0.0*
    b. Point 2, **V** = *0.1*, **R** = *0*, **G** =*250.0*, and **B** = *10.0*
    c. Point 3, **V** = *0.4*, **R** =*0*, **G** = *0.832*, and **B** = *1*
    d. Point 4, **V** = *1*, **R** = *1*, **G** =*0.19*, and **B** = *1*
13. Select the **Sprite Renderer** Module, change the **Alignment** to **Velocity Aligned**.
14. Click the Orange + Stage Button at the top of the **Emitter** Stage Stack and select *Event Handler*.
15. Select the **Event Handler Properties** Module. Change the **Execution** Module to *Spawned Particles*. Then enable **Random Spawn Numbers**, finally set the **Spawn Number** to 250 and the **Min Spawn Number** to *225*.
16. Click the Green + Button next to the **Event Handler** Stage and select the *Receive Death Event* Module from the pop up menu. Select the **Receive Death Event** Module, change the **Acceleration** parameter to *Output*.

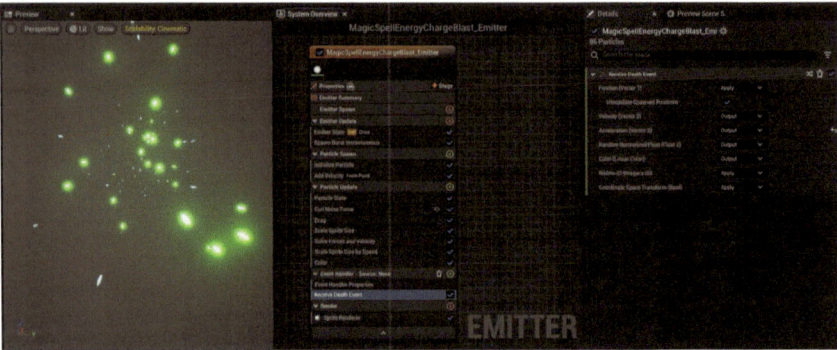

FIGURE 13.4 Magical spell energy charge blast emitter.

17. Click the **Save** Button and close the **Niagara Editor**. An example of the finished Emitter can be seen in Figure 13.4 for you to review.

In our final **System** Asset, we need to adjust the **Energy Charge Blast Emitter**. System Assets allow us to connect the spawning and looping of **Emitters** to other Emitters. This is very helpful when we want Events like Death and Location to impact different Emitters.

When building connected Emitters it can be helpful to still spawn particles while building the systems look. This allows you to set up the look and feel of a particle effect before finalizing spawning and events. After look dev is complete, you can then easily remove or disable any **Spawn** Modules.

Magic Spell – Energy Charge Ring Emitter

We'll now move onto the creation of our final Emitter before joining everything together in our Niagara System.

1. In the **Content Browser**, navigate to the **Content | VFX** folder.
2. Right click anywhere in the **VFX** Folder and create a **FX \ Niagara Emitter** asset. From the pop up menu choose to create a new Emitter and set the Template to be **OmniDirectionalBurst** and Label the asset *MagicSpellEnergyChargeRing_Emitter*.
3. Double click the **MagicSpellEnergyChargeRing_Emitter** to open the **Niagara Editor**.
4. Self the **Initialize Particle** Module and set the **Lifetime Min** to *0.1* and the **Lifetime Max** to *1*. Then change the **Uniform Sprite Size Min** to *2.5* and the **Uniform Sprite Size Max** to *5*.
5. Delete/Disable the **Shape Location** Module.
6. Delete/Disable the **Add Velocity** Module.
7. Delete/Disable the **Gravity** Module.
8. Delete/Disable the **Drag** Module.

9. Delete/Disable the **Scale Color** Module.

10. Next, click the Green + Button next to the **Particle Update** Stage and add a *Curl Force Noise* Module.

11. Select the **Curl Force Noise** Module. Set the **Noise Strength** to *400* and the **Noise Frequency** to *50*.

12. Next click the Green + Button next to the **Particle Update** Stage and add a *Shape Location* Module.

13. Select the **Shape Location** Module. Set the **Shape Primitive** to *Ring* and the **Ring Radius** to *55*. Change the **Rotation Mode** to *Axis Angle*. Lastly change the **Offset mode** to *Default*. We will override the Offset Parameter in the System asset later on.

14. Next click the Green + Button next to the **Particle Update** Stage and add a *Point Attraction Force* Module.

15. Select the **Point Attraction Force** Module. Set the **Attraction Strength** to *−1250*, this will push the particles away and set the **Attraction Radius** to *400*. This module creates the movement of our ring particles, we will change the Attractor Position Offset later on in our final Niagara System.

16. Then click the Green + Button next to the **Particle Update** Stage and add a *Color* Module. Using the Upper Gradient track, add 4 color values using the list below.

    a. Point 1, **V** = *0*, **R** = *544*, **G** = *5000.0*, and **B** = *0.0*

    b. Point 2, **V** = *0.1*, **R** = *28.0*, **G** = *250.0*, and **B** = *0.0*

    c. Point 3, **V** = *0.4*, **R** = *0.25*, **G** = *1*, and **B** = *0.12*

    d. Point 4, **V** = *1*, **R** = *0.6*, **G** = *1*, and **B** = *0.5*

18. Select the **Sprite Renderer** Module, change the **Alignment** to *Velocity Aligned*.

19. Click the Orange + Stage Button at the top of the **Emitter** Stage Stack and select *Event Handler*.

20. Select the **Event Handler Properties** Module. Change the **Execution** Module to *Spawned Particles*. Then enable **Random Spawn Numbers**, finally set the **Spawn Number** to 300 and the **Min Spawn Number** to *250*.

21. Click the **Save** Button and close the Niagara Editor. An example of the finished Emitter can be seen in Figure 13.5 for you to review.

We have now created all of the **Emitters** required for our **Magic Spell System**, we will create the **System** asset next.

When working in a team you'll often find two workflows when dealing with effects that have many Emitters; (1) Which follows what we have done here building separate **Emitters** that we connect into a final system and (2) Building **Emitters** in the System asset itself with no separate Emitter assets in the Content Browser. Both of these workflows are fine, the first affords you the opportunity to share Emitters easily across Niagara Systems and the other creates less assets in the Content Browser. Best practice will normally be decided by your Technical or VFX lead, always be as adaptable as you can.

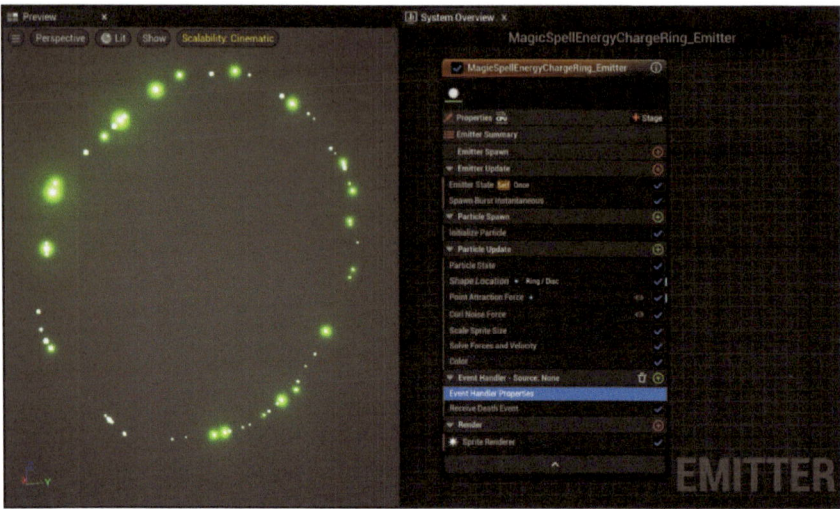

FIGURE 13.5   Magical spell energy charge ring emitter.

Magic Spell System

Let's now create the System asset to control our Magic Spell!

1. In the **Content Browser**, navigate to the **Content | VFX** folder.
2. Right click in the **VFX** Folder and create a **Niagara System Asset**. From the pop up menu select **New system from selected emitters(s)**. Then enable **Parent Emitters** to change the filter of what templates we can select. Ctrl click on the Five **Magic Spell Emitters** and press the Green **+** Button and click **Finish**.
3. Label the created System Asset *MagicSpell_System*.
4. Double click on the **MagicSpell_System** asset to open up the Niagara Editor. You might find the five Emitters are bunched together in the System Overview. If they are you can use the left mouse button to select Emitters and drag them around until you can clearly see properties.
5. Select the **Blue MagicSpell System Niagara Overview** Node. Set the **Loop Duration** to *0.1*. We are now going to let the System asset take charge of much of the particle spawning and also reposition some of the Emitters..
6. To do this locate the **User Parameters** menu on the left. Press the **+** Button next to the **Edit Hierarchy** Button. From the search options look for the type **Vector**. Label this *Vector Beam End* and set its value to **X** = *500*, **Y** = *0*, *and* **Z** = *0*. With this parameter created we can drag and drop the **Beam End** Parameter onto Emitters to allow us to edit locations easily.
7. Next select the **Magic Spell Beam** Emitter and then select the **Emitter State** Module, change the **Life Cycle Mode** to *System*. Next click on **Beam Emitter Setup** Module, drag and drop our **BeamEnd User Parameter** onto the **BeamEnd** parameter on the **Beam Emitter Setup** Module.

8. Select the **Magic Spell Sparkling** Emitter and then select the **Emitter State** Module, change the **Life Cycle Mode** to *System*. Next click on **Initialize Particle** Module, drag and drop our **BeamEnd** User Parameter onto the **PositionOffset** parameter on the **Initialize Particle** Module. Make sure **PositionOffset** is enabled and set the **Position Offset Coordinate Space** to *Local*. You'll know that this has worked correctly as a Sparkling emitter will update to the correct location at the end of the Beam.

9. Select the **Magic Spell Energy Charge Blast** Emitter and then select the **Emitter State** Module, change the **Life Cycle Mode** to *System*. **Disable** the **Spawn Burst Instantaneous** Module. Select the **Event Handler Properties** Module and set the Source to be *MagicSpellEnergyCharge_ Emitter DeathEvent*.

10. Select the **Magic Spell Energy Charge Ring** Emitter and then select the **Emitter State** Module, change the **Life Cycle Mode** to *System*. Disable the **Spawn Burst Instantaneous** Module. Select the **Event Handler Properties** Module and set the **Source** to be *MagicSpellEnergyCharge_ Emitter DeathEvent*.

11. Select the **Magic Spell Energy Charge Ring** Emitter and then select the **Emitter State** Module, change the **Life Cycle Mode** to *System*. Disable the **Spawn Burst Instantaneous** Module. Next click the **Shape Location** Module. Locate the **Offset Mode** settings, you'll see an **X**, **Y** and *Z* value for **Input Position**. Drag and drop our **Beam End** User Variable onto the **Offset Parameter** and set the **Offset Coordinates** to *Local*. You'll now see the ring of particles spawn in the correct place in the viewport. Select the **Receive Death** Module, set the **Position Value** to *Output*, this will stop the particles being overriding by the location of the particles that die.

12. Lastly select the **Point Attraction Force** Module. Drag and drop the **Beam End** User Parameter onto the **Attractor Position Offset** Parameter and set the **Attractor Position Offset Coordinates** to *Local*.

13. Click the **Save** Button and close the **Niagara Editor**. An example of the finished System can be seen in Figure 13.6 for you to review.

FIGURE 13.6 Magical spell system.

There's been a lot of steps with this effect, but hopefully you can see how awesome it is! We've created a **Niagara System** to control the final particles, which is fantastic for previewing and look dev but in a games pipeline you would be required to create several **Niagara Systems**. For example:-

    a. A Niagara System for a weapon/spell charging
    b. A Niagara System of the weapon/spell firing
    c. A Niagara System for the impact of the weapon/spell firing.

The reason for this is that the VFX would need to spawn randomly based on game code executing, to adapt to the above it is mostly a matter of taking the **Niagara Emitters** we've created and separating them out into the required **Niagara Systems** a production team might request. Creating a **Niagara Single System** like we have is great for concepting and testing out shapes, color and speed. Don't get too concerned with separations and complicated Niagara Systems when you are trying to develop a look it can slow things down.

Magic Spell – Attaching System Assets

We are now going to add a preview mesh to help us test our Particle Effect. Using additional meshes outside of Niagara is useful as it lets us debug things like transforms, spawn locations and colors. Niagara VFX are often used in conjunction with many other assets so it's important to see how they interconnect with other systems in Unreal.

    Let's preview **MagicSpell_System** in the level next using a wand mesh.

1. In the **Content Browser**, navigate to the **Content | Meshes** folder.
2. Locate the mesh **WandVFX_Mesh**, drag and drop the asset into the level.
3. Using the **Details** panel set the **Location** value to be (**X** = 1516.5, **Y** = −889.5, **Z** = *−142.4*).
4. In the **Content Browser**, navigate to the **Content | VFX** folder.
5. Locate the **MagicSpell_System**, drag and drop the asset into the level anywhere you please..
6. Locate the **MagicSpell_System** in the **Outliner**. Right click on the **Niagara System** and search for the **WandVFX_Mesh**. This will allow us to drag the spell around the level by manipulating the wand.
7. Select the **MagicSpell_System** in the outliner and set its location to be (**X** = *46.9*, **Y** = 0.0, **Z** = *3.0*).
8. You should now be able to see the Magic Spell next to the Wand Mesh, cool! An example can be seen in Figure 13.7.

We are now going to continue with the magical theme and create some background firework effects, this will continue to develop our use of Events and explore the development of different types of movement to create patterns.

FIGURE 13.7   Magical spell system in the level.

Fireworks

Fireworks – Head Emitter

The first Emitter we are going to build will represent the head of our **Firework effect**. It will be a singular particle that will launch at different angles over time. As the **Firework Head Emitter** moves through space it'll leave a colored trail of particles behind it and eventually explode resulting in the Firework pattern we love to see in the sky. The first **Emitter** will be very bright to ensure we see the initial movement through the sky.

Let's start building our Fireworks!

1. In the **Content Browser**, navigate to the **Content | VFX** folder.
2. Right click anywhere in the **VFX** Folder and create a **FX \ Niagara Emitter** asset. From the pop up menu choose to create a new Emitter and set the Template to be **Single Looping Particle** and Label the asset *FireworksHead_Emitter*.
3. Double click the **FireworksHead_Emitter** to open the Niagara Editor.
4. Select the **Initialize Particle** Module, click the reset value arrow next to the **Lifetime** Parameter and set the value to *3*. Change the **Uniform Sprite Size** to be a *Random Range Float* using the arrow to the right of the Parameter. Then set the **Uniform Sprite Size Min** to *20* and the **Uniform Sprite Size Max** to *25*.

5. Now click the Green **+** Button next to the **Particle Spawn** Stage and select the **Add Velocity** Module from the Menu. Change the **Velocity Parameter** to be a **Random Range Vector** using the arrow to the right of the **Velocity** Parameter. Set the **Velocity Minimum** to be **X** = −450, **Y** = −450, and **Z** = 1400. Set the **Velocity Maximum** to be **X** = *450,* **Y** = *450, and* **Z** = *150.*

6. Now click the Green **+** Button next to the **Particle Update** Stage and select Add **Color** Module from the Menu. Set the **Color** value to **R** = *0,* **G** = *1.5, and* **B** = *25.*

7. Click the Green **+** Button next to the **Particle Update** Stage and select Add **Generate Death Event** Module from the Menu. We will use this to spawn the **Fireworks Bang Emitter**.

8. Click the Green **+** Button next to the **Particle Update** Stage and select **Add Generate Location Event** Module from the Menu. We will use this to spawn the **Fireworks Trail** Emitter.

9. Now select the **Properties** Module at the top of the Emitter and Enable **Persistent IDs**.

10. Click the Green **+** Button next to the **Particle Update** Stage and select **Add Curl Force Noise** Module from the Menu. Set **Noise Strength** to *55* and enable **Pan Noise Field**.

11. Click the **Save Button** and close the **Niagara Editor**. An example of the finished Emitter can be seen in Figure 13.8 for you to review.

The first **Emitter** isn't particularly exciting, the particle fires upwards randomly with a very bright intensity. It does however lay the groundwork for the other emitters to connect to the events it generates. To expand on the **Fireworks Head Emitter** you could try to create some textures for the Sprite Renderers Material, however given the

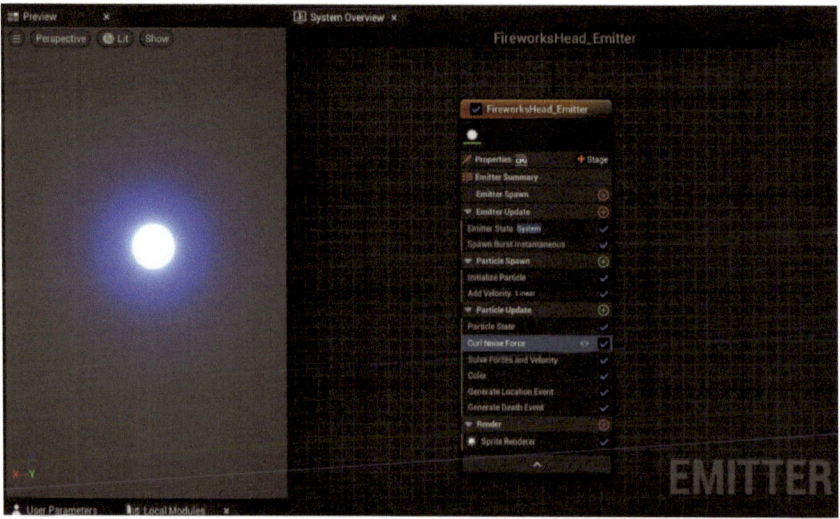

FIGURE 13.8   Fireworks head emitter.

distance that you'll view this effect from any changes would need to be bold to stand out. We'll now move onto our **Trail Emitter**.

Fireworks – Trail Emitter

The **Trailer Emitter**, consists of a spawned particle that is quite short lived. It follows the **Head Emitter** with a subtle intensity across the sky before the Firework explodes. To create interest with the **Trail Emitter** you could look into varying the colors and add noise to the particle's position to make the trails cool.

Let's get started!

1. In the **Content Browser**, navigate to the **Content | VFX** folder.
2. Right click anywhere in the **VFX** Folder and create a **FX\Niagara Emitter** asset. From the pop up menu choose to create a new Emitter and set the Template to be **Single Looping Particle** and Label the asset *FireworksTrail_Emitter*.
3. Double click the **FireworksTrail_Emitter** to open the Niagara Editor.
4. **Delete** or **Disable** the **Spawn Instantaneous** Module.
5. Select the **Initialize Particle** Module, change the **Life Time** to a *Range Float Range*. Set the **Lifetime Min** to *0.1* and the **Lifetime Max** to *0.6*. Set the **Uniform Sprite Size** to a **Range Float Range**. Set the **Uniform Sprite Size Min** to *8* and the **Uniform Sprite Size Max** to *12*. This will make the particles very short lived and smaller than the Fireworks Head Particle.
6. Click the Green + Button next to the **Particle Update** Stage and select **Add Scale Sprite Size** Module from the Menu. Set the Template to **Smooth Ramp Down**.
7. Click the Green + Button next to the **Particle Update** Stage and select **Add Curl Force Noise** Module from the Menu. Set **Noise Strength** to *64* and enable **Pan Noise Field**.
8. Click the Green + Button next to the **Particle Update** Stage and select **Add Gravity Force** Module from the Menu. Set **Noise Strength** to *64* and enable **Pan Noise Field**.
9. Click the Green + Button next to the **Particle Update** Stage and select **Add Color** Module from the Menu. Using the Upper Gradient track, add 3 color values using the list below.
   a. Point 1, **V** = *0*, **R** =*0*, **G** = *1.21*, and **B** = *15.0*
   b. Point 2, **V** = *0.5*, **R** = *15.0*, **G** = *0*, and **B** = *15.0*
   c. Point 3, **V** = *1*, **R** =*1*, **G** = *1*, and **B** = *1*
10. Click the Orange + Stage Button at the top of the **Emitter** Stage Stack and select *Event Handler*.
11. Select the **Event Handler Properties** Module. Change the **Execution** Module to *Spawned Particles*. Set the **Spawn Number** to 5.
12. Click the Green + Button next to the Event Handler Stage and select the Add **Receive Location Event** Module from the Menu. Change the **Velocity** Parameter to **Apply**.

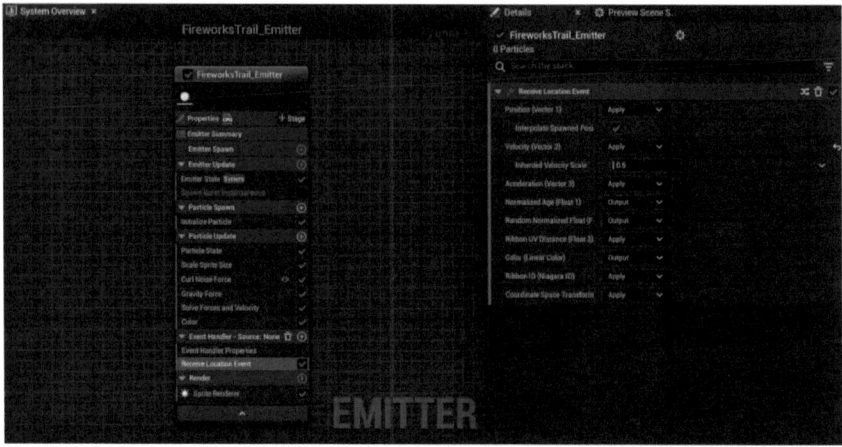

FIGURE 13.9   Fireworks trail emitter.

13. Click the **Save Button** and close the **Niagara Editor**. An example of the finished Emitter can be seen in Figure 13.9 for you to review. Note that at this
point the Emitter will not be spawning any particles, we need to integrate it
into a System for it to work. Let's do that next to check everything is OK.

Fireworks – System 1

To test what we've created so far let's create a System asset. We can come back and
edit this later as we build the Fireworks explosions. Let's get started!

1. In the **Content Browser**, navigate to the **Content | VFX** folder.
2. Right click in the **VFX** Folder and create a **Niagara System Asset**. From
   the pop up menu select **New system from selected emitters(s)**. Then enable
   Parent Emitters to change the filter of what templates we can select. Ctrl click
   on the two **Fireworks Emitters** and press the Green + button and click **Finish**.
3. Label the created **System Asset** *Fireworks_System*.
4. Select the **Event Handler Properties** Module on the **FireworksTrail_
   Emitter** and set the Source to be *FireworksHead_Emitter LocationEvent*.
5. Click the **Save Button** and close the Niagara Editor. An example of the
   System so far can be seen in Figure 13.10 for you to review.

If everything has gone correctly you should now see a variety of particles following the Fireworks Head Emitter. You can customize the effect quite dramatically by
manipulating the Noise, Size and Color. However, to get the best sense of what's going
on it's worthwhile testing the effect in the level.

Try placing the System Asset in the Level at Location near the shoreline. The location we used is $X = -2684.6$, $Y = 92.3$, $Z = -1099.5$

Press 1 on the keyboard to pull back to the Bookmark view of the exterior tower.
You should now see the Fireworks fire in the background. It's likely that the Fireworks

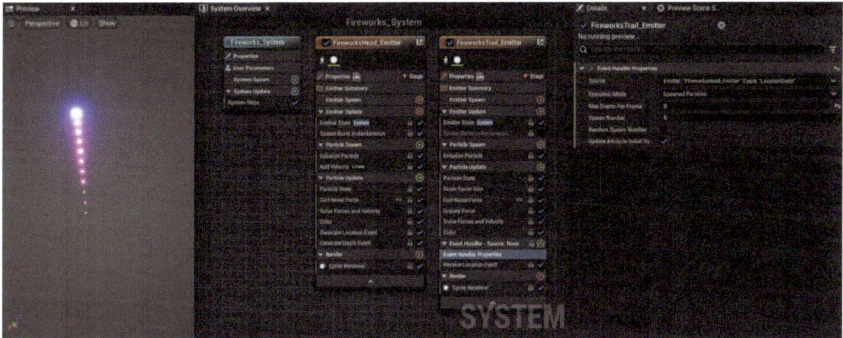

FIGURE 13.10 Fireworks system 1.

might be culled and not visible at this distance. You could try viewing the effect at a closer range or you could select the System in the Outliner and locate the Bounds Parameter in the Details panel. Try increasing the Bounds Parameters to 5 as shown in Figure 13.11. Once you are able to see the effect, you may wish to go back to the **Head / Trail Emitters** and tweak **Sprite Sizes** and **Color** Parameters.

Fireworks – Bang Emitter

Let's now move on with our fireworks effect and create the first explosion, this will continue to help us preview the effect's presence in the level. There's a great many types of patterns and styles of explosions you could create. To begin with we are going to create something similar to our **Magic Spell Emitters**, with particles frantically moving in all directions. This will require a wide range of velocities and noise to move particles over a large distance.

FIGURE 13.11 Level fireworks system.

Let's get started!

1. In the **Content Browser**, navigate to the **Content | VFX** folder.
2. Right click anywhere in the **VFX** Folder and create a **FX\Niagara Emitter** asset. From the pop up menu choose to create a new Emitter and set the Template to be **Omni Directional Burst** and Label the asset *FireworksBang_Emitter.*
3. Double click the **FireworksBang_Emitter** to open the **Niagara Editor**.
4. Select the module **Add Velocity**. Set the **Minimum Value** to be *700* and set the **Maximum Value** to *1500*.
5. Delete or disable the **Scale Color** Module.
6. Then click the Green **+** Button next to the **Particle Update** Stage and add a *Color Module*. Using the Upper Gradient track, add four color values using the list below.
   a. Point 1, **V** = *0*, **R** = *500*, **G** = *0.0*, and **B** = *350.0*
   b. Point 2, **V** = *0.1*, **R** = *5*, **G** = *0.0*, and **B** = *3*
   c. Point 3, **V** = *0.4*, **R** = *1*, **G** = *0*, and **B** = *0.65*
   d. Point 4, **V** = *1*, **R** = *1*, **G** = *1*, and **B** = *1*
7. Select the **Event Handler Properties** Module. Change the **Execution** Module to *Spawned Particles*. Finally set the **Spawn Number** to 125.
8. Click the Green **+** Button next to the **Event Handler** Stage and select the *Receive Death Event Module* from the pop up menu.
9. Now that our Event has been implemented for controlling spawning Disable or Delete the **Spawn Burst Instantaneous** Module.
10. Click the **Save Button** and close the **Niagara Editor**. An example of the finished Emitter can be seen in Figure 13.12 for you to review.

Fireworks – Radial Emitter

We are now moving onto the **Radial Emitter**, this pattern will be very similar in construction to the Bang Emitter so we will begin by duplicating our Bang Emitter asset. The difference in this effect will be the way the particles are emitted, instead of a spherical pattern, the **Radial Emitter** will push particles in a ring-like motion. Combining and using forces in different ways is a great approach to creating something very different with only minor tweaks.

Let's get started!

1. In the **Content Browser**, navigate to the **Content | VFX** folder.
2. Right click anywhere on the asset **FireworksBang_Emitter** and select **Duplicate** from the menu. Label the new asset *FireworksRadial_Emitter.*
3. Double click the **FireworksBang_Emitter** to open the **Niagara Editor**.
4. Select the **Initialize Particle** Module, set the **Uniform Sprite Size Min** to *15* and the **Uniform Sprite Size Max** to *25*.
5. Disable or Delete the **Add Velocity** Module.

FIGURE 13.12   Fireworks bang emitter.

6. Next click the Green **+** Button next to the **Particle Spawn** Stage and add a *Vortex Velocity Module*. Set the **Velocity Amount** to *1500*. You should now see an error, click the **Fix This** Button. If you do not see the **Fix This** Button, you can instead use the Green **+** Button next to the **Particle Spawn** Stage to add an **Apply Initial Forces** Module under the **Vortex Velocity** Module.

7. Next click the Green **+** Button next to the **Particle Update** Stage and add a *Vector Noise Force Module*. Set the **Force Amount** to *1000*.

8. Select the **Color** Module. Adjust the first two points on the upper gradient as follows:

   a.   Point 1, **V** = *0*, **R** = *1500*, **G** = *0.0*, and **B** = *1000.0*

   b.   Point 2, **V** = *0.1*, **R** = *500*, **G** = *0.0*, and **B** = *340*

9. Click the **Save Button** and close the **Niagara Editor**. An example of the finished Emitter can be seen in Figure 13.13 for you to review.

FIGURE 13.13   Fireworks radial emitter.

Fireworks – System 2

We are now going to revisit our Fireworks System asset, adding in our explosion Emitters. We need to tweak a few minor settings to ensure everything syncs up properly so we can test the final effect in our level.

1. In the **Content Browser,** navigate to the **Content | VFX** folder.
2. Double click on the **Fireworks_System** asset to open the **Niagara Editor**.
3. Use the **Content Browser** to drag and drop our **FireworksBang_Emitter** and **FireworksRadial_Emitter** assets into our **Fireworks_System** Overview space.
4. Select the **Event Handler Properties Module** on the **FireworksRadial_ Emitter** and set the **Source** to be *FireworksHead_Emitter DeathEvent*.
5. We next need to select the **Emitter State** Module on the **FireworksRadial_ Emitter**. Set the **Life Cycle Mode** Parameter to be handled by the *System*. Without doing this the Emitter will only activate once and not when each particle death occurs.

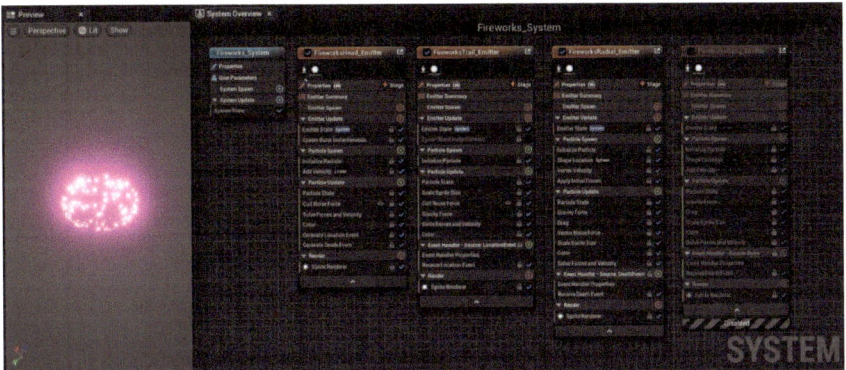

FIGURE 13.14 Fireworks system 2.

6. Select the **Event Handler Properties** Module on the **FireworksBang_ Emitter** and set the **Source** to be *FireworksHead_Emitter DeathEvent*.

7. We next need to select the **Emitter State** Module on the **FireworksBang_ Emitter**. Set the **Life Cycle Mode** Parameter to be handled by the *System*.

8. We can now toggle the Radial and Bang Emitters to see different explosions when the Head Emitter's life ends.

9. Click the **Save Button** and close the **Niagara Editor**. An example of the finished Emitter can be seen in Figure 13.14 for you to review.

You will almost certainly want to tweak the properties of the system, Figure 13.15 shows the final System in the Level exploding above the tower. In your own time, you

FIGURE 13.15 Final fireworks system in the level.

could experiment with other Emitters to create different explosion patterns. Perhaps look into different System locations in the level, Shape Locations, Velocities and Forces to create cool-looking explosions. It's also possible to daisy chain Events so that exploding particles could generate location events to create their own trails.

Conclusion

In this chapter we've built two multi-tiered Systems exploiting features such as Beams and Events. The two systems have bags of options for customization and parameters. Use your creativity to expand on what we've tried to make your own fireworks and spell shapes.

In our next chapter we'll be exploring Waterfall effects. Before we move on let's test our knowledge with a quick quiz!

Chapter 13 Quiz

Question 1: What type of Effects do Ribbon Renders work for?

    a. A series of connected particles for example Wispy Smoke, Trails or Beams.

    b. Small debris particles for explosions.

    c. Underwater bubbles and water ripples.

Question 2: What does a Jitter Module do?

    a. It allows us to distort particle positions, in this chapter we used it to add wavy noise to the beam's position.

    b. It generates material noise that makes our particle color change over time.

    c. It creates random life times for our particles.

    d. All of the above.

Question 3: What does a Kill Particles in Volume Module do?

    a. It creates particles that Kill other Unreal Actors.

    b. It removes all particles within a volume.

    c. It stops particles spawning within a set volume.

Question 4: What's a good way of spawning particles behind a leading emitter?

    a. A Delay Event.

    b. A Transform Event.

    c. A Generate Location Event.

Answers

Question 1: a
Question 2: a
Question 3: c
Question 4: c

14

The Waterfall

Introduction

In this chapter, we are going to create our Waterfall Effects and Systems, you'll learn about:

- Creating flowing water materials.
- Creating Water Splash SUB UV materials.
- Animating Water Foam Materials.

Water VFX often requires many different types of ingredients to create a particular effect. We'll begin by creating several materials to help power our effect. After this we'll apply these Materials to Meshes and Particle Systems. In addition to what we try in this chapter, you might also enjoy looking into packages such as Houdini, 3ds Max and Blender to learn about fluid simulation and generating water textures.

It's helpful to break down water VFX into different stages. The stages can include flowing water, splashes and ripples. We'll be tackling water crashing over a short drop, creating a waterfall that splashes down into a pool.

Waterfall Flowing Water

In this section, we'll begin by exploring the ingredients needed to power our Flowing Water.

Flowing Water Meshes

Let's begin this process by looking at our Water Meshes.

1. In the **Content Browser**, navigate to the folder **Content | Meshes**.
2. Double click on the asset **Waterfall_Mesh** to open the Mesh in the Static Mesh Editor.
3. With the Mesh Open let's look at some important things to consider for your own projects.

Let's explore the Waterfall Mesh and its use. Figure 14.1 shows the Mesh open in the Static Mesh Editor, the mesh is quite low in polycount and is designed to follow the

DOI: 10.1201/9781032663852-14

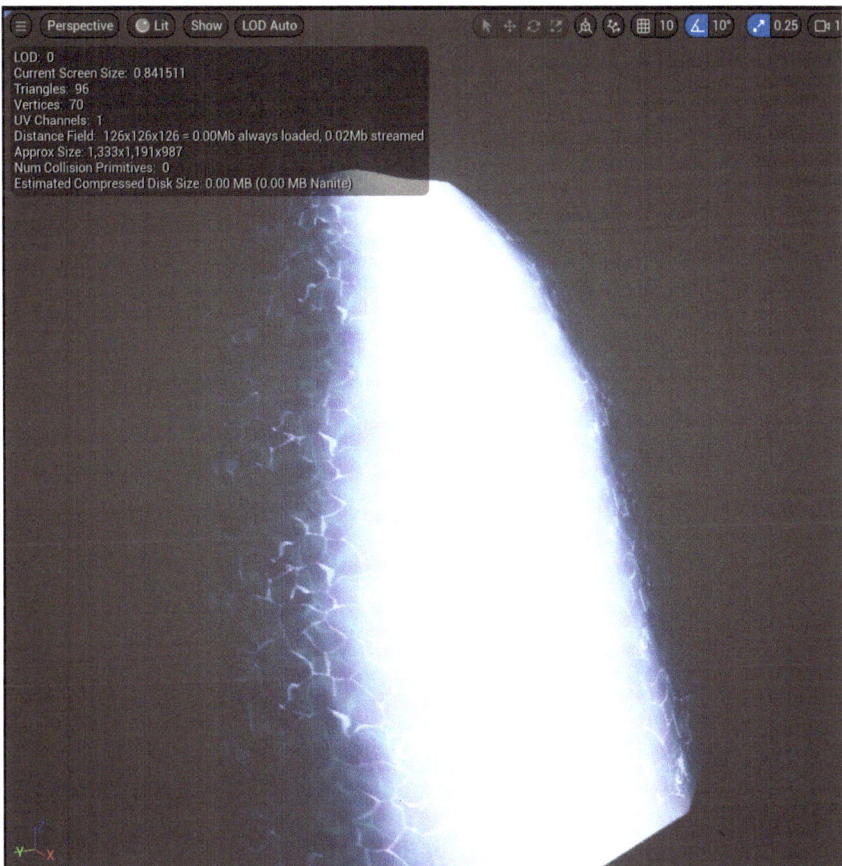

FIGURE 14.1 Waterfall mesh.

rough shape of a waterfall, this is done by tracing the geometry in a DCC Tool like 3ds Max and or Blender using polygon modeling tools. The Mesh needs to have some thickness with the idea of the mesh being placed several times along the path of a waterfall. Unfortunately, this approach does mean that each waterfall in a level/game may need a unique mesh if the shape of the waterfall is unique.

Animated Flowing Water Material

We are now going to build a Flowing Water Material which will apply to our Waterfall mesh. The idea behind this material is that it will add bright fast moving details to showcase the speed of the water flowing over the falls. The idea is that the mesh will sit just on top of the Unreal Water and add to the overall thickness and speed creating a more volumetric effect.

The result of this material can be made more realistic with different textures, the example in this project will be quite stylized and has a cut out look to the water lines.

A softer opacity and a bit of refraction can help make this material a bit more realistic if required for your own projects.

1. In the **Content Browser**, navigate to the folder **Content | Materials | Master**.
2. Right click in the **Master** folder and select **Material** from the menu.
3. Call the new Material *M_FlowingWater*.
4. Double click on **M_FlowingWater** to open the Material.
5. Navigate to the **Details** panel, locate the **Blend Mode** Parameter and select **Additive** from the down menu.
6. Set the **Shading Mode** to **Unlit**, this will lower the overall cost of the Waterfalls Material. We need to do this as we'll be animating several large meshes with position offsets, translucency and blends. You can of course try more costly lighting modes but do keep an eye on your PC's performance.
7. Our first nodes to create are two **Texture Coordinate** Nodes. Place these by right clicking in the **Material Graph** and searching for the *Texture Coordinate Node*. Place one of the nodes and then repeat the process and place the second below with a bit of space in between. Select the first **Texture Coordinate** Node and set the **UV tiling** to *2* for both **U** and **V**. Select the second **Texture Coordinate** Node and set the **UV tiling** to *6* for both **U** and **V**. We want plenty of space to the left of our Material Output Node, when placing these first nodes make sure you have a good amount of room, if you placed them quite close, move them to the left to leave space between them and the output.
8. Next create two Panner Nodes that connect to our **Texture Coordinate Nodes**. Do this by using the right click approach in the **Material Graph** and search for *Panner*.
9. Connect the first **Texture Coordinates** Node to the first **Panner** Node, set the first **Panner** Node's **X Speed** to *0.26* and **Y Speed** to *−0.59*.
10. Connect the second **Texture Coordinates** Node to the second **Panner** Node, set the second **Panner** Nodes **X Speed** to *0.1* and **Y Speed** to *−2.0*.
11. Now create a Time Node by using the right click and search approach in our Material Graph, searching for *Time*. Place the **Time** Node in between both **Panner** Nodes and connect its output to the Time input slot on both **Panner** nodes. We now have some large and small UV coordinates that are falling vertically over time.
12. Using the **Content Browser**, navigate to **Content | Textures | VFX_Waterfall**, select and drag the Texture **WaterfallStream1_BaseColor** into our material graph.
13. Place the new **Texture Sample** next to the first **Panner** node and connect the output pin of the **Panner** into the **UV** input of the **Texture Sample**.
14. Again, using the **Content Browser** Navigate to **Content | Textures | VFX_Waterfall**, select and drag the Texture **WaterfallStream2_BaseColor** into our material graph. Place the new **Texture Sample** next to the second

Panner and connect the output pin of the **Panner** into the **UV input** of the **Texture Sample**.

15. Add a **Multiply** Node by holding M and left clicking after the **Texture Sample** that has the texture **WaterfallStream2_BaseColor** plug the **RGB** output pin of the **Texture Sample** into the **A** input of the **Multiply** Node. Create a **Scalar Parameter** Node nearby by holding S and left clicking and connect it to the **B** input of the **Multiply** Node. Rename this **ScalarParameter** to *Line Strength* and set its **Default Value** to *3*. This section of the Material will control the very fine water highlights that move fast and pop at the edges.

16. After the **Multiply** Node, place an **Add** Node by holding A and left clicking. Connect the output of the **Multiply** into the **A** input of the **Add** Node and set the **B** value to *0.2*. This will raise all the values of the pixels up, we are doing this as there's a bit too much black in the texture and adding a tiny bit more white will help with later blends.

17. Add a **Multiply** Node by holding M and left clicking after the **Add** Node. Connect the **Add** Nodes Output into the **B** input of the **Multiply**. Connect the **RGB** output of the **Texture Sample** that uses the texture **WaterfallStream1_BaseColor** into the **A** input of the **Multiply** Node.

18. We've now constructed the Panning section of the material, you can review the node setup in Figure 14.2.

19. Click the **Save** Button in the Material Editor.

Now that we've created panning water noises, we can start to work on other sections of our material such as Color. To this we'll create ways to mask and add further contrast to the results of our panning node chains before blending in a color water texture. Let's hop back into the Material Editor!

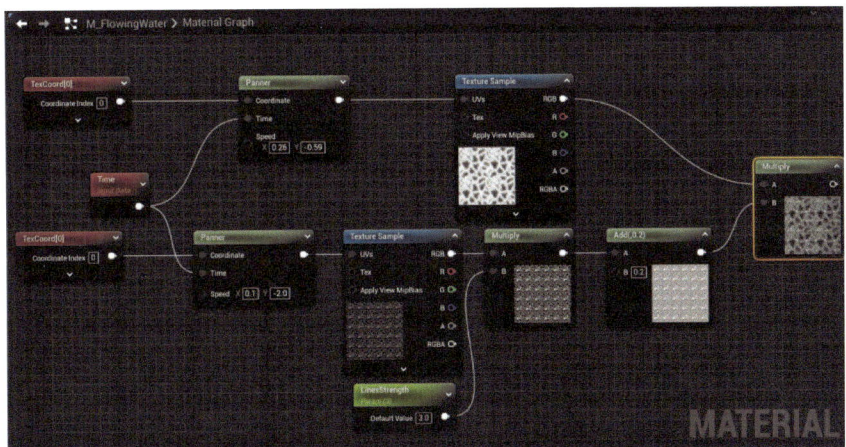

FIGURE 14.2 Animated flowing water material panning chains.

1. Using the **Content Browser** Navigate to **Content | Textures | VFX_ Waterfall**, select and drag the Texture **WaterMask** into the **M_ FlowingWater** Material. Place the new **Texture Sample** slightly above our two **Panner** Node chains. This texture will be used to add extra brightness in the middle of Material and fade out the opacity near the edges.

2. Place an **Add** Node by holding A and left clicking in the Material Graph. Connect the **RGB** output of the **Texture Sample** into the **A** input of the **Add** Node**.** Then connect the **Multiply** Output (from **Panner** chains) into the **B** input of the **Add** Node**.** Clicking the dropdown Preview on the **Add** node should now show the Panning water textures with the extra brightness added to the middle.

3. Next we need to mask out the edges. To do this place a **Multiply** Node after the **Add** Node by holding M and left clicking in the Material Graph. Connect the output of the **Add** Node into the **B** input of the **Multiply** Node. Connect the **RGB** output of the **WaterMask Texture Sample** Node into the **A** input of the **Multiply** Node. If all's gone well the edges of the texture should now be darker while the center section remains bright.

4. We'll now use this Node chain to create the color for our Material. To do this first add a **Saturate** Node by right clicking in the Material Graph and searching for *Saturate*. Connect the **Multiply** Nodes output into the **Saturate** Node's input. This will limit the Grayscale values to 0–1 which will help us ensure we don't over inflate our color values.

5. Next hold L and left click in the Material Graph to create a **Linear Interpolate** Node. Connect the **Saturate** Node's output into the **B** input of the **Linear Interpolate** Node. Set the **Alpha Value** to *0.5*. Don't worry about the **A** input, we will come back to that shortly.

6. Hold M on the keyboard and left click to place a **Multiply** Node. Connect the output of the **Linear Interpolate** Node into the **B** input of the **Multiply** Node. Hold V on the keyboard and click to place a **Vector Parameter** Node. Label this **Vector Parameter** as *Color Tint* and set its **Default Value** to be White (**R**=*0.29*, **G**=*0.37*, and **B**=*0.88*).

7. Connect the **RGB** output of the **Vector Parameter** into the **A** input of the **Multiply** Node. Finally connect the output of the **Multiply** Node into the **Emissive Color** input on our Material Result.

8. We now have to back track a bit to the **Linear Interpolate** Node. We need to create four nodes to create the logic that plugs into **A**. The idea here is that we will Blend a blue water texture with the animated panning mask. This will create a white volume of water in the middle with blue finer details near the outer sections.

9. Place a **Texture Coordinate** Node by right clicking in the **Material Graph** and searching for *Texture Coordinate*. Place the node a bit to the left of the **Linear Interpolate** Node and leave a bit of space in between. Select the **Texture Coordinate** Node and set the **UV tiling** to *6* for both **U** and **V**.

10. Now, using the right click approach in the **Material Graph**, search for *Panner*. Connect the **Texture Coordinates** Node to the **Panner** Node, set the Panner Node's **X Speed** to *−0.3* and **Y Speed** to *−2*. Then create a **Time**

Node and connect the **Time** Node's output to the **Panner** Node's **Time** input.

11. Using the **Content Browser** Navigate to **Content | Textures | VFX_ Waterfall**, select and drag the Texture **Water_basecolor** into our **M_ FlowingWater Material**. Place the new **Texture Sample** slightly to the right of the **Panner**. Connect the **Panner** Node's output into the **UV** Input of the **Texture Sample** Node.

12. Lastly connect the **Texture Sample** Node's **RGB** output into the **A** input of the **Linear Interpolates** node. We should now see the blue water color apply to the material.

13. Click the **Save** Button in the Material Editor.

We've now constructed the color section of the material, you can review the node setup in Figure 14.3. We have two small sections left to build (1) The Opacity Nodes and (2) The World Position Offset Nodes.

1. Firstly, locate the **TextureSample** that has our **WaterMask** texture applied and scroll until you see the **Multiply** Node. Drag out of this **Multiply** Node and create another **Multiply** Node from the Menu. For Input **B**, create a **Scalar Parameter** by holding **S** and left clicking in the Material Graph. Label the **Scalar Parameter** as *Opacity Strength* and set its **Default Value** to *0.75*.

2. After the **Multiply** node, right click in the Material Graph and choose to create a *Depth Fade* node from the popup menu. Connect the output from the **Multiply** into the **DepthFade** input and the output of the **DepthFade** into the Material Results **Opacity** Input slot. You should now see the edges of our Material go transparent.

3. We are now going to make a couple of nodes that will animate the Water Meshes vertices in the level. To do this locate the **TextureSample** that has our **WaterfallStream1_BaseColor** texture applied. Drag out of the **RGB** output and create a **Multiply** Node toward the lower section of the Material Result Node.

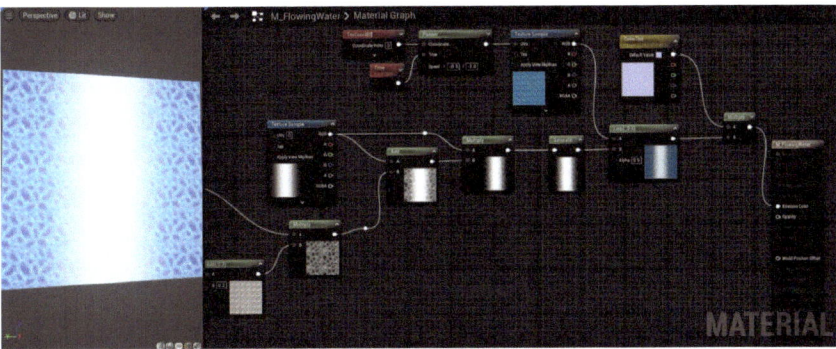

FIGURE 14.3 Animated flowing water material generating color.

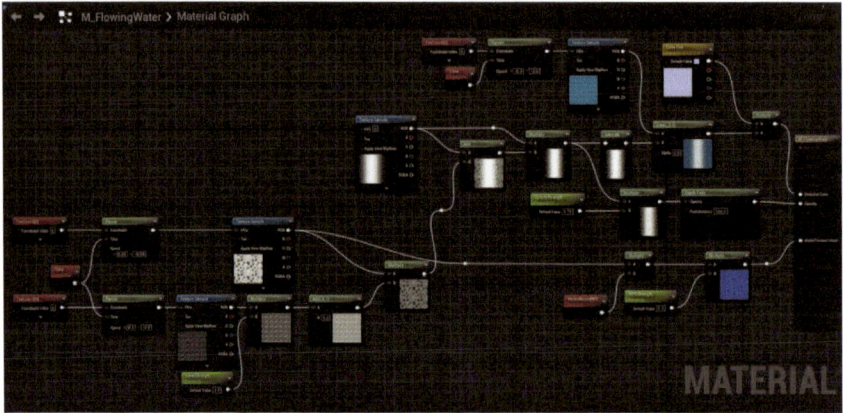

FIGURE 14.4   Animated flowing water material opacity and WPO.

4. For the **B** input of the **Multiply** Node, right click in the Material Graph and search for a **VertexNormalWS** Node. Connect the output of the **VertexNormalWS** Node into the **B** input of the **Multiply** Node.

5. Now create another **Multiply** Node, feed in the previous **Multiply** Node's output into the **A** Input of the New **Multiply** Node. Then Hold S and left click to create a **Scalar Parameter** in the **Material Graph**. Label the **Scalar Parameter** as *WPOStrength* and set its **Default Value** to *5*.

6. Connect the **Output** of the **Multiply** Node to the **World Position Offset** input of the **Material Result** Node.

7. You can review the overall placement of nodes in Figure 14.4.

8. Click the **Save** Button in the Material Editor.

We've now completed our Flowing Water Material, if you'd like to see its results in the Level Select the Meshes labeled as **"Waterfall_Mesh"** in the World Outliner and use the Details panel to set the **Element 0** Material to *M_FlowingWater*. You could expand what we've done here in many ways. For example you could:

- Make a Material Instance of the Material and tweak the properties
- Parameterize the Panner sections of the Material to afford greater tweaking and customization, and
- Add a **Desaturation** Node just before the **Emissive** Input to allow you to lower the amount of color as there's always a chance that the water could become quite vibrant in daylight scenes and look toxic.

We'll now move onto another Material that will help drive our particle effects.

Waterfall Splash Effect

To build our Splash Effect we first need to build our particle effect. You should find many of the operations and nodes similar in this Material. Let's get started!

Waterfall Splash Material

We are now going to build our Splash Material, this will be very similar to Materials that we created for our Fire and Smoke Effects earlier in the book. The material will represent water, foam and particles bouncing up from the river as the waterfall fall crashes downwards. The effect is often quite bright and white with a very thick water vapor appearance.

We will begin by creating the basic requirements such as SUB UV control, blend modes and parameters. In a later section we'll also explore adding refracting control to the effect to help distort the look, this will be optional and maybe something you'd like to add for a more realistic setting. Let's begin:

1. In the **Content Browser**, navigate to the folder **Content | Materials | Master**.
2. Right click in the **Master** folder and select **Material** from the menu.
3. Call the Material *M_WaterfallSplashSubUV*.
4. Double click to open the Material.
5. Navigate to the **Details** panel.
6. Locate the **Blend Mode** Parameter, select *Additive* from the down menu.
7. Set the **Shading Model** to **Unlit.** If you require better lighting you could also use the Translucent Blend Mode but it is more expensive.
8. Make sure there's a good bit of distance between the Material Result node and where your cursor is in the Material Graph. Then right click in the Material Editor Graph and place and search for a **Particle Color** Node.
9. Just to the right of the **Particle Color** Node, hold **M** and left click to create a **Multiply** Node. Connect the **RGB** output of the **Particle Color** node into the **A** input of the **Multiply** Node.
10. Right click just below the **Particle Color** node and search for a *Texture Sample Parameter Sub UV* Node. Set the **Parameter Name** to *Texture Map*. Set the **Texture Map** to our *Splash Atlas* texture. Connect the Red channel pin from the **Texture Sample Parameter Sub UV** Node to the **B** input of the **Multiply** node.
11. Connect the output of the **Multiply** to the **Emissive Color** input on the **Material Result** Node.
12. Place another **Multiply** node to the right of the **Texture Sample Parameter Sub UV** Node. Connect the Red channel pin from the **Texture Sample Parameter Sub UV** Node to the **A** input of the **Multiply** node.
13. Hold **S** on the keyboard and left click below the **Texture Sample Parameter Sub UV** Node, this will create a **Scalar Parameter** Node. Rename the **Parameter** node *OpacityStrength* and set the **Default Value** to *0.84*. Connect the output of **OpacityStrength** to the **B** input of the **Multiply** Node.
14. With both of the **Multiply** inputs created, place another **Multiply** node and connect the output of the original **Multiply** Node into the **B** Input of the new **Multiply** Node.
15. Connect the **Alpha Output (A)** of our **Particle Color** Node into the **A** input of the new **Multiply** Node.

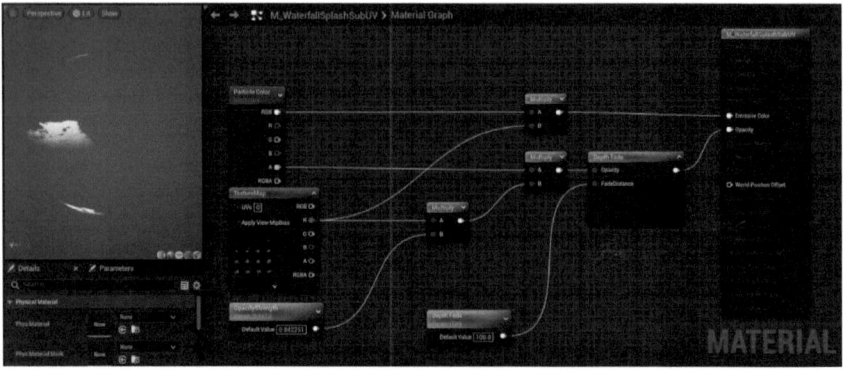

FIGURE 14.5   Waterfall splash material.

16. Drag out from the new **Multiply** Node and select **Depth Fade**. This will help blend our particle seams when translucent objects overlap. The default value of *100* is fine for the fade distance, we can parametrize this by right clicking on the **Fade Distance** text and selecting **Promote to Parameter** from the options menu.

17. Check that the **Default Value** of the **Fade Distance** parameter node is set to *100*.

18. Connect the **Output** of the **Depth Fade** Node into the **Opacity** Input of our **Material Result Node**.

19. Click the **Save** Button in the Material Editor and use Figure 14.5 to review your work.

Waterfall Splash System

Let's now incorporate our Splash Material into a Niagara System. This Particle Effect will use our Splash Sub UV image to drive particles spawning at the base of our waterfall. We will spawn several sprite particles that will display the Sub UV animation and create a water vapor look. As this effect will normally be white/a bright hue, be mindful of the overall amount of particles you create as it's quite easy for it to become overpowered and too bright. We also want to be careful with particle overdraw, try to minimize the overlaps created when the effect is placed in the world and use the Unreal Optimization View modes to debug any particular performance hit areas.

Let's get cracking!

1. In the **Content Browser**, navigate to the **Content | VFX** folder.

2. Right click anywhere in the **VFX** Folder and create a **FX\Niagara System** asset. From the pop up menu choose to add *Fountain Template* to the asset, click Finish and then Label the asset *WaterfallSplash_System*.

3. Double click the **WaterfallSplash_System** to open the **Niagara Editor**.

4. Disable or delete the **Shape Location** Module.

5. Disable or delete the **Add Velocity** Module.

6. Disable or delete the **Gravity Force** Module.

7. Disable or delete the **Drag** Module.

8. Disable or delete the **Scale Color** Module.

9. Select the **Spawn Rate** Module and set the **Spawn Rate Parameter** to *5*.

10. Select the Initialize **Particle** Module. Set the **Lifetime Min** to *1* and set the **Lifetime Max** to *3.5*. Change the **Position Offset** to *Random Range Vector*, set the **Minimum** offset to (**X**=*5,* **Y**=*−25,* and **Z**=*0*) and set the **Maximum** offset to (**X**=*5,* **Y**=*25,* and **Z**=*0*). Set the **Sprite Size Mode** to *Random Non-Uniform*. **Sprite Size Min** to **X**=*300* and **Y**=*250* and **Sprite Size Max** to **X**=*500* and **Y**=*350*. Lastly set the **Sprite Rotation Mode** to *Unset.*

11. Click the Green+Button next to the **Particle Spawn** stage and from the popup menu select the **Add Velocity** Module. Set the **Velocity** to be *Linear* and *Random Range Vector.* Set the **Velocity Minimum** to (**X**=*−0.001,* **Y**=*−0.001,* and **Z**=*0*) and Set the **Velocity Maximum** to (**X**=*0.001,* **Y**=*0.001,* and **Z**=*5*).

12. Click the Green+Button next to the **Particle Update** stage and from the popup menu select the **Sub UV Animation** Module. Set the **Sprite Renderer** Parameter, to match the *Sprite Renderer* Module.

13. Click the Green+**Button** next to the **Particle Update** stage and from the popup menu select the **Scale Sprite Size** Module. Set the **Template** to *Linear Ramp Up.*

14. Then click the Green + Button next to the **Particle Update** Stage and add a *Color* Module. Using the Upper Gradient track, add 1 value using the list below and remove any existing points.

    a.   Point 0, **V**=*0,* **R**=*3,* **G**=*3.35,* and **B**=*4*

    For the Lower Gradient track (Transparency) the default values are fine.

15. Select the **Sprite Renderer** Module. Set the **Material** Parameter to be **M_WaterfallSplashSubUV**. Next enable *SubUVBlending Enable* and set the **Sub Image Size** values as **X**=*4,* and **Y**=*4*. Set the **Default Pivot** in **UV Space** to be **X**=*0.5* and **Y**=*1*. Change the **Alignment Parameter** to *Velocity Aligned.*

16. Click the **Save** Button in the Niagara Editor.

An example of the completed System can be seen in Figure 14.6. We've now created the Splash System which will help reinforce the flowing materials to add further volume to our waterfall. We now need to place several Niagara System assets to test the visual appearance of the effect. While placing the assets try to avoid overly straight lines, this can make the particles stand out in a negative way.

Let's now test the system in the level.

1. To do so, Open the **Content Browser** and navigate to the **Content | VFX** folder.

2. Drag and drop a copy of the **WaterfallSplash_System** into the level.

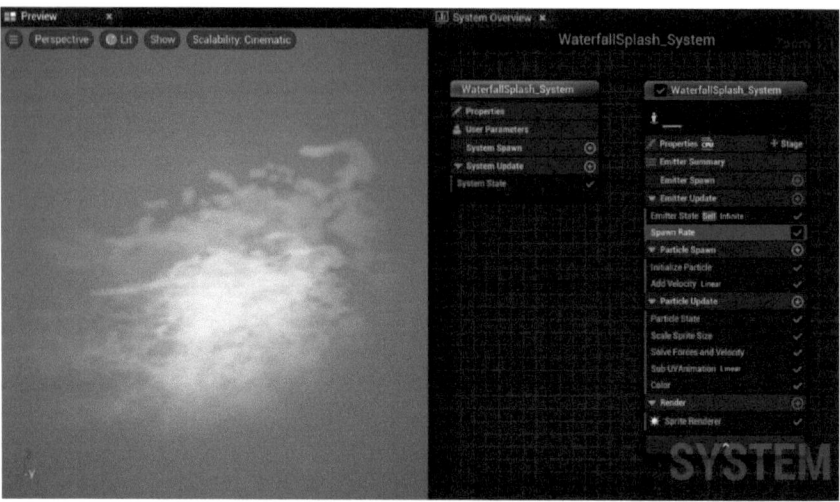

FIGURE 14.6 The waterfall splash system.

3. Make **11** copies of the System asset in the Level, you can do this by selecting the **WaterfallSplash_System** Actor in the **World Outliner** and pressing Ctrl+C to Copy and Ctrl+V to Paste.

4. Next use the following list of Transform details to copy onto the **12 WaterfallSplash_System** assets. You can ignore this step if you wish and place the assets manually.

   1. (**X**=*-1113.846045*, **Y**=*2724.862805*, **Z**=*-1036.710008*)
   2. (**X**=*-972.615325*, **Y**=*2634.514838*, **Z**=*-1036.710008*)
   3. (**X**=*-1293.932305*, **Y**=*2835.394939*, **Z**=*-1036.710008*)
   4. (**X**=*-1219.562994*, **Y**=*2770.405043*, **Z**=*-1036.710008*)
   5. (**X**=*-1481.886380*, **Y**=*2953.154465*, **Z**=*-1036.710008*)
   6. (**X**=*-1126.667301*, **Y**=*2712.653719*, **Z**=*-1036.710008*)
   7. (**X**=*-1270.996560*, **Y**=*2834.005726*, **Z**=*-1028.606186*)
   8. (**X**=*-1357.941813*, **Y**=*2848.463432*, **Z**=*-1036.710008*)
   9. (**X**=*-1126.899513*, **Y**=*2744.975742*, **Z**=*-1036.710008*)
   10. (**X**=*-1032.500229*, **Y**=*2647.314502*, **Z**=*-1036.710008*)
   11. (**X**=*-1433.943521*, **Y**=*2867.016492*, **Z**=*-1036.710008*)
   12. (**X**=*-1433.943521*, **Y**=*2879.572079*, **Z**=*-1054.089428*)

The above locations are guides, by all means tweak and adjust to what you think looks cool. If your computer struggles to render lots of transparent particles you may also create less particle systems to improve performance. Before moving onto the next section a completed version of the placed Waterfall Effect can be seen in Figure 14.7.

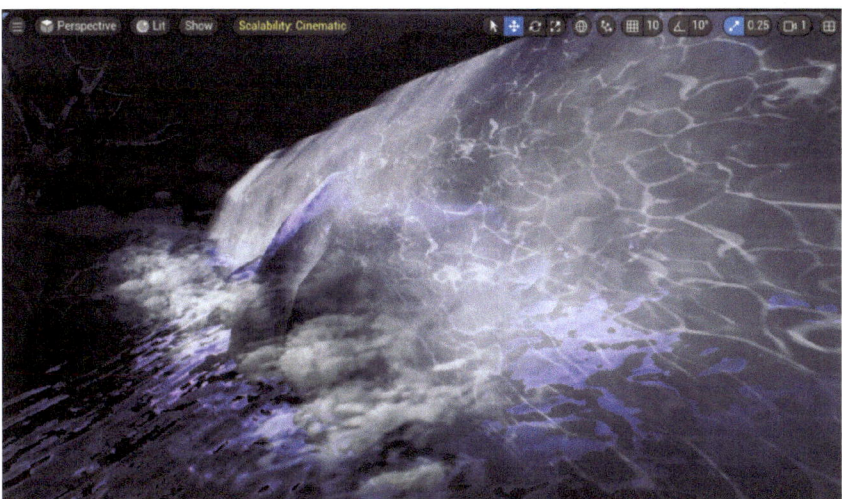

FIGURE 14.7 The waterfall splash system in the level.

Waterfall Splash Material 2

As mentioned earlier we are going to make a slight tweak to our Splash Material to make things a bit more realistic. We are going to add just a couple of nodes to enable refraction, this is quite a costly step in regards to performance so do feel free to skip it if your PC is struggling to run the effects thus far.

1. Open the **Content Browser** and navigate to the **Materials | Master** folder and open the Material **M_WaterfallSplashSubUV**.
2. Create a Copy of the **TextureMap Node** using copy and paste or right click duplicate approaches and adjust the **Parameter name** to *Normal Map*. Change the **Normal Map Texture Parameter** to be *SplashAtlasNormal*. Connect the **RGB** Output into the **Normal Map** input of the Material Result.
3. Next, create a **Fresnel** node in the **Material Graph** by right clicking and searching for the *Fresnel* Node. Connect the **Normal Map RGB** output into the **Normal Map** input of the **Fresnel** node. Connect the output of the **Fresnel Node** into the **Refraction** Input of the **Material Result** Node.
4. In the **Details** panel, search for the Parameter **Refraction Method** and set it to *Index of Refraction*. By default this option is **Disabled**.
5. To improve Performance a little you could change the **Shading Model** to *unlit*. To see the tweaks to the Material please review Figure 14.8 and 14.9 to see the effect in the level.
6. You can always disable the **Refraction** Parameter in the **Details** panel if you wish to turn it off.
7. Remember to click **Save** before Closing the **Material Editor**.

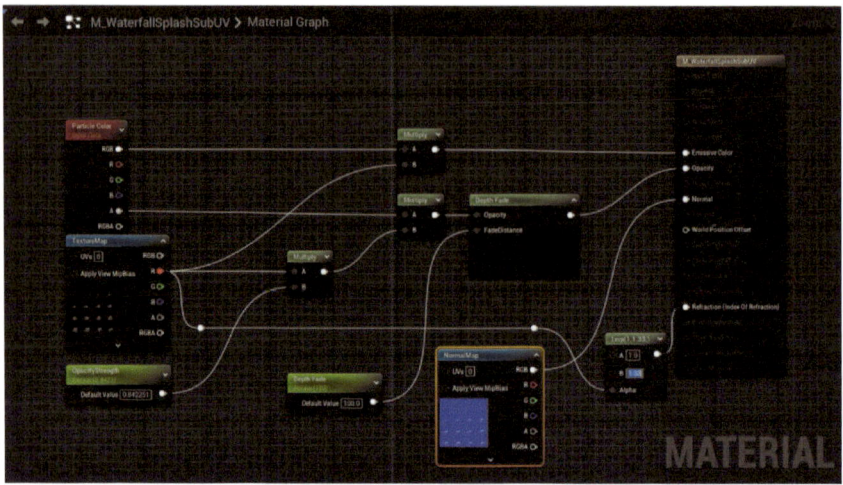

FIGURE 14.8   The waterfall splash material refraction.

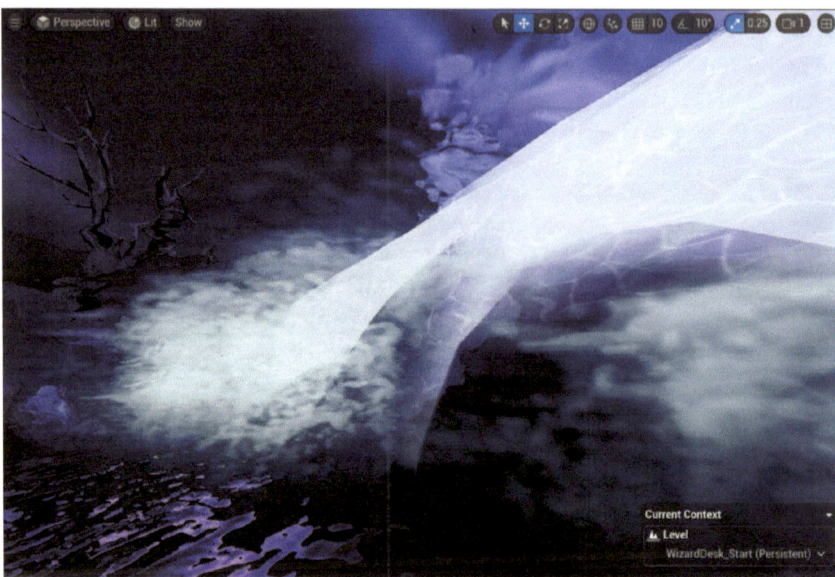

FIGURE 14.9   The waterfall splash refraction in the level.

Waterfall Foam Effect

Water Foam Material

In this next section we are going to build a Material that will power our Water Foam Particle Effect. This Material will use several of the effects we've used in previous chapters to create a foam pattern which we will animate in Niagara via the use of Particle Color and Dynamic Parameters.

1. In the **Content Browser**, navigate to the folder **Content | Materials | Master**.
2. Right click in the **Master** folder and select **Material** from the menu.
3. Call the Material *M_WaterFoam*.
4. Double click to open the Material.
5. Navigate to the **Details** panel.
6. Locate the **Blend Mode** Parameter, select **Additive** from the down menu.
7. Set the **Shading Model** to *Unlit*.
8. Create two **Texture Sample** Nodes in the Material Graph by Holding T and left clicking. Set the **Texture** Parameter to be **WaterfallStream1_ BaseColor** on both **Texture Sample** Nodes.
9. To the left of the **Texture Sample** Nodes create two **Texture Coordinate** Nodes by right clicking in the Material Graph and searching for **Texture Coordinate**. On the upper **Texture Coordinate** Node set the **U** and **V** tiling to *2.5* and on the lower **Texture Coordinate Node** set the **U** and **V** Tiling to *0.75*. The idea here is to have one water texture that repeats a few times and one that is at a very large scale.
10. Above the **Texture Samples** place a **Particle Color** Node by right clicking in the **Material Graph** and searching for **Particle Color** from the popup menu.
11. Create two **Multiply** Nodes to the right of the Texture Samples, on the first **Multiply** Node connect the **R** output of the **Particle Color** Node into the **A** input of the first **Multiply**. Connect the **R** output of the upper **Texture Sample** into the **B** input of the first **Multiply** node.
12. On the second **Multiply** Node connect the **G** output of the **Particle Color** Node into the **A** input of the second **Multiply** node. Connect the **R** output of the upper **Texture Sample** into the **B** input of the second **Multiply** node.
13. Create a new **Multiply** Node and set the **A** value to be *0.5* and connect the upper output of the first **Multiply** node into value **B**. This will darken the repeating water texture. We do this as combining textures can lead to really bright values very easily.
14. Next create an **Add** Node and connect the output of the upper **Multiply** Node into the **A** Input of the **Add** Node and the output of the second **Multiply** Node into the **B** input of the **Add** Node. An example of what we've done so far can be seen in Figure 14.10.

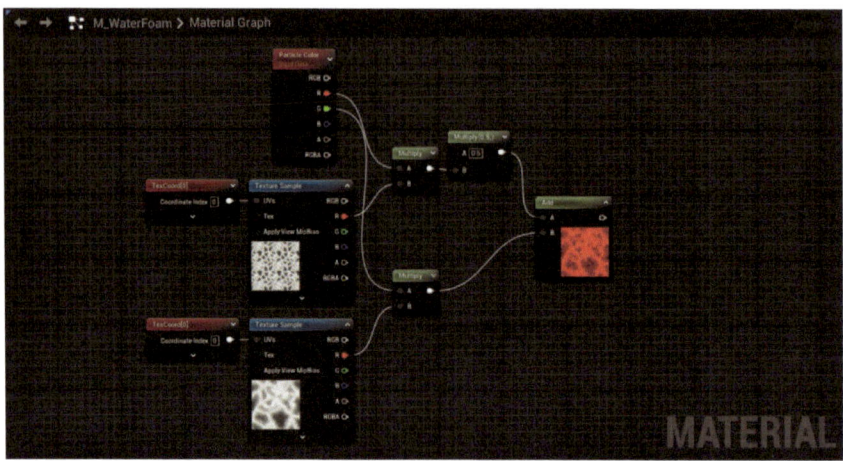

FIGURE 14.10   The water foam material WIP.

15. Next, we need to create a Power Node, by right clicking in the **Material Graph** and searching for *Power* from the pop up menu. Connect the output of the **Add** Node to the **Base** Input on the **Power** Node. Set the **EXP** input on the **Power** Node to *2*. This will raise the contrast a bit and create a few more dark values in our water texture.

16. Now we are going to mask the texture with a Radial Gradient. To do this first create a Constant Node by holding **1** and left clicking in the Material Graph. Set the value of the Constant Node, which is currently labeled as **0**, to be *0.5* This will represent our **Radius**.

17. Then right click in the Material Graph and search for the node *Radial Gradient Exponential*. Connect the **Constant** to the **Radius** Input on the **Radial Gradient** Node.

18. Now create a **Multiply** Node by holding the M key and left clicking in the Material Graph. Connect the **Radial Gradient Exponential** Node to the **B** Input slot on the **Multiply** node and then connect the output of the **Power** Node to the **A** Input slot of the **Multiply**. If you preview the **Multiply** Node you should now see a texture that looks a bit like a spotlight being shone on a patch of water.

    We now have a couple of choices, to complete the Opacity Input we could add Erosion, Depth Fade and a Saturate to control the final values. We will go through each step but it's up to you if you wish to utilize all of the above. The setup so far creates a nice water mask with good UV control, each feature we add should allow for further customization to help create a cool water foam effect. The first thing we'll do is build the Erosion functionality.

19. Underneath the **Multiply Node** in the Material Graph right click and Search for *DynamicParameter*.

20. Select the **DynamicParameter** node and using the **DetailsPanel** type the name *FoamErosion* into the **ParamNames Index[0]** and Set its **Default Value** to *1*.

21. Next to our **DynamicParameter** node, right click and Search for the node *SmoothStep*.

22. Drag out from the **Multiply** Node output and search for a *OneMinus* node.

23. Place the **OneMinus** Node just before our **Smooth Step** Node. Connect the **One Minus** Nodes output into the **Smooth Steps Min** Input.

24. Connect the **FoamErosion** output from our **DynamicParameter** Node to the **Value** input of our **Smooth Step** Node.

25. Drag out from the **Multiply** Node and let go of the left mouse button, from the menu create a New **Multiply** Node.

26. Connect the output from the **ValueStep** node to the **B** input of the **Multiply** Node.

27. To the right of the **Multiply** node, right click and search for a *Saturate* node.

28. Connect the Output of the **Multiply** Node to the **Saturate** Node. An updated preview of our Material can be seen in Figure 14.11 for you to compare against.

29. From the **Saturate** Node drag out from the output and create a *Depth Fade* Node from the popup Menu. Now connect the output from the **Depth Fade** Node into the **Opacity Input** of the Material Result Node.

30. From the **Saturate** Node drag out from the output and create a **Multiply** Node. Lastly, hold V and left click to create a **Vector Parameter**. Label the **Vector Parameter** as *Color Tint*. Set the **RGB** values as (**R**=*0.13*, **G**=*0.17*, and **B**=*0.52*). This allows us to control the final color of the water foam if we wanted to create a Material Instance.

31. Press **Save** and Close the **Material Editor**.

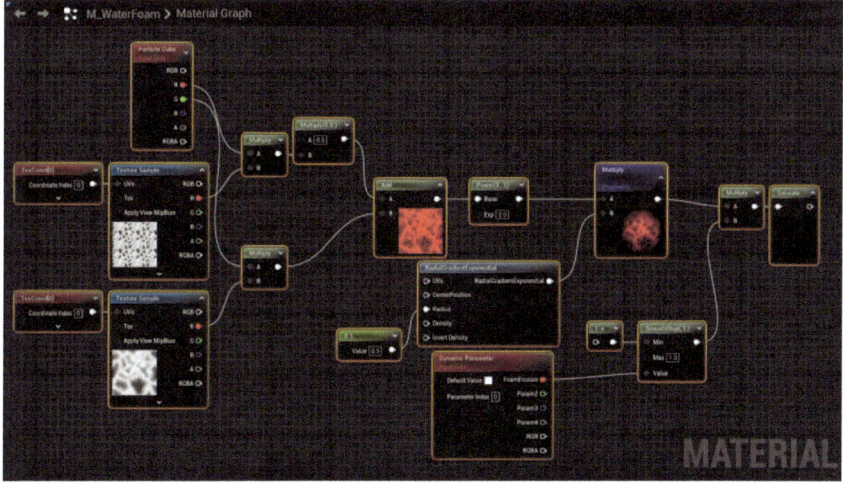

FIGURE 14.11 The water foam material WIP 2.

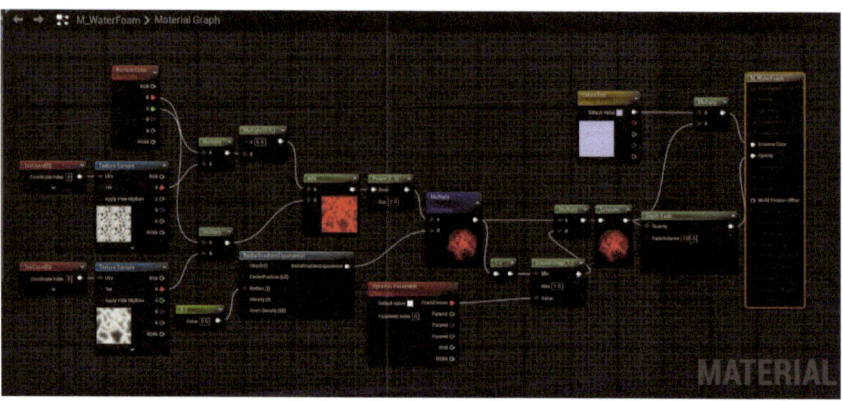

FIGURE 14.12 The water foam material final.

A final preview of the material can be seen in Figure 14.12. If you find the foam to be too colorful you may wish to add a **Desaturation Node** right before **Emissive Input** as a bonus addition.

Water Foam System

1. In the **Content Browser**, navigate to the **Content | VFX** folder.
2. Right click anywhere in the **VFX** Folder and create a **FX \ Niagara System** asset. From the pop-up menu, choose to add *Fountain Template* to asset and Label the asset *WaterFoam_System*.
3. Double click the **WaterFoam_System** to open the **Niagara Editor**.
4. Disable or delete the **Shape Location** Module.
5. Disable or delete the **Add Velocity** Module.
6. Disable or delete the **Gravity Force** Module.
7. Disable or delete the **Drag** Module.
8. Disable or delete the **Scale Color** Module.
9. Select the **Emitter State** Module and set the **Loop Duration** to *1*.
10. Click the **Spawn Rate** Module and set the **Spawn Rate Parameter** to *5*.
11. Select the **Initialize Particle** Module. Set **Lifetime Min** to *1.5* and **Lifetime Max** to *2*. Increase the **Alpha** value on the **Color** Parameter to *1.5*. Reset **Mass Mode** to *Default*. Set the **Uniform Sprite Size Minimum** to *225* and the **Uniform Sprite Size Maximum** to *300*.
12. Click the Green + Button next to **Particle Spawn** and add a *Sprite Facing and Alignment* Module. Set the **Sprite Facing** parameter to **X** = *0*, **Y** = *0* and **Z** = *1*. This makes our Particles always face up.
13. Click the Green + Button next to **Particle Update** and add a *Sprite Rotation Rate* Module. Change the **Rotation Rate** Parameter to be a *Random Range Float*.

14. Click the Green+Button next to **Particle Update** and add a **Scale Sprite Size** Module. Set the **Template** to *Linear Ramp Up*, select the last keyframe and increase the value to *2*. This will grow the foam effect over the particle's life.

15. Click the Green+Button next to **Particle Update** and add a **Color** Module. Set the **Color** Parameter to be a *Color from Curve*. Using the Upper Gradient track, set the following 3 values using the list below:

    a. Point 1, **V**=*0*, **R**=*2*, **G**=*2*, and **B**=*1*

    b. Point 2, **V**=*0.8*, **R**=*0.78*, **G**=*0.916*, and **B**=*1*

    c. Point 3, **V**=*1*, **R**=*0.29*, **G**=*0.327*, and **B**=*1*

    For the Alpha/Lower Gradient Track leave 1 input set to full white so there's no fade This series of values may look strange; however, the Color setup in the Material is such that the Red and Green channels control the alpha/visibility of the two water textures. So rather than tinting the Color of the overall particle effect this will either darken or brighten the water's grayscale values.

16. Next select the **Sprite Renderer** Module, set the **Material Parameter** to *M_WaterFoam*. Now we've added our Material, we can add our **Dynamic Material Parameters** Module.

17. Click the Green+Button next to **Particle Update** and add a **Dynamic Material Parameters** Module. Change the **Foam Erosion** to be a *Float From Curve*. Then select a *Smooth Ramp Down Curve* as the Template. Select the first key frame and set its **Value** to be *4*. This gives the erosion a longer time length before the foams texture becomes hidden.

18. Click **Save** to complete the Niagara System. Figure 14.13 shows an image of the completed System's overview in the Niagara Editor.

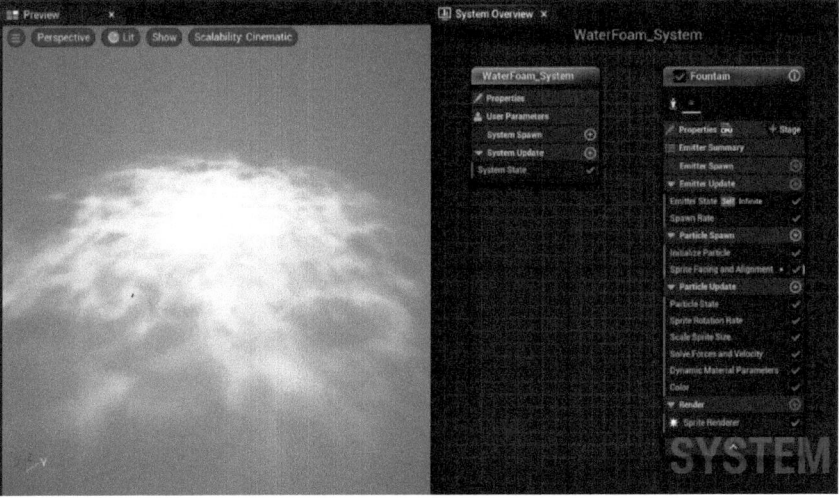

FIGURE 14.13   The water foam system in the Niagara editor.

FIGURE 14.14   The water foam system in the level.

To preview our final effect in the level you can drag and drop the **WaterFoam_System** asset from the **Content Browser** into our level. It needs to sit just above the water, so you may need to experiment with the Z height of the particle asset to get it to look right. The Foam effect is quite large, but you will likely need to duplicate it several times across the waterfall to cover all the necessary ground. Figure 14.14 shows five foam assets duplicated and translated across the waterfall.

Conclusion

In this chapter we've built several water assets to help create our WaterFall effect. This is very much a start in this area of VFX, water can become very complicated depending on art style. It's worth looking into other material features such as refraction, normal map ripples and simulations to help build up your knowledge for more complex results.

You have now reached the chapter quiz, be sure to attempt the four questions below to test your knowledge.

Chapter 14 Quiz

Question 1: What Material node is commonly used for animating Water textures in Materials?

    a.   Rotator
    b.   Transform
    c.   Panner

Question 2: What Material node helps blend unwanted edges when geometry overlaps?

    a.   Depth Fade

    b.   Pixel Offset

    c.   Specular Vector

Question 3: What View Mode is helpful when working with lots of Transparent VFX-like Water Systems?

    a.   Draw Calls

    b.   Lighting Complexity

    c.   Overdraw

Question 4: What Module is best suited to spawn Waterfall Splashes?

    a.   Spawn Rate

    b.   Spawn Instantaneous

    c.   Spawn Per Unit

Answers

Question 1: c

Question 2: a

Question 3: c

Question 4: a

15

The Fire Tornado

Introduction

Welcome to our final chapter! In this chapter, we are going to create our Fire Tornado System, you'll learn about:

- Creating Lava Materials for Mesh Particles.
- Setting up Mesh Particles in Niagara.
- Creating a Fire Tornado with multiple emitters.

Mesh Particles offer another alternative to the Sprite and Ribbon Emitters we've looked at already. The major benefit of a Mesh particle is they offer better shape, form and depth thus increasing the overall realism of the effect you are creating. We can use them in two main ways, the first, where a Mesh Particle can represent an object, in this chapter, we will use a rocky-shaped Static Mesh to be a Lava Rock, and the second, where the Mesh Particle represents a Track/Runway for a material to trace creating a complex animation.

In order to begin creating Mesh Particles, you will need a Static Mesh and a Material. Try to be mindful about the amount of polygons and Materials used in the construction of your Mesh. It can be quite easy to overwhelm lower end systems if your work is not optimized.

Rock Meshes

In this section, we'll begin by exploring the ingredients needed for our Fire Tornado. Let's begin this process by looking at our RockMeshes.

Rock Meshes

1. In the **Content Browser**, navigate to the folder **Content | Meshes**.
2. Double click on the asset **Pebble_Stone_Mesh** to open the Mesh in the Static Mesh Editor.
3. With the Mesh Open, we can look at some important things to consider for your own projects.

DOI: 10.1201/9781032663852-15

The pebble stone mesh has a low polycount of 192 triangles. The structure of the mesh is angular and chunky with a plain material. We can swap the Material with something more dynamic to take this very basic shape and make it into something much cooler.

Lava Material

The first Material we are going to make is the Lava Material. This material is designed for one main function, to make our rocks look like awesome lava and add some variety to the mesh. We are going to add variety by blending between two similar sets of textures. We have provided a lava and a non-lava texture set, our Niagara System will dynamically blend between the two, creating a mixture of hot and cold rocks. We are going to apply this effect to several stages of the Material Graph so it won't just alter the Color but the Emissive, Normal and other textures to create a complete effect.

This is but one way of adding some variety to the final Niagara System. In addition to blending materials we could also have several mesh emitters that spawn slightly different geometry. With this approach we could use random floats to add variety to spawning and speed to create variation.

Let's now build our awesome material!

1. In the **Content Browser**, navigate to the folder **Content | Materials | Master**.
2. Right click in the **Master** folder and select **Material** from the menu.
3. Call the Material *M_Lava*.
4. Double click to open the Material.
5. Right click in the Material Graph and search for the *Dynamic Parameter* Node.
6. Select the **Dynamic Parameter** Node and, in the **Details** panel, label **Index 0** as *Emissive* and **Index 1** as *Lava*.
7. Drag out of the **Emissive** Output of **Dynamic Parameter** and from the menu create a *Named Reroute* Node. Label this Node *EmissiveParam*.
8. Drag out of the **Lava** Output of **Dynamic Parameter** and from the menu create a *Named Reroute* Node. Label this Node *LavaParam*.
9. You can review the structure so far against Figure 15.1, the two reroute nodes shall help us keep the Material Graph clean. They will allow us to place nodes independent of connection lines whenever we want to call the nodes. It's great to use these nodes when you have a value that's needed frequently in several places.
10. Next create two **Texture Sample** Nodes by holding T and left clicking in the Material Graph, you can convert them to Parameters if you'd like to make instances of this Material later. But for this tutorial it's not required.
11. Set the **Texture** property of the first **Texture Sample** to **Textures | VFX_ LavaRock | NonLava_BaseColor** and Set the **Texture** property of the second **Texture Sample** to **Textures | VFX_LavaRock | Lava_BaseColor**.
12. Now create a **Linear Interpolate** Node by holding L and left clicking in the Material Graph.

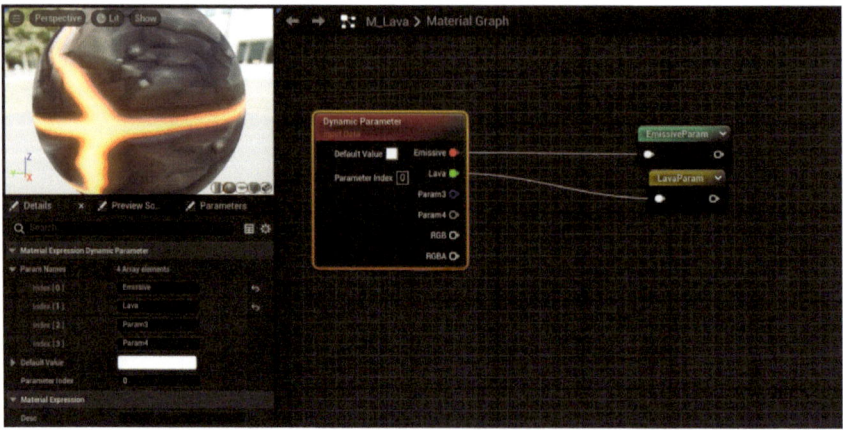

FIGURE 15.1   Dynamic parameter setup.

13. Connect the first **Texture Sample** into the **A** input of the **Linear Interpolate** Node and connect the second **Texture Sample** into the **B** input of the **Linear Interpolate** Node.

14. Right click in the Material Graph and search for the *LavaParam* reroute node from the popup menu, Then connect the **LavaParam** Node to the **Alpha** input of the **Linear Interpolate** Node. Finally drag out from the **Linear Interpolate** Node and connect it into the **Base Color** Input of the Material Result Node. You can review this stage against Figure 15.2.

The rest of the Lava Material will build on the above approach. The Roughness and Normals stages will duplicate the approach almost exactly, whereas our Emissive input needs a little more variety to allow us to toggle between a pure black (off emissive) and a Lava Texture. Let's build the rest of the material.

1. Create Two **Texture Sample** Nodes like we did previously. Set the first **Texture Sample** to **Textures | VFX_LavaRock | NonLava_ORM** and Set the second **Texture Sample** to **Textures | VFX_LavaRock | Lava_ORM**.

2. Create a **Linear Interpolate** Node and Connect the **Texture Sample** Nodes to the **Linear Interpolate** Inputs.

3. Create a **LavaParam** Node and connect it to the **Alpha** input on the **Linear Interpolate** node.

4. Then Connect the **Linear Interpolate** Output to the **Roughness** Input of the Material Result Node.

5. Now Create Two more **Texture Sample** Nodes like we did previously. Set the first **Texture Sample** to **Textures | VFX_LavaRock | NonLava_ Normal** and Set the second **Texture Sample** to **Textures | VFX_LavaRock | Lava_Normal**.

6. Create a **Linear Interpolate** Node and once again Connect the **Texture Sample** Nodes to the **Linear Interpolate** Inputs.

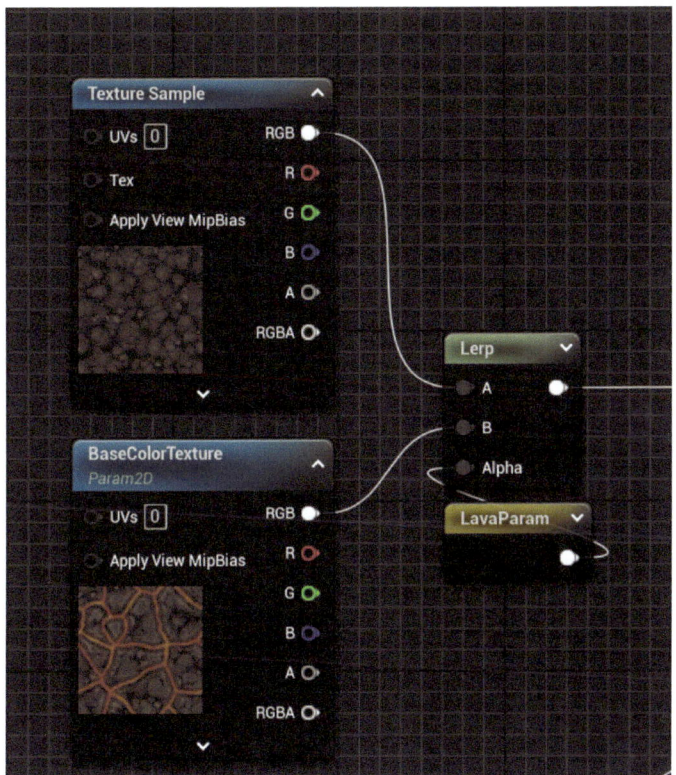

FIGURE 15.2   Lava Lerp.

7. Create a **LavaParam** Node and connect it to the **Alpha** input of the **Linear Interpolate** node.

8. Then Connect the **Linear Interpolate** Output to the **Normal** Input of the Material Result Node.

9. Now create one final **Texture Sample** and set its **Texture** property to **Textures | VFX_LavaRock | Lava_Emissive**.

10. Above the **Texture Sample** create a **Constant**, by holding 1 and left clicking in the Material Graph.

11. Create a **Linear Interpolate** Node, connect the **Constant** into the **A** input and the Emissive **Texture Sample** into the **B** input.

12. Drag out of the **Output Pin** of the **Linear Interpolate** node and create a *Multiply* Node from the Popup Menu. Then right click in the Material Graph and create an *EmissiveParam* Node, connect this into the other **Multiply** Node Input.

13. Finally Drag out of the **Multiply** Node into the **Emissive** Input of the Material Result Node.

14. **Save** the **Material**.

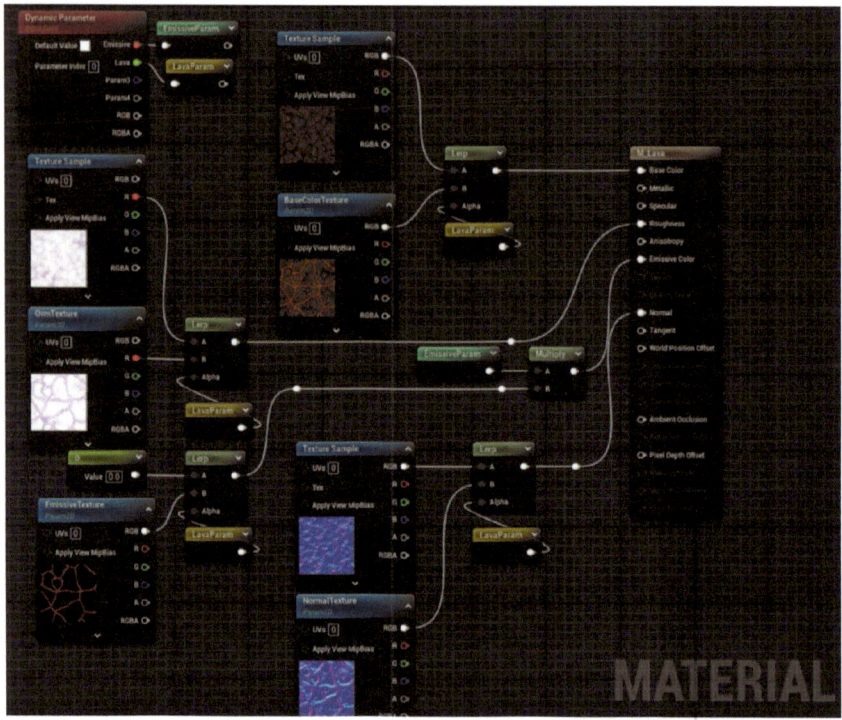

FIGURE 15.3   Completed lava material.

You can compare your work against the example in Figure 15.3, we've kept the Graph quite compact via the use of Reroute Nodes and swapped the inputs on the Multiply Node, this is not necessary but made the Graph fit a little better. We can now move on to the other Materials needed for the effect.

Linear VFX Distortion Material

In this next section, we are going to build a material that will add a distorted fall off to a Ribbon Particle. The idea is to add a very stylized trail that has a bit of noise in its tail to help add a bit of energy to the effect. We'll first start by creating some panning textures and then move onto modifying some UV coordinates, this will be similar to some of the materials we built earlier on in the book. Let's get cracking!

1. In the **Content Browser,** navigate to the folder **Content | Materials | Master**.
2. Right click in the **Master** folder and select Material from the menu.
3. Call the Material *M_VFXDistortLinear*.
4. Double click to open the Material.
5. Right click in the Material Graph and search for the **Texture Coordinate** Node. Select the **Texture Coordinate** Node and set the **X** and **Y Tiling** Values to be *0.5* in the **Detail Panel**.

6. Then Drag out from the **Texture Coordinate** Node's **Output** pin and search the *Panner Node* from the Popup Menu.

7. Select the **Panner** Node and set the **Speed X** Value to −*0.4* and the **Speed Y** Value to *0*.

8. Now **right** click in the Material Graph and search for a *Time* Node. Connect the Output Pin of the **Time** Node into the **Time** input of the **Panner** Node.

9. Drag out from the **Panner** Node and from the menu search for a *Texture Sample Parameter 2D* Node.

10. Select the **Texture Sample Parameter 2D** Node. Set the **Parameter Name** to *ParticleTexture* and Set the **Texture** property to **Textures | EnergyOrb | Particle2**.

11. Select all of the nodes we have created and make a copy of the nodes below using Ctrl + C and Ctrl + V.

12. Select the copied **Texture Coordinate** Node and set the **X** and **Y Tiling** Values to be *1.5* in the **Detail Panel**

13. Select the copied **Panner** Node and change the **Speed X** Value to −*0.1*.

14. Now Create a **Multiply** Node after the **Texture Sample Parameter 2D** Nodes using **M** and **left click**. Connect the **RGB** Output pins from both **Texture Sample Parameter 2D** Nodes into the **A** and **B** Inputs of the **Multiply** Node.

15. Drag out from the **Multiply** and create a *Component Mask* from the Popup menu. Select the **Mask** and enable only the **R & G** Channels.

16. Create an **Add** Node just after the **Mask** just **A** and left click. Connect the **Output** from the **Mask** Node into the **B** Input of the **Add** Node.

17. Then create another **Texture Coordinate** Node by right clicking in the Material Graph and searching for the node.

18. Connect the **Output** pin of the **Texture Coordinate** Node into the **A** Input of the **Add** Node.

19. Review your progress against Figure 15.4 and Save your progress.

We have now constructed the UV distortion part of the Material. To improve this section further you could parametrize the Panner Node's Speed inputs and add a Multiply Node after the Mask to adjust the strength of the panning coordinates. To finish the Material, we'll now move onto combining what we've done so far with Gradient and Particle Color nodes.

1. Drag out of the **Add** Node and search for a **Linear Gradient** Node.

2. Drag out of the **Linear Gradient** Node and search for a **One Minus** Node.

3. Next, create two **Multiply** Nodes, using **M** and **left click**. Connect the **One Minus** Node into the **A** Input of Both **Multiply** Nodes.

4. Now Create a **Particle Color** node by right clicking and searching for *Particle Color*.

5. Connect the **RGB** Output Pin of the **Particle Color** Node into the **B** Input of one of the **Multiply** Nodes.

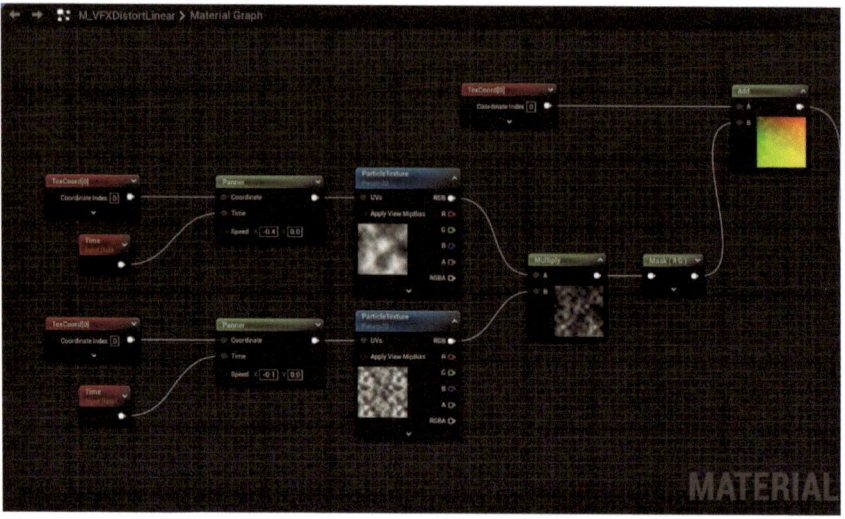

FIGURE 15.4   UV distortion chain.

6. Connect the **A** Output Pin of the **Particle Color** Node into the **B** Input of the other **Multiply** Node.

7. Connect the **Multiply** Node Output that has the **RGB** Output value in **B** to the **Emissive Color** input of the Material Result Node.

8. Connect the other **Multiply** Node Output to the **Opacity** input of the Material Result Node.

9. Now make sure no nodes are selected and in the **Details** panel, Set the **Blend Mode** to *Additive* and the **Shading Model** to *Unlit*.

10. Finally Save your Material and compare your overall results against Figure 15.5 to compare the Material Result Connections and Figure 15.6 to see an overview of the Material Graph.

We've created our Linear VFX Distortion Material which we will borrow from in the next section. The UV manipulation provides a lot of variety which will help add textural detail to our effect. You could also try adding your own noise textures to the Material/alter the tiling to see how the UV manipulation changes.

Radial VFX Distortion Material

We are now going to create a very similar material that will swap out the mask for a radial mask instead of linear fall off. We'll start by copying over the previous Materials nodes and then customize the new Material.

1. In the **Content Browser**, navigate to the folder **Content | Materials | Master**.

2. Right click in the **Master** folder and select Material from the menu.

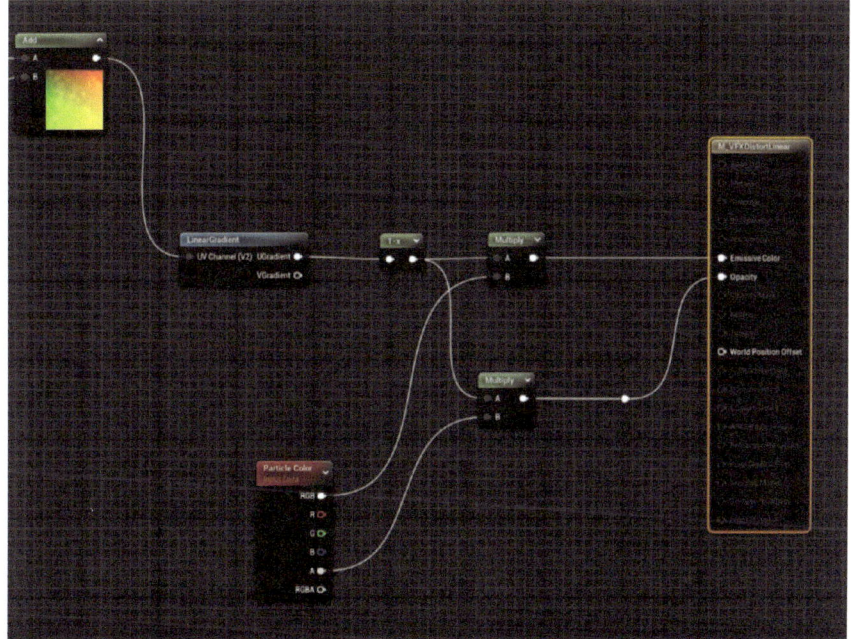

FIGURE 15.5 Material result node connection.

FIGURE 15.6 Linear VFX material overview.

3. Call the Material *M_VFXDistortRadial*.
4. Double click to open the **Material**.
5. Now go back to the **Content Browser** and double click on the **Material** *M_VFXDistortLinear*.

6. Drag a selection across all nodes and press Ctrl+C to copy the Nodes.

7. Then go back to the *M_VFXDistortRadial* Material Editor and Press Ctrl+V to paste the Nodes.

8. Connect the nodes to the Material Result Nodes **Emissive** and **Opacity** Inputs.

9. Now scroll to the left of the graph and select the Upper **Panner** Node. Set the **X** value to be −0.3 and the **Y** Value to be 0.2.

10. Next Select the Lower **Panner** Node. Set the **X** value to be 0.1 and the **Y** Value to be 0.3.

11. Now scroll to the right of the graph and select the **LinearGradient** Node, use the **Material Function** Dropdown in the **Details** panel and from the menu select *Radial Gradient Exponential*.

12. This will update the node and disconnect it, hook up the **UV** input of the **Radial Gradient Exponential** Node to the nearby **Add** node.

13. Next remove the **One Minus** Node and replace with a *Power* Node (right click in the Material Graph and select *Power* from the Menu), be careful to connect the **Power** Node exactly as the **One Minus** Node was set up.

14. Set the **Power** Node's **Exp** value to 5 and link the **Radial Gradient Exponential** Node with the **Power** Node as shown in Figure 15.7.

15. You may also review the overall structure/layout of the Material against Figure 15.8. After doing so, Save the Material.

We have now built all of the Materials required for the Fire Tornado. As with any of the materials we've built please adjust and tinker with the values until you are happy.

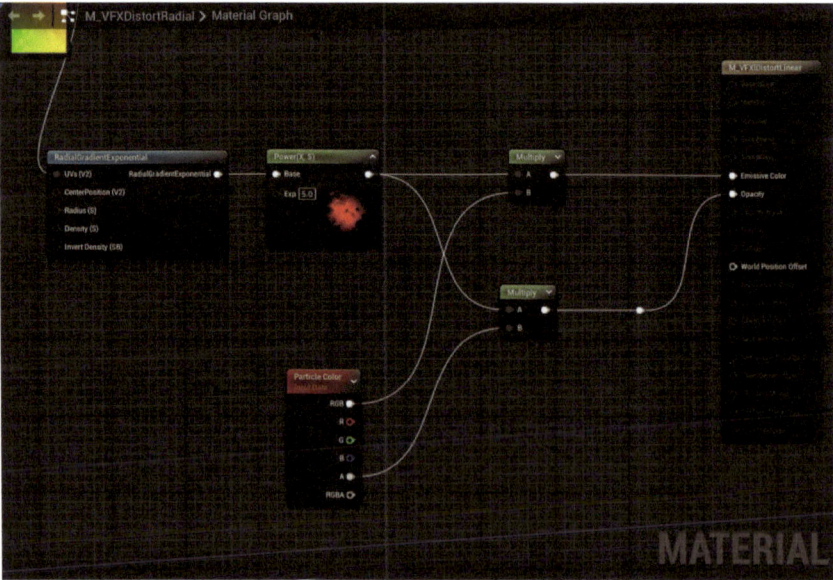

FIGURE 15.7 Radial material result node connection.

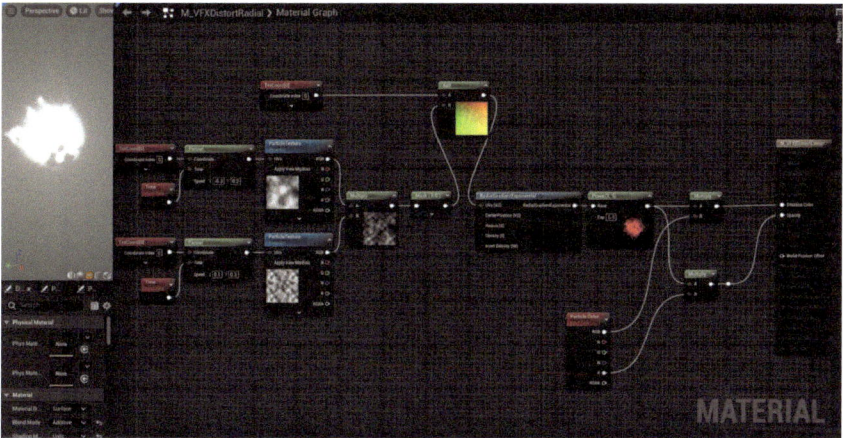

FIGURE 15.8 Radial VFX material overview.

If you'd like to take these materials further you could look at replacing the radial and linear gradient nodes with texture masks created in another DCC such as Photoshop. The trade off by doing this would be texture memory instead of Material Instruction Count. For now though, let's move on to the Niagara part of the chapter.

Fire Tornado System

We are now going to build our Particle Effect, the Fire Tornado will be built from several emitters that contribute to the overall system. You'll first learn how to work with meshes as we spawn our rock particles. After this you'll add internal swirling fire embers to add further heat to the central column of the effect. We'll then add spawning orbital ribbons to add a further sense of speed. By the completion of the effect you will have used the three main types of renderers and created a very cool effect. Let's begin!

Spawning the Rock Particles

We are now going to set up our Swirling Mesh System. The idea is that the particles will float upwards and then spin in a vortex. We'll make use of our Lava material to apply random amounts of emissive glow and texture values to the rock pieces to help make them look powerful and cool as they move upwards. We'll also generate a location event for the rocks to help connect with the Ribbon Effect later.

An important consideration at this point is to keep an eye on the Spawn Rate and amount of particles on the screen. On lower-end systems, a high value can end up slowing down performance. Feel free to spawn less rocks if your hardware runs slow while testing this effect.

Let's get building!

1. In the **Content Browser,** navigate to the **Content | VFX** folder.

2. Right click anywhere in the **VFX** Folder and create a **FX \ Niagara System** asset. From the pop up menu choose to add *Upward Mesh Burst* to the asset, click **Finish** and then Label the asset *FireTornado_System.*

3. Double click the **FireTonardo_System** to open the **Niagara Editor.**

4. Disable or delete the **Gravity Force** Module.

5. Disable or delete the **Scale Color** Module.

6. Disable or delete the **Scale Mesh Size** Module.

7. Disable or delete the **Spawn Burst Instantaneous** Module.

8. Select the **Emitter State** Module and set the **Loop Behavior** Parameter to *Infinite* and set the **Loop Duration** to *8.*

9. Click the Orange + Button next to **Emitter Update** and select the *Spawn Rate* Module from the Popup Menu.

10. Select the **Spawn Rate** Module and Set the **Spawn Rate** Parameter to *25.*

11. Set the **Initialize Particle** Module. Set the **LifeTime Max** Parameter to *6.* Change the **Color Module** Parameter to *Direct Set* using the dropdown menu arrow. Next **Reset** the **Color** Parameter to **White** using the Arrow Button. Set the **Mesh Uniform Scale Min** Parameter to *0.1* and the **Mesh Uniform Scale Max** Parameter to *0.42* and finally reset the **Mesh Renderer Array Visibility Mode** Parameter to *Unset.*

12. Select the **Add Velocity** Module. Set the **Minimum Velocity Speed** to *450* and the **Maximum Velocity Speed** to *750.* Increase the **Cone Angle** to *35.*

13. In the **Particle Update** Section, press the Green + Button and from the Menu search for the *Vortex Force* Module.

14. Select the **Vortex Force** Module, set the **Vortex Force Amount** to *2500* and the **Origin Pull Amount** to *1500.*

15. In the **Particle Update** Section, press the Green + Button and from the Menu search for the *Generate Location Event* Module.

16. Click the **Emitter Properties** at the top of the stack and enable **Requires Persistent ID's** and **Compile.**

17. In the **Particle Update** Section press the Green + Button and from the Menu search for the *Dynamic Material Parameters* Module. We'll revisit this shortly.

18. Now select the **Mesh Renderer,** delete **Meshes Index** [1] and change **Index[0] mesh** to be **Meshes | Pebble_Stone_Mesh | Pebble_Stone_Mesh.** Next change the **Override Material Explicit Mat** value to be *M_Lava.*

19. Now select the **Dynamic Material Parameters** Module. Change the **Emissive** type to be a *Random Float Range* using the right dropdown arrow, set the **Minimum Value** to be *3* and the **Maximum Value** to be *15.*

20. Change the **Lava Value** to be a *Multiply Float by Int,* then change the **Integer** value to be a *Random Range Int.*

21. Compile and Save the Niagara System.

22. If you review against Figure 15.9, your Niagara System should look similar.

FIGURE 15.9   Upward burst rock mesh emitter.

Spawning the Fire Particles

Among the swirling rock particles, we are going to add some embers/fire VFX. These particles will add further color to help break up the brown rocks. We'll make use of many of the same modules as well as some additional ones to add color and some stretching to the particle sprite size to add more sensation of speed.

1. Open up the **FireTornado_System** in the **Niagara Editor**.
2. Select the **UpwardMeshBurst Niagara System** Stack and press Ctrl+C to copy in and Ctrl+V to Paste a copy of the entire emitter. We'll now customize this to spawn our Fire Particles.
3. Select the **Emitter State** Module and set the **Loop Duration** to *1*.
4. Select the **Spawn Rate** Module and set the **Spawn Rate** to *15*.
5. Scroll to the bottom and delete the **Mesh Renderer** Module.
6. Then use the Red+Button next to the **Render** Stage and add a *Sprite Renderer*.

7. Select the **Sprite Renderer**, set the **Material Value** to **Content | Materials | Master | M_VFXDistortRadial** and set the **Alignment Parameter** to *Velocity Aligned.*

8. Next select the **Initialize Particle** Module, reset the **Mesh Scale Mode** Parameter. Change the **Sprite Size Mode** to *Random Uniform* and set **Uniform Sprite Size Min** to *7* and **Uniform Sprite Size Max** to *15.*

9. Now select the **Add Velocity** Module and change the **Velocity Speed Maximum** to *650.*

10. Select the **Velocity Force** Module, set the **Velocity Force Amount** Parameter to *1275.*

11. Delete or disable the **Generate Location Event** Module.

12. Delete or disable the **Dynamic Material Parameters** Module.

13. Press the Green+Button next to the **Particle Update** Stage and from the **Menu** search for the *Scale Sprite Size by Speed* Module.

14. Select the **Scale Sprite Size by Speed** Module, set the **Max Scale Factor** to **X** = *1* and **Y** = *8.*

15. Press the Green+Button next to the **Particle Update** Stage and from the Menu search for the *Color* Module.

16. Select the **Color** Module, set the **Color Parameter** to be *Color from Curve* using the dropdown arrow. Create 3 points on the upper curve track
    a. Point 1, **V** = *0.2*, **R** = *125*, **G** = *27*, and **B** = *0*
    b. Point 2, **V** = *0.4*, **R** = *15*, **G** = *1*, and **B** = *0*
    c. Point 3, **V** = *1.0*, **R** = *1*, **G** = *0.7*, and **B** = *0*

17. For the lower curve track, move the white Alpha value to about *0.8.*

18. **Save** and **Compile** the **Niagara System** and compare against Figure 15.10 for a System overview.

Spawning the Orbiting Ribbons

For our final effect, we are going to use the location of our vortex-swirling Lava rocks to create a cool trail. We'll work within the same System and start with a simple fountain system, making a few changes to help connect the ribbons to the Lava rock. The idea behind this system is to create almost an outline silhouette to the overall effect and add further speed. We'll also link in our linear distortion material to help break up the ribbon's appearance.

Let's get started!

1. Open up the **FireTornado_System** in the **Niagara Editor**.

2. Move to the right of the Niagara Graph, right click and select **Add Emitter**. From the menu select a **Fountain** as the Emitter template.

3. Delete or disable the **Spawn Rate** Module.

4. Delete or disable the **Shape Location** Module.

5. Delete or disable the **Add Velocity** Module.

6. Delete or disable the **Gravity Force** Module.

FIGURE 15.10 Upward burst fire emitter.

7. Delete or disable the **Scale Color** Module.

8. Delete or disable the **Sprite Renderer** Module.

9. Use the Red+Button next to the **Render** Stage and select the *Ribbon Renderer* Module from the menu.

10. Select the **Ribbon Renderer** Module and set the Material to **Content | Materials | Master | M_VFXDistortLinear**.

11. Select the **Emitter State** Module and set the **Life Cycle Mode** to *System*.

12. Use the Orange+Button next to the **Emitter Update** and select *Beam Emitter Setup* Module from the menu.

13. Select the **Initialize Particle** Module, change the **Lifetime Mode** to *Direct Set* and change the **Lifetime** Parameter to *0.66*. Any sprite and mass parameter values can be reset. Set the **Ribbon Width** Module to *Direct Set* and set the **Ribbon Width** Parameter to *11.7*.

14. Next, use the Green+Button next to the **Particle Update** Stage and select the *Scale Ribbon Width* Module. Select the **Ribbon Width** Module and change the **Ribbon Width Scale** to *Float from Curve* using the dropdown arrow. Use the **Template** options to change the curve to a *Smooth Ramp Down*.

15. Next, use the Green+Button next to the **Particle Update** Stage and select the *Color* Module. Select the **Color** Module. Create 5 points on the upper curve track

    a. Point 1, **V**=*0.0*, **R**=*255*, **G**=*100*, and **B**=*0*

    b. Point 2, **V**=*0.2*, **R**=*15*, **G**=*4*, and **B**=*0*

    c. Point 3, **V**=*0.5*, **R**=*5*, **G**=*0.0*, and **B**=*0*

    d. Point 4, **V**=*0.75*, **R**=*1*, **G**=*0.0*, and **B**=*0.8*

    e. Point 5, **V**=*1.0*, **R**=*0*, **G**=*0*, and **B**=*1*

16. For the lower curve track, move the white Alpha value to about *0.5*.

17. Now, for the last section, use the+Stage button at the top to add an *Event Handler* Stage.

18. Select the **Event Handler Properties** Module, set the source to be our *UpwardMeshBurst* Emitter and our **Location** Event. Set the **Execution Mode** to *Spawned Particles*. Set **Max Events Per Frame** to *10* and **Spawn Number** to *1*.

19. Next click on the Green+Button next to the **Event Handler** Stage and from the menu search for a *Receive Location Event*. You should now see Trails coming from our Lava rocks, huzzah!

20. **Save** and **Compile** the **Niagara System** and compare against Figure 15.11 for a System overview.

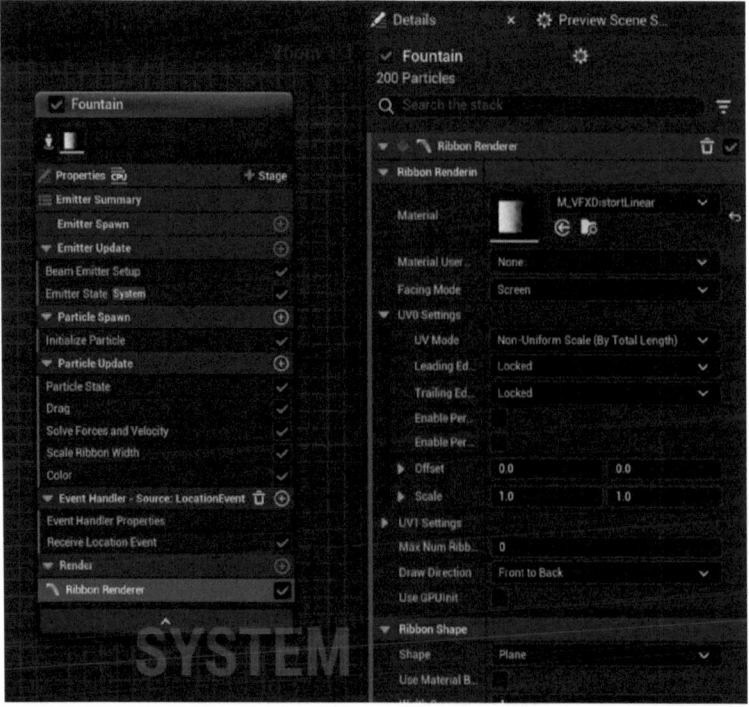

FIGURE 15.11   Fountain ribbon emitter.

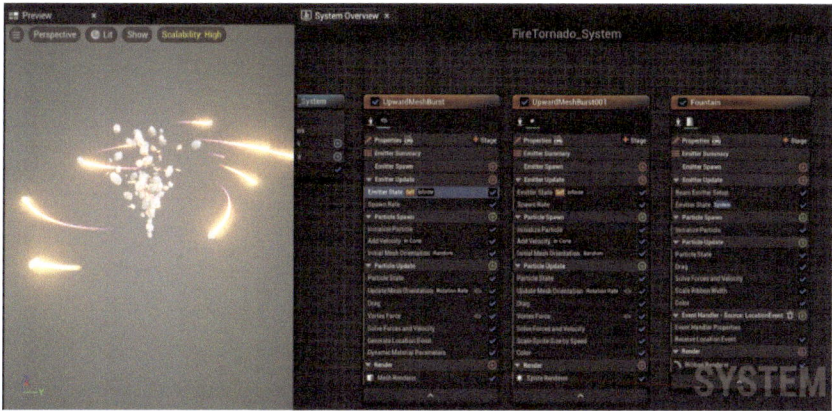

FIGURE 15.12   Fire tornado system overview.

FIGURE 15.13   Fire tornado level preview.

Figures 15.12 and 15.13 showcase the Emitters appearance in the Niagara Editor and Game Level for comparison. We've now completed our final effect, well done!

Conclusion

In this final chapter we've explored how we can build Mesh Renderer Niagara Systems with the ability to change material appearance via particle update. We've then combined these meshes with trails to add extra speed and character to our effect. Building up VFX effects out of different Renderers is a great way to leverage their strengths to do a specific job.

We've now introduced many of the major systems of Niagara throughout the book and hope that you have enjoyed trying the exercises and seeing them come to life in Unreal. Keep trying to build more complex and challenging VFX and incorporate the latest and greatest materials within your Niagara Systems.

For the final time now, why not partake in the Chapter Quiz?

Chapter 15 Quiz

Question 1: What does a Mesh Renderer do in a Niagara Emitter?

    a.   A Mesh Renderer allows us to use Static Mesh Geometry in Niagara Emitters.

    b.   A Mesh Renderer allows Niagara to collide with other Niagara Emitters.

    c.   A Mesh Renderer creates Sprites for use in Niagara.

Question 2: How did we create variety in our Mesh Particle Appearance?

    a.   We used a Color node to vary the texture of our Rock Meshes.

    b.   We used a Dynamic Material Parameters Node that helped blend two Textures together in a Material.

    c.   We used a Material Fracture to add damage to our Rock Meshes.

Question 3: What approach was used to create trailing particles?

    a.   A Sprite Renderer

    b.   A Mesh Renderer

    c.   A Ribbon Renderer

Question 4: What's a benefit of using separate Emitters to create a Niagara System?

    a.   We can generate more particles.

    b.   We can use different Emitters to target precise particle behaviors.

    c.   A Multi Emitter System loads faster.

    d.   More Emitters equals more fun.

Answers

Question 1: a

Question 2: b

Question 3: c

Question 4: b

Index